Travels with Teddy Bear

Travelogues of a Woman with Asperger's Syndrome with Her Teddy Bear

Debra Schiman

www.bearsac.com

Pen Press

First published in Great Britain by Pen Press
All paper used in the printing of this book has been made
from wood grown in managed, sustainable forests.

ISBN13: 978-1-906206-92-5

Printed and bound in the UK
Pen Press is an imprint of Indepenpress Publishing Limited
25 Eastern Place
Brighton
BN2 1GJ

A catalogue record of this book is available from
the British Library

Cover design by Jacqueline Abromeit

This book is dedicated to
my niece Aliyah

About the Author

Born 1967, in North London within a 'dysfunctional family', Debra boarded at a 'Special Needs' school with her brother. Despite her schooling, Asperger's syndrome – a high functioning form of Autism – was not picked up.

Unimpressed by mainstream employment and society Debra found hope within the learning difficulty and disability rights fields and more recently a voice within the Aspie community. At 38 she was diagnosed with Asperger's syndrome. This put her life in to perspective and set her free.

The combination of two passions 'Bearsac' her beloved teddy bear and travel has become the mainstay preoccupation and, like many Aspies, her preoccupation has become more than just a hobby, thus this book.

Acknowledgements

I would like to thank my Cousin Madeleine for believing in me; Jason Cook - Author of 'There's No Room for Jugglers In My Circus' - for his information; Sue Grossman for her teachings.

For their hospitality and/or assistance, I would like to thank: The Jakeljs in Slovenia; the woman in the fur hat in Moscow, and the man; train attendants on the Trans-Mongolian; Orsta and family and Mejet and family in Mongolia; the young lady from Cardiff for her Vaseline in Beijing.

For the tales and memories I have of them, I would like to thank: the man with the pimp stick in Newark; the man with large red buttons on his coat in Geneva; the Pigeon Devil-Woman of Zagreb; the penguin in the mobile phone advert in Japan; Salty (Mikal) on the Trans-Mongolian; the Dead Teddy Bear Hat Seller on the Great Wall of China and the waiter in Beijing, to whom I would also like to apologise. Apologies also to the scorpion-wielding man also in Beijing, and to the silkworms I ate.

I would also like to thank the many people whose names I do not know that have assisted me, inspired me or shared food, drink or a smile with me on my travels.

Last but not least, I would like to thank Bearsac and Choc-Ice for being there for me as my teddy bears.

Contents

Introduction

Travel is one of my favourite topics of conversation; I can talk about it for hours, if permitted. However, I often find it very challenging to converse with people once the subject matter digresses from travel and national culture, to popular culture. I suddenly feel a little alienated and unsure of what to say to continue being part of the conversation; not that I felt that comfortable being part of it in the first place. Even on the subject of travel itself, I sometimes feel like I am sitting on the outside, trying to squeeze bits in. On subjects that are not my thing, any hopes of being part of a conversation are near pointless. I am comfortable just listening and observing people, or prefer going off into my own thoughts, from which I do not like to be distracted.

My favourite subject of all is my travelling companion and teddy bear, *Bearsac*. I know he is not alive, but Bearsac has really become a live 'character', and to not animate him would be to kill him. He evokes in people many emotions and reactions: affection, friendliness, laughter, openness, curiosity, intrigue, concern, fear, prejudice, snobbishness, confusion, comfort, discomfort, reflection, inspiration; and the list goes on. How, seen in this light, can he not be real?

I am entertained by, and get a real kick from, the different ways people react to Bearsac; and I love the way he is spoken about by people face to face, on their mobile phones, and on the Internet. I am not bothered by the bad things people might say about him or me; I am a great believer in Oscar Wilde's quote "There is one thing worse than being talked about, and that's not being talked about."

It amuses me how I have taken a teddy bear rucksack, animated it, and turned it into a near cult status figure. It is a fabulous way of sharing something with other people. Bearsac is great at getting people to be more open-minded. He inspires them; they learn things from him; and because of his ability to inspire others to share something with us, I learn from them.

Another topic of conversation I feel comfortable with is Asperger's syndrome. Why? Because I have been diagnosed with it. Rather, I should say I *am* an 'Aspergian' or 'Aspie', and am proud to be different!

> *Asperger's syndrome is a condition on the high func-tioning end of the autistic spectrum. It manifests in various ways and can have both positive and nega-tive effects. It is typically characterized by issues with social and communication skills. Some people with AS experience varying degrees of sensory overload and are extremely sensitive to touch, smells, sounds, tastes, and sights. They may prefer soft clothing, familiar scents, or certain foods and may dislike being touched.* (sourced from http://en.wikipedia.org/wiki/Asperger%27s_ Syndrome)

Having used that Internet sourced explanation, which will maybe explain certain things that come up in the book, I would now like to point out that lots of Aspies simply understand our brain as being wired in a 'different' way from that which the medical world sees as 'normal' (or, as we Aspies more correctly say, 'typical').

It is society's barriers that are the main issues for us: attitudes of people and establishments that do not understand us and our needs; exclusion; sensory stimuli of everyday happenings that don't hinder neuro-typicals. (A neuro-typical is someone with 'typical' brain wiring, or what the medical world and most people incorrectly call 'normal'). Aspies tend to have to manually learn things that are natural for other people, like understanding non-verbal communication and unwritten social rules.

Of course, not having the same natural social understandings as the majority of the population means we may find it harder to fit into society's often illogical social constructions. Without understanding and acceptance of our differences, we might feel isolated by the expectations of fitting into a society to which we don't have the neurologically built-in instruction manual.

So I am not denying that some Asperger traits are barriers, as they often are. But Aspies have lots of strengths: logical thinking not weakened by emotion or swayed by society's views; deep focus on things that interest us; loyalty; and ability to spend long periods of time alone. Some Aspies have unusually intense skills and some have unusual unique interests. These things are strengths but are often portrayed as weaknesses by the 'Medical Model of Disability' way of looking at Asperger's, which portrays us as not having empathy; being too literal, having 'obsessional' interests and being aloof. I am not denying that we are ever like these portrayals, but this is certainly not the case for all of us. All Aspies have similar 'Asperger's' traits, but not all have them all, nor all at high degrees. An Aspie-wired brain processes information differently to the typically-wired brain; this can give us advantages, disadvantages or purely differences. When I experience sensory overload, it can be very hard for me to process information, whether it be through the senses, thought or movement. I can become disorientated and panicky – especially in unfamiliar environments or situations like those met abroad.

Five months after diagnosing myself as an Aspie, at 38 years old, I was officially diagnosed. For me it was an answer to what had gone before and why I was 'different' in a way not understood or tolerated. It put my life into context and is still doing so. I celebrate being an Aspie and having a better understanding of myself; I also celebrate my growing understanding of others and of this peculiar world we live in.

Asperger's syndrome is a wonderfully strange and misunderstood creature. She is thought always to be geeky, self-centred, shy, retiring and shunning of others not from her small planet. Yet for some Aspies (like me), she allows us to be uninhibited by social rules and to be at ease in our own company, not needing to be seen with another person, not fearing being seen to be alone. To this day I still do not really understand why so many people are scared to be seen alone. I can understand them maybe being scared of 'being on their own', but it is the being 'seen' to be alone that bothers people so much. Why?

As is often part of Asperger's syndrome, I do not understand a lot of society's unwritten rules, and have no time for some that I do. I care nothing for the rule of not talking to strangers about things outside the range of acceptable small-talk. I am not the stereotypical shy retiring type of Aspie; I find it quite easy, in my own way, to approach strangers and talk about things deeply with them. I do, though, have difficulty sustaining conversations if I have little interest or understanding of the subject. I am not good at, and have no interest in, general chit-chat, but I have 'manually' learnt small-talk to a small degree; and although I don't like it much, it enables me to approach people in a way more comfortable for them than launching into something too deep.

A lot of people think that Bearsac is a prop I use to allow myself to be able to talk to people. Bearsac is a hobby. He is more a prop for 'them' maybe, as he breaks down their fear and taboo of talking to strangers and makes me seem approachable.

I tend to get on better with people of a different culture from mine, maybe as I am not expected to take part in, and conform to, the British unwritten rules that I do not understand. Maybe the cultural difference means they do not perceive me in the way I am perceived by British people. Maybe it is because more effort is needed on both sides to communicate where there is a language barrier. It could be that language barriers mean I don't appear 'odd different' to people of other nationalities the way I so often do to British people.

Before I travel anywhere, I always study the culture of the country I am to visit, so as to try not to offend; and to learn some of the language. I feel more at ease with people of a different culture; I feel more accepted for being me. Having said that, travel can be stressful and stress can cause me sensory overload and mild OCD-type traits, you may recognise some in the book.

Most of the countries I visited were before I knew I had Asperger's, so I make no direct reference to them being AS traits until further on into my travels, when I knew of my status as an Aspie.

I find it harder to identify fake positivity in people, such as false smiles and kindness, than fake negatives; it is, after all, easier to hide real thoughts behind a false smile than to fake anger or negativity.

The Aspie strength I hold most dear is the ability not to be inhibited by what I think other people think about me. Too many people – and I think it is the *majority* – allow themselves to miss out on doing things they want, and some also do things they don't want, because they are worried about what others will think of them, or they feel the need to impress and keep up. Sometimes I am inhibited by my own self-doubt, like anyone else; but mostly I get on despite the fear. I love my Bearsac hobby and never let criticisms of the ignorami stop me pursuing my hobby and being myself.

Apologies if, in parts, I am rather repetitive, over explanatory, or too detailed; these are Aspie tendencies, which I thought would maybe give a bit of perspective on my traits.

Chapter One

Annapolis – America
July 2000

It was July 2000, not long into a promising new millennium. I had been sent by my employer of the time to Annapolis, America, to help open a new office. How could I go without trusted teddy bears Bearsac, who goes everywhere with me, and Choc-Ice, who I sleep with? Well I couldn't, could I? So, with Bearsac on my back and Choc-Ice travelling in my easily identifiable purple suitcase with furry teddy bear patch glued on, we set off for the States. This was to be my first trip of many with Bearsac, and the first of a few with Choc-Ice, who is falling apart.

Anticipation pumped my every breath as the engines fired and the plane sped down the runway; I had not been airborne for some years and love flying. My enthusiasm, though, was soon eaten by the tasteless in-flight food. Having to endure the over perfumed stench of the over-made-up lady two rows in front of me made the journey seem twice as long; she must have over-done it with the samples in duty-free. I sniffed at Bearsac's fur from time to time to recover from said stench, but still suffered dizziness and blurred vision brought on by it, which made sure my head ached most of the journey. The close proximity of the flickering personal video screen, even the insane flashing of my neighbour's screen, tore at my nerves, so I was unable to pass the time watching films. I must have appeared somewhat odd, sitting there wearing an eye-mask, tissue in my ears, cuddling Bearsac, kissing and sniffing his fur whilst muttering repetitively

1

under my breath: 'Wash that stench of a woman'; 'Coffee should be made illegal' and by thinking hard about the usual order of the players from numbers 1 – 11 of the Arsenal team in the mid 1980s, the order of the planets from the sun, or the release order of Gary Numan's singles. With my focused mind now taken away from my environment, food time came around again. The flight attendant gave me an extra cake for Bearsac; he didn't like the smell of it so I had it instead.

My boss picked me up from Baltimore Airport. Bearsac and I walked right past him, even though he was the only person in the waiting area of this local flight arrivals lounge. I had seen him but just did not recognise him, and was already thinking of phoning the London office as I didn't even have the address of the condo. The boss had said before leaving the UK that there was no need for me to know the address as he would pick me up; he couldn't see any reason for me needing to know it. He is such a weird and naïve Mr Bean-like man, but with practically no clear personality. He had studied astrology and based his every decision on it. An astrologer - for whose services he had been paying - had told him to set up the business and that opening a branch in the States would make it very successful. The astrologer even told him which star-signs his employees should be. Aries was one of them, and I'm Aries.

However, my boss did have his own mind in some ways, and used it to decide that my being Jewish (gleaned, I assume, from my surname) meant – as he explained to me one day – that I would be an honest and hard-working employee! I am, but it has sod all to do with my ethnicity! The funny thing about his 'positive' prejudice was that he was not Jewish himself. Anyway, with a good basic salary and reasonable commission rate, I could not afford to take offence; principles don't pay my rent. I was not going to be dictated to by society's expectation (assumed, rightly or wrongly, on my part) that I should leave because of his ignorance. Oh what politically correct rules society forces itself to live by!

Anyway, my colleague, who had come with the boss to meet me, approached me with open arms in 'long lost friend' greeting stance; I had only last seen him a few days ago, and was unsure whether to take on the hug or whether it was a joke. Awkwardly, I mirrored his gesture and gave a light hug. My boss, when we went back to where he was sitting, said he'd seen a woman carrying a suitcase with a teddy bear on it and thought of me, but he had not recognised me!

We drove to the condo-cum-office in which I was to spend the next two weeks. There were no tattooed bikers in headscarves; no surgically enhanced guys or broads waving from open-top cars; not even any mirrored skyscrapers along palm-treed avenues - This was the route to Annapolis.

However, at traffic lights the hire car stood beside an enormous Mack truck with shiny pipes. Now I knew I was in America. The sight of the driver using his CB radio took my mind back to just a few years earlier, when I used to spend hours in a bedsit on my CB. That was before I had Bearsac. If I'd had him at that time then Bearsac would have spoken on it like Choc-Ice often did. The rumble of the truck's engine kicking in shook me from my memory and we were off down the near-empty carriageway.

The condo was simple and clean, and the complex had its own pool, which myself and colleague used after work each day - apart from one day when it was really, really raining, thundering and lightning, and the roads had turned to river within less than a minute. The heavy rain of that day was short-lived and the water soon evaporated, and within minutes the roads were bone dry and all was quiet once more.

About 5am on my first morning, just as daylight was opening its eyes, I crept out with Bearsac, trying not to wake my colleague, who was sleeping in the sitting room I had to pass through. I went first to the waterfront and admired the boats that held the bells that I had lain listening to most of the night before. The boats' gentle bobbing created shimmering ripples of silver-blue on the water. The sun was rising on the horizon, the scene beautifully calm. The surrounding quiet left me feeling I was the only human on earth, so I felt quite content to just sit and take it all in with Bearsac sat beside me. There was a patch of green mould on the bench; it somewhat resembled the shape of the UK; I sat Bearsac on it so as to put the UK out of my mind.

Back on my feet I walked out of the tree-lined condo complex; birdsong filling my ears quite beautifully. I found us on a road gently dotted with small wooden houses, each with porch and customary rocking chair. There were squirrels darting erratically around that scurried into the trees as Bearsac greeted them. Squirrels are mad.

I was stopped in my tracks by this weird, almost quacking sound coming from above me. I looked up towards the sound, turning up Bearsac's head at the same time, both of us scanning the tree for a duck, wondering how a duck had got so high up in a tree. I saw no duck, but Bearsac pointed out that the sound was emitting from a squirrel. This demented squirrel was performing repetitive circular acrobatics around the same three branches, and was making the noise that had stopped me: *whirrrrr wuack wuack wuack wuack wuack wuack wuack whirrrrr wuack wuack wuack wuack wuack wuack wuack*. I had never noticed or thought about the sound squirrels make before; it really is the most peculiar noise of any creature on the planet. I became a little intrigued with squirrels for a while after that and would bore and annoy people by repeatedly doing impressions of them. I was reminded of a cuddly toy I once had that I thought looked like a squirrel without a tail; I used to have it handcuffed to my bag a few years before I had Bearsac, but I lost it at a Gary Numan concert when the handcuffs broke. This beautiful, cheeky-faced, cuddly creature was called Sid, and I still miss him.

I turned down a road with a singular small shop that had caught my eye; it had a faded Pepsi cola sign outside and I felt inspired to photograph it. Surprised that this grocery and liquor shop was open so early, I stepped inside. The shop descended into silence, its staff and three customers stared at me, looked at each other and then back at me:
   'Good morning,' I chimed with a smile.

The woman behind the counter nodded slowly and four pairs of eyes cautiously penetrated my back as I looked around, picking up and smelling items I had seen in American films but not in real life, such as Oreo biscuits and Hershey bars – not that I expected to smell much through the wrapping, but I tend to sniff at things anyhow. Spotting some lovely-looking cherries, I stuffed a couple of handfuls into a brown paper bag, which I opened with a flick, to break the deafening silence. For the entire three or four minutes I was in there, not a word was spoken other than by myself and by the woman who told me the price of my purchase.. I put the cherries inside Bearsac's tummy (he's a rucksack, after all), looking forward to having them for breakfast, and continued further down the road.

I passed what must have been a council-type housing estate and went into a laundrette to check out what coins it took, as I knew I would have to wash my clothes at some stage, and didn't realise then that the condo complex had its own laundry facilities. Again the chat turned into silence as I walked in and all activity ceased. There were several people eyeing me. It was not clear which coins the machines took, so I enquired, to no-one in particular. During the long silence that followed, which I thought would never be broken, I realised I was the only white person in there and that I had been in the shop too. Maybe, unspokenly, I was not meant to be there! Informed at last about what coins to use, I thanked my informer, bid good-day to everyone as a whole, and laughed gently to myself once outside.

Further down, the road came to an end; a whistling black man returned my good morning with a look I took to be confusion but could have been wind.

'Good morning,' he eventually replied.

'We don't get many of your folks around these parts.'

I laughed, and told him of my reason for being in Annapolis, and of my company's cyberspace exhibition.

'I don't get all this cyberspace stuff; it's a bit too space-age for an old man like me, I can just about use the microwave.'

With that, he bid me good day and walked off, picking up in his whistling where he had left off.

I came to a small wooded area; by now I was in dire need of using the lavatory. I took a quick look to make sure there was no one around, squatted between some bushes and made like a bear and shat in the woods. I had checked first that I had some tissue to wipe my bottom with. I took pride in the thought that for some time, there would be a part of me still in America once the rest of me was back home in the UK. I thought of my poo as fertiliser and wondered if anything would grow from it. Smiling on this thought, I made my way back to the condo, swinging Bearsac by his straps.

After breakfast, and the offensive smell of the boss's and colleague's coffee, I sat in the fitted wardrobe in my bedroom to chill out, reminding myself it was a closet, as I was in America.

The smell of the wood in the darkness of the closet took me within myself and calmed me, as this type of environment usually does. Calm, I was now ready to go out computer and stationery shopping with the boss and his weirdness.

He enthused about the ins and outs of the construction of the car, oblivious to my lack of interest. Conveniently, boss-man opened bank accounts for my colleague and I, as his intention was for us to take turns working for the duration of a three-month work visa after this initial two-week trip, to open the office and set it up.

In the town centre, nearly every person we passed said hi to us, and lots of people made a fuss of Bearsac, stroking him, tickling him under the chin or speaking to him. There was one person that wanted to buy him and offered me $50; I still have him though.

The main street in the centre of Annapolis is colourful, with charming little shops. At the top of town, and visible from most parts, is the State Capital Building, which is the oldest state capital building in continuous use in the USA. Built between 1772 and 1779, it was designated a National Historic Landmark in 1960.

Later in the day the boss went back to London, leaving my colleague and me without a car in a town where public transport finishes at about 7pm. Annapolis reminded me of the small town in the film 'Back To The Future', during the scenes in the 1950s. I took lots of photographs of water hydrants, road signs, overhead cables that web the town and suspended trafficlights in my enthusiasm to record anything that showed any difference to the UK.

Annapolis is in the state of Maryland and is renowned as the sailing capital of America; but there were no sailing events during our stay. About 33 miles east of Washington and about 26 south of Baltimore, Annapolis sits on the edge of Chesapeake

Bay, which is the largest of the USA's 130 estuaries. The bay is about 200 miles long, so we saw just a tiny part of it. The water in the Chesapeake Bay is shallow; its average depth is only about seven metres. Annapolis became Maryland's capital in 1695, though this was only for a year.

As well as sailing, Annapolis is famous for the arrival of the African slave trade. In 1767, a ship called 'Lord Ligonier' sailed into the Annapolis City Harbour with Gambian Africans brought over to be sold as slaves. One of the Africans was apparently Kunta Kinte, an ancestor of Alex Haley (the man who wrote *Roots)*. There are life-size bronze sculptures of Alex Haley reading to some eager children. The sculptor was Ed Dwight, America's first African-American astronaut trainee. He has had a highly varied career, including, amongst other things, Air Force test pilot, restaurateur, and construction entrepreneur; but in the mid 1970s he began an artistic career and has done many sculptures, including ones of Louis Armstrong, Ella Fitzgerald, Charlie Parker and Miles Davis.

I got my colleague to take a photograph of Bearsac and me lying next to the bronzed children as bronze Alex Haley read to us. My colleague must have thought me really odd when I sniffed the bronze after stroking it, but who cares. I felt the usual strong urge I feel after touching something I think must be dirty to wash my hands; so he must have thought me even odder when I used some bottled water and tissues to wash off the copper smell and dirt I imagined enfilthed my hands after my urge to touch and sniff it in the first place.

Sunset saw Bearsac and me sitting on the dock of a small crab-bery, eating small soft crabs and a larger hard-shelled crab. The soft crabs are eaten complete, shell and legs as well as flesh; both types were deliciously fresh.

My boss had left behind a book called *Chesapeake*; which in the evenings I read. Not that I have much of an attention span for reading, but I was happier to be in my room than spend hours sitting with my colleague watching American TV, making awkward small-talk or conversing on things of no interest to me. The book transported me back some 400 years to the time of the Native Americans. It covered the lives of several fictional men or families living along or exploring the bay, from 1583 until the late 1970s. My attention waned as it approached the more modern end of the timescale; but the book was 1000 and a half pages long. Why the extra half page? I wondered, when I turned to the end of this doorstop of a book to see how many pages it was. The complete unevenness of the extra half page after such a round number as 1000 annoyed me; so I tossed the book aside.

One day, when I had got my photographs out of the printers and was taking more photos, a white man came over from his condo nearby and suggested a good vantage point for a photograph. I showed him the ones I had just got printed. His neighbour, an old white woman, invited me into her condo to see her pride and joy, a framed photo she had taken at Cape Cod. I showed her and the man the rest of mine in her sitting room and when they saw the photograph of the grocery shop with Pepsi sign, the man said that it was the only place he did not recognise from the photos. The old woman slurred through the side of her mouth:
  'That's the coloureds storrrrrre.'

Suddenly, the man got up and left without a word, and the old woman went quiet. It was then it dawned on me fully that there was an unspoken apartheid in town, and race was a taboo area of conversation. I did not know how to take the way she spoke, or her neighbour's sudden departure, which I don't think was down to his finding offence at her.

9

However, I was too wary that I might have misunderstood her intonation and the strange atmosphere that seemed to clothe the residential part of this town to say anything. Indirect comments, especially in accents I am a stranger to, confuse me. In England, race - although not a comfortable or very honestly discussed subject of conversation - is not quite such a taboo subject, and racism is more direct; so it is a bit easier to deal with and confront. I doubt all of America is like this tiny part of its vast nation. However, it did come across as being like the way the more southern parts of the States are portrayed in some American films.

I took the small, infrequent bus to 'Mammoth' (about half the size of a UK Tesco store before it has been made bigger), just outside Annapolis. This inaptly named store is what passes for a supermarket. There is little fresh fruit and vegetables, but there are piles of plastic-looking, carelessly wrapped processed hard cheeses, available in all manner of colours, even some like slabs of congealed vomit. In the queue the man in front of me wears a company ID badge on his XXXL shirt (I had vacated the first queue I had got in because the woman in front had dropped a jar of mayonnaise on the floor and I guessed it would hold things up). Spotting the company name on his badge and having not long before read the book *The Celestine Prophecy*,[1] I took this situation as a cue to speak to the man in this second queue. The large aviation company for which he worked was one of the main US targets of the company I was working for. Calming down my butterflies and willing Bearsac to stay quiet, I introduced myself, the company and what we do. He seemed very interested in the prospect of having a virtual stand in a virtual aviation exhibition

---

1   *The Celestine Prophecy* by James Redfield in part speaks of society evolving due to the realisation that coincidences are not always accidental, but have deeper meanings that should be followed up with action.

in cyberspace. He gave me his card and said to send him some details.

Laden down with shopping I looked for the nearest bus-stop for the bus back to the condo. The nearest was way down on the other side of the road. There was no crossing and the traffic way too fast to risk crossing without one. The only thing was to walk. I lost count of the amount of people that looked out of their windows at me walking with my bags, quite a few people stopping and asking if I needed a lift, even though they were going the other way. I think people were more confused than offended when I turned down their offers. A bit further down, the only other pedestrian around asked if I needed a hand with my bags. The only place he could have been going on foot was into Annapolis, so I accepted his offer with great gratitude. I told him how strange I thought it that there was not a bus stop from the supermarket to get back, and about the number of lifts I had been offered, even though the people had been driving in the opposite direction. He laughed with great throatiness, tilting back his head and then said,

'They would have thought it very odd that someone was walking, especially such a little lady with so much shopping, as near on every damn person drives around here.'

The man spoke to Bearsac as though he was oblivious to the fact he is a teddy bear and of course Bearsac replied in the same nature; they spoke for some 20 minutes.

When I had arrived back at the condo and knocked at the door, there was no reply. There was only one key at this stage and my colleague, who had it, was meant to be waiting in for the telephone engineer. I went to sit outside, leaving my shopping in the hall to avoid it being in the sun.

A few minutes later, a man walking by said hi and we had a short conversation about what I was doing in Annapolis. I went on to tell him of the reason I was sitting there and he offered to put my food in his fridge in his condo, which was in the same block as ours. Unsure at first of what to do, I weighed up the situation. I took him up on his offer of the fridge and to wait in his condo, saying I would first have to put a note under the door of my condo, telling my colleague the number of his. He didn't seem to understand why but didn't argue.

Once I had put the note under the door, I grabbed my shopping and went to his condo, where he told me all about Annapolis. He had spent some time in the UK so I asked his opinion on the differences in culture, words, and about how race and racism is viewed in both countries. He agreed with what I thought, that race is less of a taboo and racism more direct in the UK than in Annapolis. He was not from Annapolis and said he thought the atmosphere between black and white was quite strange when he first came to live there. I don't remember which part of the States he was from, but he said the racism faced by blacks and whites in his home town was easier to see, and agreed that this makes it easier to deal with. (He was white, by the way, for anyone that needs to know.)

After an hour or so of me asking him about the differences be-tween the US and UK he said he needed to get on with some work but I could still keep my stuff in his fridge until I could get back in to my own condo (I think I must have got on his nerves, but I was absorbed in how words are different). I tried knocking at my condo again in case my colleague had arrived back but not seen the note. He opened the door, sleepy-eyed. He had been in all day but must have been in a deep sleep when I'd knocked earlier. I went and got my food and started cooking, setting the smoke detector off.

After work and at the weekends, Bearsac would sit on the sun-lounger, watching me in the pool; this must have bored him silly. Not over keen on swimming anyway, I preferred to make up my own aqua-cise moves and practise my Thai Boxing using the water as resistance. This, for some reason, caused my colleague some embarrassment, though none of the American residents seemed to be embarrassed, so God only knows why my colleague was. The floor of the pool was quite rough, and by the end of the day the soles of my feet were as smooth as a baby's. I woke suddenly one night, as I couldn't get out of my head the idea of other people's dead skin being in the pool. The heat of the next day made me forget about all that though.

On one of the weekends, Bearsac and I went to the United States Naval Academy; we sat on a cannon and watched the navy boys march around. Open since 1845, it is where Navy & Marine Corps cadets train to become officers. We met a large stone duck with a yellow plastic rain-hat on its head in the pretty street where all the high-ranking officers live; we stopped so Bearsac could speak to it. The navy's mascot is a ram. A real ram actually escorts the football team during the games, and it is as well known throughout Annapolis as Bearsac is in Borehamwood.

After this we walked around the town and to the harbour, and from City Dock we took a boat trip out to Thomas Moore Lighthouse, which is in the middle of the bay and on wooden stilts, and not at all tall like the ones in Britain. Bearsac was proud to have lots of people take photographs of him in front of the lighthouse and gave his best poses to the clicking cameras whilst the boat wobbled as people all came to our side. The rocking proved too much for two people, and once they started, about half the boat-load joined them in puking their guts up on either side of the boat; still, I'm quite sure any fish would have made a good meal of it. Bearsac and I spent time most evenings sitting in companionable quiet taking things in at City Dock.

Once we had the Internet set up I received an e-mail from my boyfriend, Alan, saying he had been to get a passport, as he was worried about me being out in America. He was concerned I might get shot and wanted to come and rescue me! Luckily, his mother talked him out of it. He got on my nerves insisting that I chat on messenger with him on-line all evening until I went to bed, so I couldn't get shot. I explained that Annapolis is far safer than Borehamwood. He was also concerned that I was sharing the condo with a male, so I think he thought that if I was on-line, I couldn't be getting off with him. My colleague could have been under the table pleasuring me as I typed, for all he knew! One evening that I was out, my colleague used messenger; Alan thought he was talking to me, so my colleague had a bit of fun with him! Alan would not respond once he was told who it really was, and when I later went on-line, I had to convince him it was really me before he would reply.

Whilst taking the post to the post office one day, I met an old woman in the street with a 'Vote for Bush' poster safety-pinned to her shirt. She handed me a poster, but I told her I couldn't vote as I was from England. She took no notice and explained, with great passion through her over-white, saliva-covered dentures, why I should vote for Bush in the 2000 elections, come November.

Later, in the evening, Bearsac and I were invited to have dinner outside in the communal gardens that overlook the boats, with some of the other residents of the complex we had met by the pool. None of them said they were going to vote for Bush when I asked, desperately trying to think of something to offer in inter-action. They didn't trust Bush and voiced their reasons as being to do with oil being the sole base for his wanting to be in control. Bush had started his own oil and gas company in the 1970s, called Arbutus Energy (*arbutus* means 'bush' in Spanish). One lady happily pointed out that 'George Bush' is an anagram of 'He bugs Gore'; this brought a round of laughter to the table. I wondered whether Gorge Bush and Al Gore were aware of the anagram as I tucked into some sweet potato pie, happy that I was able to interject on a subject of conversation amongst strangers 20 to 40 years older than me.

This was my last night and I was sorry to be going back home and leaving such nice people. I didn't want to go home the next day and back to the office with my boss; it had been so nice working without him and his weird ways and I had a new perspective on my life.

Before leaving, Bearsac and I had a look around Baltimore, home of The Baltimore Orioles baseball team, and Baltimore Ravens American Football team, and spent some time people-watching at the harbour, eating Baltimore Crab. In Baltimore, crab is a speciality and is a fast but tasty option when you are only in town for a couple of hours. No frills seemed to be the way to go in Baltimore. Sat at a table overlooking the harbour, brown paper for a table cloth, I tucked in, all tooled up for the messy job, the steam from the crabs misting up my glasses. I sat Bearsac well away so he wouldn't get splattered. It was meatier than the crab I had tried in Annapolis but had a peppery coating, unlike the sheer nakedness of my Annapolis crab. The sweetness of the flesh seemed not possible on a savoury food, but then I remembered the Cromer Crab I'd once tried as a teenager on holiday in Norfolk, and the fuss father made when I dropped a bit on the table. Laughing at the memory, I rubbed into the brown paper table covering the bits of crab meat I had dropped on this occasion and sent my laughter up to my father in spirit. My taste buds and stomach satisfied, I looked out over the harbour, inhaling the scene and exhaling it as a contented drawn-out sigh.

We got back to the airport in time for a short flight to Newark (New Jersey), where I was to get my flight back to England. I had a couple of hours to spare and went into Newark Town. Newark's main street reminded me of the main shopping street in Wood Green in London, for some reason; cheap underwear shops, cheap and tacky jewellery/pawn shops, overpriced trainer shops and too many fast food joints. Newark is New Jersey's biggest city. It resides about eight miles west of Manhattan and about two miles north of Staten Island. However, we didn't have time to go find the Staten Island Ferry and take a ride, so we just had a quick look around, finding nothing of much interest. The people though were friendly and asked all about Bearsac when he waved at them.

Turning a corner, I near collided with a very dapper and hip black man who was approaching the winter of his life but strutting like he was in his prime and knew it too well. I realised I was laughing out loud at him, but he took it to be with admiration. . He said:
　　'Hi there, young lady, what a *fiiiiine* day we see ourselves having today.'

My eyes watered with laughter as he walked round his shiny, expensive, gold-capped carved walking stick, doffing his hat as he said this. He shared with Bearsac and me stories of his time in the Vietnam War, his gold-capped tooth glinting in the sun as he spoke. A few days later, in England, when showing my photographs to someone, they said he might have been a pimp, or a wannabe pimp! Pimp or not, his was the easiest and most friendly interaction I had during my visit to the States. But don't get the wrong idea; most people I came across were very friendly, but many seemed to be more than a little intrigued to know what carrying a teddy bear and animating it 'means'.

On my first day back at the office I sat on the stairs for a few minutes sniffing Bearsac's fur before going in. A colleague came to me and asked what was up. I explained I wanted to pack the job in, but couldn't until I got another as I would not get benefits if I just left of my own accord; and also, I didn't want to let the boss down after he had spent money sending me out to Annapolis. She told me I might not have to worry, and to go in and I would find out why. I welcomed the immediate news that we were all to be made redundant, as the business had gone bust. I sorted out my desk and then went to the job centre to get benefit forms with a spring in my step and Bearsac on my back.

A week after leaving, I found out that in the end, the only company in the world that was interested in having a virtual stand at our virtual exhibition was the aviation company the man I'd met in Mammoth, near Annapolis worked for!

Bearsac on a Water Hydrant Annapolis

Chapter Two

Italy
May 2002

Day 1

There is something about the sound of the word *Italy* that had always drawn me to the idea of going. In 2002 having not yet heard of EasyJet, I saw a coach trip - advertised in a travel agent window in Barnet - as my only affordable option. I always liked the shape of Italy, looking at it on maps as a kid. It is said to be like a boot, and I think it has a frilly garter sticking over the top, which seems a shape more suited to France, with its Moulin Rogue in Paris.

The coach to Dover was fine, but the holiday coach failed to turn up and the replacement was totally inadequate. This unluxury coach was cramped, with little leg space and the air conditioning had packed in – not ideal conditions for a coach trip of some 22 hours. Uncomfortably hot all day and most of the night, it cooled down to a chill when going through the French and Swiss Alps in the early hours. The discomfort was worth it though, as we passed the lakes in the Swiss Alps at the break of dawn, where the mist flirted with the glistening water in the cool sunshine.

We had plenty of stop-offs en route, which was just as well, as Bearsac could not handle the heat too well with his fur. I had to agree with Bearsac that the food in the French, Swiss and Italian service stations was almost as bad as in the UK, but at least we weren't overwhelmed by the smell of fry-ups. However, the strong coffee aromas gave me a headache, so we spent most of the stop-off breaks outside, getting away from it. Behind one service station was a sewage farm; for some reason, when back on the coach I told the others all about it and the photographs I had taken of it, they expressed how odd they thought it was to photograph such a thing as part of my holiday snaps. Even odder, they must have thought, that I photographed my teddy bear beside the sewage farm!

The coach trundled past wild flower-touched fields, soft rolling hills and featureless landscapes, many towns and villages, but it was hard to stay interested when it was so hot and stuffy, and some twat nearby was playing with some game that bleeped and flashed. Sat in front of us were a mother a daughter, though they seemed more like three generations of females, with the daughter in her late teens to early 20s but going on 50 years old one moment and dropping down to ten years old the next. She stuck her little nose up in the air when Bearsac spoke to her, and sulked that I wasn't bothered but rather just laughed; she sulked further when her mother showed appreciation of Bearsac and winked at me as if to apologise for her daughter. Hording her battery-operated fan to cool herself, only occasionally holding it up to her mother's flushed face, Little Miss Sulk folded her arms across her chest in a huff once the battery had run down.

It occurred to me that there were rather a lot of turquoise vehicles frequenting the Italian roads. Some looked most strange, like what one would maybe expect Barbarella to drive and convert to flight mode at the flick of a switch. I wanted to get the driver to speed up so we could catch them up and I could take photographs and wave Bearsac's paw at the people in the strange vehicles, but I decided to just count them instead. Once bored with counting turquoise vehicles, I just decided to catch up on writing notes of the trip so far – not that I found writing too easy in motion; it was as though a spider had got its legs covered in ink and had darted about all over the paper.

The coach met with a traffic jam and stood for some time beside a cattle truck full of creatures. Just like us, they stood stuck in traffic, in wide-eyed innocence, a rack of lambs. They knew not of the ordeal facing them at their journey's end, they knew not the plates that they were destine to grace once they had been chopped up, sold to humankind and burnt. Bearsac knew all too well their destiny, and he was quiet for a while, at least until sweets found their way to him by way of another of the tour group. The throaty chugging of a tractor in a field on the other side of the road distracted us from the animals.

'I've never seen a turquoise tractor before,' calls out Bearsac. 'How many vehicles in this colour does this country possess.'

Day 2 - Fiuggi

Arrival at the hotel in Fiuggi was on the afternoon of the following day. Although basic, it was very clean and the staff superb, very friendly and helpful. Bearsac's teddy friend (Rizla), who had been travelling in the confinement of the suitcase, was immediately let out. After hugging the three bears and taking them to have a quick look around the hotel, I had a much-needed cold shower; I luxuriated in its coolness, refreshing my scorched body.

With Bearsac I had a quick explore of the hotel's surrounding area before returning to see who amongst the tour group wanted to go into town for food. We headed into Fiuggi town with Anne, a lovely lady, with whitish-blond hair from Glasgow, who was on the coach trip alone.

Whilst we were looking at postcards we asked the nice lady in the shop where we could get some tasty but inexpensive pizza.
'Yummy yum yum pizza,' Bearsac added.

We didn't understand the woman's directions, so she very kindly locked up and took us. The warm, intoxicating aroma of garlic greeted us well before we even entered. My *zucchini* (courgette), thin-based pizza was simple and not smothered in thick strands of rubbery cheese; it tasted better than anything in the pretentious places in London that claim to serve 'the best Italian pizza in the world'. I offered some to Bearsac and Rizla but was thankful that they couldn't really eat it. I later had to give in to temptation and devour some *gelato* (ice-cream). The sweet fresh scent of strawberry hit my senses first, preparing my palate for the coming delights as I raised the soft cool *gelato* to my anticipant tongue. The first tongueful tasted like heaven and filled me with warmth as it slithered sexily, caressing its way slowly down my orgasmic throat. Intoxicated by its spell, I *uuummmmed* my way to another tongueful, letting it melt and drip down the sides of my mouth just so I could lick my lips with a smack and *uuummmmm* some more.

A stray cat sat in the middle of a road, its ear cut. It was not moving, so fearing it might be badly injured, Anne suggested I put some ice-cream just out of reach to see if it would move. After some hesitance, it did and lapped up the ice-cream whilst an agile old man came rushing over saying,

'No give cat *gelato*, no good.'

He proceeded to spoon out some cat food, which brought forth an onrush of stray cats in an assortment of colours. The man stroked and greeted some, telling us their names. I should think these are cats of many names.

The sinking sun draws people to mingle, the air heady with flirtations. As darkness closes in deeper, the street scene changes its rhythm to suit, and the aroma of garlic becomes more prominent on the cooling air. Couples stroll, hand-in-hand, Armani suits and Gucci handbags upon their persons. Much posing is taking place but little other action. Not that I, myself, have noticed this; but Anne points it out and together we watch and make comparative notes to the track-suit-bottomed, baseball-capped lager-louts back in the UK.

After some time Anne, myself, Bearsac and Rizla strolled slowly back to the hotel, where we escaped the group getting drunk in the bar and sought refuge in our own respective rooms. Tired from the coach and stressed at having had no time to myself, I was in bed before midnight after a wind-down session sitting in the wardrobe. Sitting in confined spaces seems to calm me down and allow me to unwind with a greater sense of solitude than just being alone at large in a room.

Day 3

I awake just before 4am and sit out on the balcony a while with Bearsac before getting dressed to take the three bears out for photographs. As the crickets slowly start to simmer down, birds fill the sound-waves they vacate.

We leave the hotel at 4.50am; it's still dark. To our surprise, we find the hotel front door locked. I find the key that I then re-member has been left aside for early risers and unlock the door, checking we can get back in without it before putting it back. We come to the gate only to find that locked too. It is too dark to see the keyhole to know if any of the keys will unlock it, so we all climb over the gate.

We stroll gently along the road, listening to the sounds of crickets, birdsong, dogs barking and howling in the distance; cats, well, you know. The gentle breeze lifts the sweet scent of flowers into the air, replacing the enticing aroma of fresh garlic from the night before. It is now just getting light, but the sun hides behind the moun-tains, so no sunrise photographs, which is what I got up early for.

Walking past a house, we spot a small dog sat using its front legs to turn itself around and around on the spot. Is this some strange ritual Italian dogs perform at sunrise? Bearsac speaks to it, asking why it is turning around like that on its bum, but the dog, for some reason, doesn't reply but just carries on this peculiar act.

The only people around are delivery men dropping off bread and newspapers. We sit on the grass in the middle of a roundabout, just for the hell of it. Choc-Ice points out that the yellow and red tulips surrounding the perimeter of the roundabout are alternated, apart from one bit where there are two yellows next to each other. Of course this really means I noticed this myself. I guess a lot of people would think it sad to notice such things, but what the hell.

Fiuggi was originally called Anticoli di Campagna. It is situated about 70 km Southeast of Roma (Rome). A hillside town nestled between two mountains with lush green forests; it is beautiful, with pretty buildings, dappled woods, and wild flowers along forgotten paths. The weather seems to be dictated by the mountains in the mid mornings when a beautiful mist hovers gracefully, but almost threatening to spoil your day. However, by late morning the soaring sun melts away the mist and a young energetic teddy bear and owner require water.

There have been claims of healing properties in the water of Fiuggi. It is said that during the 1300s Pope Boniface VIII had claimed the mineral water from the Fiuggi spring had healed his kidney stones. About 200 years later they were rumoured to have relieved the artist Michelangelo of what he called "the only kind of stone I couldn't love." Soon the miracle water *'acqua di Fiuggi'* was being bottled and was sent to all royals across Europe.

Fiuggi is really two towns on a hillside. The medieval old town, 'Fiuggi Città', is 2500 feet above sea level. The more modern spa town is called 'Fiuggi Fonte' after its fountains.

Back at the hotel I breakfasted, slightly miffed that my eggs were too hard-boiled and not as I like them, moist just in the middle of the yolk. The coach left at 8.30am for Pompeii. On the drive to Pompeii, the three bears play a game of seeing who can get the most waves from the lorry drivers we pass. They take it in turns and as nearly all the drivers wave each time, it's declared a draw. The other tourists have given up being amused by watching the three bears play the game long ago, but I am in my element.

Our first trip of the holiday was to Montecassino Monastery. It is up on a mountain, which is reached by a narrow, poppy-lined road winding round and round until you get to the top where the views are populated by poppies and the gentle breeze radiates the smell of herbs. The Monastery was founded by St. Benedict around about the year 529. Montecassino became renowned for the life of its Founder. It was seen as a holy place, and one of beautiful art and culture. It was rebuilt in the early 18th century a very long time after it was destroyed by the Longobards of Zotone, Duke of Beneventum, in about 577.

This St. Benedict geezer was born about 480 A.D. in Norcia. In Rome - where he went to live after studying - he became disgusted by the vice that was present in the city. He abandoned everything and retired to Subiaco, where he lived like a hermit. Monks living nearby asked him to become their Superior and Mentor. St. Benedict accepted, but they were none too happy when he tried to correct their far from perfect way of life. The monks tried to murder him with a goblet full of poison but failed when he smashed the goblet. After having founded 12 convents, St. Benedict left Subiaco and headed south with a few disciples in tow. He chose the mountain *Monte cassino* for the monastery. He died on March 21st 547 A.D. His body, and that of his sister,

Scolastica, rests beneath the High Altar. There is a small oratory dedicated to St. John the Baptist built at the top of the mountain, or so the information leaflet I was given by a woman in a strange bonnet-style hat told me, but I was not going to walk all the way around to find it. If I came by it on my travels, then fine.

On 15th February 1944, during the final stage of World War Two, Montecassino, a German stronghold, was on the firing line between the Germans and the Allies: this peaceful place of prayer, which served as shelter to civilians; was destroyed in about three hours. People died in what they thought of as a safe haven. The Abbey was rebuilt according to the original architectural plans under the 'Where and As Was' program of Abbot Ildefonso Rea, its reconstructor. The reconstruction took over ten years; the Italian State footed the bill.

I photographed the three bears at various sites around the monastery, where I had to cover up out of respect, and so was uncomfortably hot by the end of it. Bearsac had no trousers on, and as for the other two bears, Rizla had only a bow tie and Choc-Ice was a completely bare bear. I somehow think the rules don't apply to teddy bears though.

We returned to the coach, which was now like a sauna, to head for Pompeii ruins, continuing our game of waving at the lorry drivers. One of the lorry drivers must have used his CB radio to tell the drivers in front of him to look out for some teddies, as when we passed the next couple of lorries they were already looking out of the window, waiting to see them and wave.

Pompeii

Before entering the Pompeii ruins we browsed through the nearby market. Stallholders practically chase you down the street trying to flog you their tacky wares. A three-legged dog took a shine to the three bears and followed us around with a hobble. Thankfully the busy road saw him off as we returned to meet the rest of the group and our tour guide for the ruins.

Our guide had a flag with a picture of a witch on a broomstick; it read 'Wife on board'. He held it up for us to follow so we didn't get lost, every so often lowering it as his arm tired. I held up Bearsac in the same fashion for the stragglers at the back, who may not have been able to see the flag. Bearsac, by now, had become well known to the group, so was more recognisable than some poxy flag.

Pompeii, home to the Romans in the first century, became ruins after Mount Vesuvius, a volcano, erupted in 79AD, puking up it contents and burying Pompeii under many metres of ash and pumice. I often now think of Pompeii when using a pumice stone to rub away dead skin from my feet. The thriving city was lost for nearly 1700 years before its rediscovery in 1748. The residents of Pompeii did not know Vesuvius was a volcano, so it must have come as some surprise when it erupted.

The ruins of Pompeii are big and a good many more hours than the two we had are needed to see the place. It was athrong with tourists from all over the globe and getting people free photographs was very hard. Walking around gives a good impression of how the Romans lived their lives in the city and homes that are well preserved for their age. How many of today's buildings would still be standing in their glory after such length of time, let alone after such destruction? There were many people and animals buried under the ash; some skulls have been preserved and are on show in glass cabinets, as are casts of bodies that have left indentations where they have been covered.

I was amazed by the works of art painted onto the walls and floors. Beautifully preserved frescoes throw a light on everyday life of that long ago time. Bearsac lowered the tone by shouting 'Look at the boobies and willies!'

A small building still has its roof intact; it has a dome open at the top, where dust particles swirl and dance in the sunlight that streams through. It was a relief to take shelter from the heat for a few minutes and as I watched the dust dance, I imagined it to be the remains of dust from 79AD.

The streets of Pompeii were built so that water could flow down the roads; the paving is considerably higher than the road. Stepping stones offered pedestrians a way to cross to the other side without getting their feet wet or stepping in the horse poo and human poo that was poured out onto the roads. The gaps between the stepping stones allowed horse-drawn carts to pass through; it must have been earth-shatteringly loud to live on the most used streets. Being here brought the history of Pompeii alive to me in a way that I had not experienced from documentaries; the smell of dusty stonework set off my imagination, filling its every crevice with the smells of raw sewage, the sweat of horses and the richness of wines and foods.

Bearsac, Rizla and I paid a visit to the local Pompeii brothel. Choc-Ice would not come in on moral grounds and so stayed outside with Aunty Anne, who teddy sat him. He was still overcome by the pictures of naked ladies that Bearsac had pointed out and ogled, and without any shame. Bearsac and Rizla sat expectantly on the hard concrete bed, but to no avail; the ladies of the night had been consumed by the eruption some many hundreds of years ago. We saw such a small section of Pompeii as part of a guided tour group. If you get the chance to go, don't go as part of a tour group. As we returned to the coach, I looked up at Mount Vesuvius, realising that it had not erupted during our close proximity. I nodded it a silent thank you.

Once back in Fiuggi I went to the local Co-op, purely out of curiosity, and checked out what they had in there and the prices. The booze was cheap and had I known whilst still in Fiuggi that the warehouse in Calais was more expensive, I would have stocked up my drinks stash there rather than at Calais. The coach drivers, on our departure day, took us to a shop opposite the Co-op that has their logo in the window. They said it was a cheap place to buy drink to take home, but it was more expensive than the Co-op. They must get some back-hander from the place for taking everyone there, telling them how good it is. So if you go to Fiuggi, check out for yourself before you part with your dosh.

The evening saw Bearsac and I on a stroll as the sun kissed the sky goodnight and buried its orange head below the horizon. The woods we found ourselves passing smelt peaceful and beckoning, but I was wary of entering in the now eerie dark. A stirring in some long grass caught the corner of my eye; I stopped, holding my breath. Seconds passed, then a passing car's lights caught two eyes out in green. As my eyes adjusted to the dark, I could just make out the form of a fox. Conveniently, and as if by magic, a tree stub whispered to my awareness: I sat on it clutching Bearsac as we both strained our eyes in search of the fox we had already lost sight of.

Luck was not with us and after about two minutes of sitting and scanning, we gave up and headed back to the hotel. However, a couple of minutes later and again out of the corner of my eye, I noticed movement. Stilling my vision, I saw again green eyes staring back at me in the darkness. This time though there were tiny orange lights moving above like a galaxy of orange stars dancing. I guess they must have been fireflies or something, but the fox didn't seem to notice them, it just seemed to be following us. Bearsac got a bit scared at the prospect of being eaten, but I reassured him that the fox would be too scared to get close and would run off if we got too near.

For about a minute we all stood staring at each other, mesmerized. I suddenly wondered why I could see its eyes in the dark for all this time and realised that behind me a car was parked up in a lay-by with its headlights on. Once my eyes had adjusted to the beam from the headlights, I realised a man was stood beside the car wanking, and watching me. I tried to remember the Italian for 'you have a very small penis', which I had learned from a website listing useful Italian phrases for tricky situations like having men rub their penis up against you on crowded public transport, but my brain failed me. Instead, in English, I just told him to be careful he didn't run down his car battery and then walked at a quickened pace back to the hotel and told the manager.

Politeness took me and the three bears onto the porch to social-ise awkwardly with some others from the coach tour. A couple in their 50s wanted a go of the bears, holding them and sitting them on their laps; the bears were happy at this as they got to have a few sips of their drinks. The couple told the bears about Albert, a teddy bear of some many years that had been the woman's companion since childhood. The bear was not with his owner on this trip, but he had escorted her on past trips until he became too old to travel. Bearsac told those assembled about the wanker and the fox; the lady holding Choc-Ice covered his ears to protect his innocence.

Day 4 - Rome

Next day the coach heads out at 8.30am for Rome, about 70km north. The drive should take between 45 and 60 minutes. There is not much traffic until a little before entering Rome, but that's not as bad as London; the smell of petrol fumes though is nauseating and I cover my nose by burying it into Choc-Ice. I kiss Choc-Ice absent-mindedly but realisation means I have to kiss Bearsac and Rizla too, to make it fair for them and feel even physically for me. However, the kisses don't feel even in comparison to one another and I start a short ritual of alternating kisses on to each bear's head until I feel satisfied I have it even and I am no longer disturbed by the smell of petrol. The journey, which included a 15-minute break for no apparent reason, took about two-and-a-half hours. Lots of the group feel that the drivers have deliberately done this so as to spoil our holiday, as they both seem to begrudge other people having a life and seem to see us as an inconvenience. Neither of them have families to call home, and so spend months away from their lonely homes in a job they make a show of hating. The much bigger of the two is a complete swearword beginning with the capital letter W. But at least we can trust their driving ability, even if their people skills are totally inadequate. The big one is so ignorant and obnoxious. But one gets the feeling the other, away from the influence of Big Daddy, could, with training, be reasonably OK; after-all, monkeys can be trained to play nicely, can't they?

We are amused a number of times at various sets of traffic lights by different men, mostly on mopeds, gesturing to other drivers that have disrespected their road space. We can't hear over the loud din of the busy streets but we know they are not just making polite small-talk about the weather.

The coach was parked up in an underground coach-park and one of the drivers, the slightly nicer one, escorted us to St Peters Square and pointed out the big doors where we are to meet at 5.20pm.

It is now about 11am, so despite the long journey we still have quite a bit of time. We team up with a couple from the group and head for the Coliseum through the bustling streets of Rome, noise all around us. It's a real contrast from the quiet, laid-back Fiuggi. The drivers in Italy as a whole are terrible, but Rome must be the world's capital for bad driving. Crossing the road is terrifying; they ignore lights and have trouble steering; hundreds of mopeds zip around, many with dogs aboard. We saw one man open the tiny box on the back of his moped and take a live dog out, the dog totally unfazed by its mode of travel.

After following directions we found the Coliseum, where the couple and we parted ways. Skinny men, dressed as gladiators, charge lots of money to have their photograph taken with you using your own camera. One of them grabbed Bearsac and growled at him. Bearsac screamed *'Nonlo tocchi'* (Don't touch). Street peddlers pestered us with rubber toys that they wanted us to buy. We didn't want any but we hacked down the price from five euros to one euro for these kids behind us in the queue that were interested. The admission fee for the Coliseum was eight euros, which is about £5.

It is smaller inside than I had imagined and the 40 minutes we spent in there could have quite easily been done in 15 if you were in a rush. I was glad that I'd decided not to go on the guided tour of Rome as we could go where we wanted at our own pace. It was very easy to tag onto a group with an English-speaking guide, even standing next to the guide. We learnt a bit about the Coliseum and were free to do our own thing. The guides are so self-admiring they don't seem to notice intruders – no surprise really, seeing as they have their heads so far up their arseholes.

The Coliseum was built in 72 AD, during the reign of Emperor Vespasiano. It was originally called The *Amphitheatrum Flavium*. The name Coliseum was used because it was this huge oval shaped building stood next to the colossal statue of Roman

Emperor Nero. The arena could hold over 50,000 people. It was over 160 feet high and had 80 entrances. The events held there were: gladiator fights, animal hunts and mock battles. Slaves were used as fighters, there were even volunteers and up to 10,000 people would be killed during these fights in the name of entertainment. Seating in the Coliseum was made of marble for the upper classes and wood for the lower. Linen was used on the top storey to protect spectators from the sun.

We met one German and a lot of American and Canadian tourists who just loved the two bears – Bearsac and Rizla that is; Choc-Ice had a hangover and had stayed at the hotel. Some of them took photographs and said they would check out the website. At one stage there was a bigger crowd around the bears than the groups being guided around. It was a bit overwhelming having all this camera clicking going on around us, but nothing the bears or myself couldn't handle.

On leaving the Coliseum we headed towards the Trevi Fountain, which is not too far away. It was built and rebuilt in the first millennium, including contributions from Pietro da Cortona and Bernini. Nicola Salvi completed it between 1732 and 1751. The history of the Trevi Fountain goes back to ancient Rome. It was built where a virgin was said to have found the spring intersecting *tre vie* – three ways. White in colour, it has winged horses jumping out of the water. It's big, and it's hard to get the whole of the thing in when photographing. There were lots of people getting in the way, trying their best not to. Bearsac and Rizla dipped their feet into the cool soft water and I threw a coin in with my right hand over my left shoulder, so that one day I might come back to Rome. The song 'Three Coins in a Fountain' was about the Trevi Fountain. There were many more than three coins, as my coin joined hundreds of others on the pristine floor of the fountain.

Around the back and a couple of corners later, we were heading towards The Spanish Steps. A quick visit to a tourist information booth confirmed we were going in the right direction. My good sense of direction worked out what would likely be a short cut to the steps. We climbed some back steps which took us to the top of the Spanish steps and the Church of Trinita de Monti, where there are artists painting and sketching away. Arriving on the steps at the top looking down seemed to spoil the surprise. It would be much better, I thought, had they suddenly loomed up in front of us in their entire splendour. The moral of the story is - don't take any short cuts.

On the steps, people, mostly men, called out *'bambino'* or *'bella bambino'* as Bearsac greeted them and waved. Bearsac responded, saying in English 'I'm not a baby', and 'I'm four and three quarters' in Italian. At the bottom of the steps was a fountain, much smaller than the Trevi, but still beautiful. Shaped like a boat, it appeared to be sinking. We drank from it and a lady took a photograph of us after asking if the bears were my bambinos. Spotting three naval officers, I asked them to pose with the bears for a photograph. They obliged willingly, which led to lots of women asking them to pose for photographs. We thanked them and they chimed together *'ciao, bella bambino'* as Bearsac waved them goodbye.

The pathetic sound of mopeds has me covering my ears with my hands and shouting for them to shut up. A man looks at me and laughs as he politely steps into the road to let me pass. Spotting the Antico Caffe Greco, we head towards it. It is closed for re-decorating so we miss the chance to eat at one of the oldest cafés in the world, founded in 1760. Amongst it frequenters were once the likes of Byron, Keats, Shelley and Casanova, who no doubt pondered and flirted over a coffee or two. Judging from the menu outside, it was just as well it was closed, as it is rather expensive.

The heat takes us to the back streets, shielded from the direct sun by the buildings. Bearsac knocks on the windows of ground floor offices and receptions with his nose and gets a few startled looks, and even one wave; but most people don't even look up from their desks. It seems that this is the time of day when women file their nails. Well, there are three women doing so at their desks anyway; these ones just stick their noses in the air at Bearsac. Maybe I should have got Rizla out of my bag and had the two bears 69 each other in the window, but I didn't.

We continue walking the back streets, seeing the non tourist elements of Rome. I feel sorry for men in the UK; they don't know where they stand with us women. If they hold open a door for a woman, or step aside to let her pass on a narrow path, they risk being labelled sexist. If they let a door shut in her face, they are deemed rude (which of course it is, but rude to do to any gender). In Italy, and especially, it seems, in Rome, men know their place. Italian Women's Lib seems to mean women demand their right to be treated like 'ladies'.

Walking down a back street, a lady in a highly tailored suit stops abruptly in front of a suited man in her path. He knows what is expected of him, but it takes a while for him to come to his senses as he and Bearsac have been conversing for the last few minutes, walking side by side. Nodding at the lady and apologising profusely, the man steps into the road, at risk of getting run down by mopeds with dogs on board. It isn't even as if the path is too narrow, and she is a slender lady. Now all that stands before her and her determination to walk a straight line is scruffy little me, and a talking teddy bear.

The man has stopped – whether to wait for Bearsac and me, or to see what we will do, I don't know. For about five seconds, neither the lady nor I moves . Much tutting comes from the lady's mouth area, though it doesn't move. Bearsac suddenly takes control and growls loudly at her; she screams, steps into the road and runs as fast as her Guccis can carry her! Laughing my head off, I step into the road, even though no-one is now in my path.

I was hoping that Ms. Hoity Toity would look back and see me do so. Mr Man had gone; at least so I thought – but he was just waiting out of sight of the woman and was himself laughing when I passed the office doorway where he was waiting. Mr Man told Bearsac off, shaking his paw as he did so. We talked for a couple of minutes, (that is, the man and I) until he came by his office. He thanked me for making his day and shook my hand, bowing his head at me, maybe guessing I didn't want him to kiss my hand, and again shook Bearsac's paw.

I turned off the back streets and sauntered towards Via Condotti, swinging Bearsac triumphantly. This is where all the top designer names are: Bulgari, Giorgio Armani, Valentino, Versace, Cartier, Jean Paul Gaultier, Chanel and others – not that I'm into any of that nonsense, but for those that are it must be heaven on one street. In my scruffiness I strut into the middle of these designer shops, animating Bearsac in Italian. To our pleasant surprise, he is greeted warmly in each shop we enter, and the staff in each, if they are empty, crowd around to speak to him. It's a real shame that none of these shops have gimmicky teddy bears modelling their lines, as is often the case in opticians in the UK; I'm quite sure we could have come out with a free Bearsac-sized Armani, if that had been the case!

The far end of the street led us into Piazza del Popolo, a large round 'square'! On the other side, up high, is a beautiful park, The Borghes Gardens, where you can look down upon the Piazza del Popolo and most of Rome, or sit and listen to the relative quiet punctuated by the sounds of children at play in the distance.

After this we just roamed around Rome and had the most delicious pizza ever. A cold one, it consisted of sun-blushed tomatoes, great round slabs of marinated buffalo mozzarella, and the most gorgeous marinated mushrooms with fresh basil on a crispy thin base. The strong olive oil used must have had artichokes in it at one time, as there was a strong artichoke taste but no artichoke in sight. Oh, and plenty of garlic. It was too good to share with a teddy bear.

I found that The Roman Forum on Palantine Hill was not as impressive in real life as it looks in books and on TV, but that might be because we didn't get up close. It was, in the old days, the administrative and commercial centre of Rome. Palantine Hill is one of the 'seven hills' of Rome. Originally, the seven hills were separate small settlements and not recognised by the name 'Rome'. It was only when people started to take part in religious games and the separate groups bonded together and drained the marshes separating the hills, that the hills evolved towards becoming a city.

Now we had just over an hour to get back to St Peters Square by 5.20pm. We asked a friendly police-officer which bus to get after running down the street for ten minutes, stopping only to ask a suited man on a scooter if he'd hold the bears for a photograph. We got off the bus before the square to have a quick glance over a bridge at the river, and then sauntered down a road leading back to St Peters Square, only to find it was heavily barricaded off by a line of many police.

We needed to get through the square to visit the Vatican before going back to the coach. We found out that President Bush was in the Vatican for the NATO-Russia summit. The police, of course, could not let us through, but were very helpful and polite. One explained to me that I needed to go right around the square's surrounding buildings. We came to where there was an opening to go underground, where the coach park would be, so we cut through there, trusting my sense of direction, and came out where we expected. This was where the driver had first taken us at the beginning of the day, very near to the Vatican. However, this part too was cordoned off, and there were people ready poised with cameras. Just then President Bush's car drove past, but too soon after I'd arrived at the scene for me to get the shot. (Camera shot that is, not gun shot!) Everyone waved, apart from the bears and me. There was a long convoy of cars behind and once they had all passed, people were let free. By now there was no time to go to the Vatican. So I thought I should write a letter to President Bush, complaining that he had spoilt my chance of visiting the Vatican. (This is something I actually did, but I never got a reply. I was hoping my coin in the Trevi Fountain might have some effect and that I might get a free return flight to Rome another time, to make up for missing out. But clearly President Bush has other things to spend the money on!)

That evening I took Bearsac and Rizla to check out the old town. We walked to the bus station, but could not make out which bus went there from the time-table, as it did not seem to have bus numbers on it. I attempted to ask people, who didn't speak English, which bus went to the old town. I did not know the Italian word for 'old', so I tried to mime it by walking like an old person; much to the amusement of the straight-standing, aged locals. A driver came along and I asked him. He did not understand the word 'old' either, so I said: '*Maddonaica*', which I knew to be in the old town. This did the trick. From what I could make out of his Italian, the driver said it was his bus, and it did not go all the way but dropped passengers off a kilometre away. The driver and all of its four passengers told me this is where I needed to get off. The driver pointed the way to the Maddonaica, which was not in the main part of the old town but perched on its own up a very steep hill of about 1km.

The hill looked like good exercise. I proceeded up it, carrying camera bag and tri-pod, as well as two bears. We met a local lady who we walked with for some time, using some of the tiny Italian I had learnt. We chatted in broken Italian and broken English, then Bearsac thought he'd try out some of his Italian, so he said '*Mi chiamo* Bearsac, *sono quattro e tre quarti.*' (My name is Bearsac, I am four and three quarters) '*Avete tutti i dolci per favoure.*' (Do you have any sweets please).

After that mouthful, the lady simply laughed, 'No.' After a while she bid us '*buona notte,*' (good night) as she turned into her road and we continued upward to the top at a quickened pace, strengthened by the warm aroma of herbs.

Something stirs in the cacti; we stop and look towards where the rustling sound is coming from. The something meows, disclosing its identity, its face peeping out between the spikes. We try to coax it out but the damn cat won't come. We carry on, past an old house with weeds and tiny flowers peeping out of the nooks and crannies between the bricks. At last we are atop the hill.

There she was, all aglow, up on a pedestal, the Lady Madonna. I took a photograph of Bearsac and Rizla sitting outside behaving themselves. A couple of teenagers were hanging around and were probably wondering what this madwoman was doing photographing teddy bears by the Madonna. Their mad dog spent the whole time we were there chasing its tail. Two horses grazed in the dark, not confined to any enclosure, Bearsac took Rizla and me over to say hello and tell them about himself and Rizla. One horse whinnied, looking at the other. Bearsac's paranoia - assuming the horse's whinnying to be mocking in tone - got the better of him and he sulked until I took us into a bar, where I ordered some Italian lemon-soda and a glass of Chianti.

The bar's disco was empty, apart from the wife of the owner dancing. The bar owner looked after us as if we were his personal guests. He spoke of his childhood teddy bear and love of life. Bearsac and Rizla's charms brought to us samples of *arancini di riso* from the generous bar owner. *Arancini di riso* are rice balls coated in breadcrumbs, then fried. They are filled with various delights. The creamy spinach and cheese was my favourite; the spinach spilled out and lay on my tongue like mini hot cowpats. Bearsac preferred the saucy tomato and Rizla favoured the richness of the mushroom. Their round shape and orange colour is where the '*arancini*' bit of the name derives, as *arancia* is Italian for 'orange'. Arancini di riso are Sicilian in origin, and the bar owner spoke of his love of them; his portly belly suggested that this love might be a daily habit.

Too worn out and full up on arancini to continue exploration of the old town, I just ordered another delightful lemon-soda and then the two bears and I returned to the hotel and had a glass of Cynar, an Italian liquor made from artichokes. It was bitter and sweet at the same time. We then went to join Choc-Ice in bed.

Day 5 - Surrento

We arose, apart from Choc-Ice, at about 4.30am and sat on the balcony listening to the symphony of birds and crickets until I showered and went to breakfast at 6 o'clock. The coach left at 6.30 for Surrento in Naples. No Choc-Ice again, he had another hangover – that teddy bear drinks far too much, I'm just glad Bearsac and Rizla only take a few sips.

What a picturesque scene as we passed the Bay of Naples! Small weathered buildings, tiny trees, wild flowers and birds clung to the magnificent cliffs, looking out over the dark blue sea. All the driver could go on about was how the tunnels are frequented by ladies of the night and their punters, as the police are very strict on that sort of thing on the streets. There was a car pulled up by a red light in the tunnel, and it was not a traffic light. The driver gave them a honk. By now everyone was so fed up with the idiot, we didn't even laugh out of politeness, just pity.

Surrento is in southern Italy and is bordered by three bodies of water: the Gulf of Naples, the Gulf of Salerno and the Amalfi coast. Adorned with lemon and orange groves, the bright greens, orange and yellows contrast perfectly against the pastel shades of the buildings. We visited a small lemon grove where they sold lemon liquor, which we sampled. Childhood memories came flooding back – lemon Sherbet Dabs. Yummy, we all agreed, so I bought some in a cute little bottle; the 'sample' woman knew I would have a weakness for it. Bearsac and Rizla played hide-and-seek from me, but I don't miss a trick and photographed them from their hiding place up a lemon tree.

After our lemon delight we strolled through the maze of streets, too narrow for cars, but not too narrow for those pesky moped scooter things that seem to run rife all over Italy. I'm sure they are not meant to use half the roads they do use. Dogs lazed around, some hogging the middle of the roads asleep, dreaming of *gelato*-fed cats, no doubt. We stopped by a wall, which a man stood looking over. From there we could look out to sea. The man, who was British, told us of a little fishing village five minutes' walk away. We followed his directions and found it: Marina Grande. We spent about three hours here. We were stopped by a group of four fishermen who wanted to know 'why you take your teddy bears for a walk?' I told them they couldn't go for a walk on their own. They accepted that like it made total sense. I took the bears' photograph with them as I explained about Bearsac going everywhere with me and how I was also photographing my boyfriend's teddy as a surprise. Despite mention of a boyfriend, the three older men kept trying to match-make the young man and me. One of them wanted to buy Bearsac but, hugging him defensively, I said he was not for sale.

The two bears and I found sun loungers. I thought it would be nice to chill out sunbathing for a couple of hours, seeing as we were by the sea. There were only a few people there, so we had a peaceful couple of hours listening to the waves, the bells of the boats and the church bells that tolled every 15 minutes. I noticed a woman standing on her balcony looking out to sea over the harbour; she had been looking out for a while and had something white in her hand that I assumed was a handkerchief as she kept touching it to her eyes. A woman on a sun lounger near me saw that I was watching the woman on the balcony and told me that she was looking out for her husband, who was a fisherman who had never returned from sea. The woman came out at the same time each day to watch for his return. I'm not sure if this was a true story, but despite the sadness of it for the balcony woman, it is certainly a romantic story for a visitor to the little fishing village taking in the scene.

There was some beautiful Neapolitan Opera pouring out loudly across the waves from one of the restaurants. We went to eat there and sat in the sun eating spaghetti *vongole alle* (with clams); it was nice but not great. I only let the bears have a little taste and kept the rest all to myself; they find it hard to eat s paghetti, and prefer other shaped pasta that is more manageable for teddy bears. Bearsac asked the waiter why there are so many pasta shapes that taste the same and why don't they run out of fancy names for them. The waiter told him:

'In Italia, food should be beautiful and unique like the women and hav'a beautiful names of their own.'

The staff and a nice young man that seemed to be a regular user of their sun-deck made a big fuss of the bears. On leaving, I asked the name of the opera singer. It was Franco Corelli, and this music is specifically 'Neapolitan' opera, not Italian.

We stopped in a small square, where I reapplied some factor 25 sun-block before leaving the fishing village to look around the main part of Surrento. We perused a few shops, talked to a few people, and laughed at the funny vehicles driving around. Bearsac groaned as we came to steep stairs built against the cliffs leading down to Marina Piccolo, where the boats leave for the island of Capri.

I then went to take Rizla out of the bag to photograph the two bears against the view. To our horror, Rizla had gone. I took everything out of the bag, fear rising in my racing heart and a lump forming in my throat, but no Rizla. We looked around in a blind panic, hearts beating faster still. After some deep breathing, I clutched Bearsac tightly, his straps wrapped double around my wrist, and retraced our steps as best we could remember in the frenzied maze that was Surrento. We asked lots of people in English and broken Italian if they had seen a small brown teddy bear with a bow tie, as we had lost it. After about two hours of fruitless searching, it was time to head back for the coach. What was I going to tell my boyfriend, who owned Rizla? He didn't even know he was on holiday with me. I wanted to surprise him by taking photographs of Rizla in Italy and I'd even got him a teddy bear passport.

Back at the hotel, we had to first break the bad news to Choc-Ice, who had only just sobered up. We were all three very upset. Not feeling like going out in the evening, we had an early night. I didn't sleep much as the couple in the room above were shagging all night and it sounded like the bed was moving across the tiled floor. How could they shag when Rizla was lost?

Day 6 - Last day

On our last morning we took a couple of cabs with some of the others from the tour to the market in the old town. Preferring to be alone, we decided where to regroup later and went our own ways. Thursdays bring a market catering for the locals, who always make you feel welcome. The warmth and richness of Italian accents can be heard throughout the market as housewives gossip as they go about purchasing their daily bread and local produce of fruit and vegetables.

The housing is amazing; hidden away on small, maze-like narrow cobbled streets, with steep steps and hills. The shady streets are a welcome shelter from the heat of the day. Colourful ethnic rugs hang over the balconies, being aired. The aroma of old-fashioned Italian home cooking pours through the windows on the warm current of air and gently kisses my face before entering my nostrils and softening me with its hypnotising effect. Down one narrow lane an old woman sits in the doorway of her house making lace. Opposite her, in the lane, sits a rickety lady on a rickety looking chair. Bearsac is greeted with much warmth and kisses by the lady on the rickety chair; the lady of the house is a little more reserved and engrossed on her lace making.

We also chat to locals outside the pretty church with drinking fountains outside, attended regularly by the thirsty. It is soon time to get cabs back to the hotel and depart for the long homeward journey.

The last day was a sad day as departure days normally are. But this was marked with a profound sadness. We had to leave without our furry friend Rizla.

'He'll feel lost and lonely for a while,' I said, 'but he will soon get over it as he has the whole of Surrento to roam about in.'

'I bet he'll go to live in that lemon grove Bearsac told me they hid in,' said Choc-Ice.

'Or the Marina Grande,' Bearsac added. 'He won't forget us, will he Debra?' Bearsac asked.

'No of course he won't,' I replied, though I was not too sure.

With fast film in our cameras for the assumed early morning light, we were ready for Switzerland and the lakes. The bad news was that this time we were travelling in the middle of the night, so we had to content ourselves with looking at the lights instead. This was not such a shame for Bearsac as his camera is not real but just one of those toys that display photographs each time you click the button. Again I didn't sleep on the coach; so once on the ferry from Calais to Dover I was not in the best of spirits to join in singing with people in England shirts. Bearsac was wearing his England shirt, one that I made for him. The World Cup 2002 was to start the following day.

When the next day came, it was not the World Cup I had on my mind but telling Alan about the loss of Rizla. I didn't beat around the bush. The first thing I said on entering his room was: 'I have bad news'. He knew straight away; before I even told him. He knew, as he had realised Rizla had gone from the den where he hides the teddies I have given him when his friends come round, so they don't see them! He took the news silently at first but then voiced his anger at my taking Rizla. He was clearly upset at the loss. Later that night, he lit a candle and sat quietly playing sombre music on his PC. Bearsac was with me but there was no Rizla with Alan. I didn't even know he had liked Rizla that much, but he said that because I'd got Rizla for him he did; and now I'd taken him away and lost him, and he missed him.

I dedicate this chapter to Rizla and to Alan.

Hiding up a Lemon tree with Rizla

Chapter Three

Switzerland
November 2002

Day 1 - Saturday 9ᵗʰ November 2002

Shortly after I had heard of EasyJet, I learnt that there are youth hostels worldwide that aren't just for youths; I had thought they were only in the UK. Grieving over missed opportunities, I prepared for my first EasyJet flight.

Bearsac and Choc-Ice had to pass through the x-ray machine at Luton Airport. The metal under Choc-Ice's nose showed up very strongly and I was concerned that it might cause some suspicion as his nose has been hanging off since Alan punched him one time. Bearsac spoke to people in the departure lounge, and to two nice ladies working on the checkout in Boots, which for some reason stank of egg mayonnaise.

Waiting over an hour in the noisy departure lounge was driving me loopy. PA announcements seemed never-ending and two kids were running around squeaking nearby. I moved away to another area but they were running everywhere, so it made no difference where I sat. I tried to keep calm by hugging Bearsac and Choc-Ice, it helped a bit, but the little brats were just too squeaky, and their mother's voice could have stripped paint.

The man behind me in the boarding queue, wearing a faded brown corduroy jacket with too-short sleeves, was clearly annoyed he was not first in line. He created such a scene about people rushing to be first in the queue, even though the only reason I was first and not him was because my micro-scooter was faster than his sprinting in getting to the holding point! To emphasize his pettiness, I offered to let him stand in front of me but he stuck his nose in the air, claiming it was not important and he didn't care if he was last, which brought a cry of 'Get to the back then' from another man further back.

'I think he's calling your bluff, old bean,' I said to Mr Corduroy. Stifled laughter rose from various segments of the queue at the Mr Bean pun, which Mr Corduroy did not pick up on. Did this man not possess a mirror?

The plane was not full and we managed to get a seat each, I think mainly because people avoided sitting next to me; they probably thought me insane in the membrane as I had belted both bears into the seats next to me. The woman sitting on the other side of the aisle seemed to be trying to attract my attention; but when I looked at her she went red. Bearsac asked her if she was OK; she hid behind the in-flight magazine. Bearsac suggested she join him in a sing-song; she cleared her throat, flicked the magazine and crossed her legs. Bearsac told Choc-Ice that that meant she fancied him. I'm not quite sure of her expression, but I don't think she was too amused. Maybe she was suffering cold turkey on the non-smoking plane. The crevice like creases surrounding her mouth bore testament to the fact that she had clearly been loyal to cigarettes for most of her life.

The number 10 bus rattled its way to the centre of Geneva, which is where we were to stay in a hostel. My efforts at speaking the tiny bit of French I had taught myself before coming seemed to be appreciated here, unlike in France. (Although in most of Switzerland they speak German, Geneva, is known as 'Romandy', or the French-speaking part of Switzerland). English is widely used as a common language, since about one third of Geneva's population is foreign due to Geneva being home to many international establishments.

Bearsac immediately conversed with a cuddly toy vulture that sat on the reception desk at City Hostel. A number of people were watching a film in the sitting room; I guess the rain had put them off going out.

We explored the hostel before excitedly going to see Lake Geneva, which is really Lake Léman but called Lake Geneva in Geneva. I had Bearsac strapped to my back whilst I set up the camera and tri-pod, but he moaned until I strapped him to my front instead so he could see the coloured lights, which appeared to slip into the water and take a gentle swim.

Switzerland is said to be the country of three Cs: cheese, chocolate and clocks. Some would say four Cs, thinking of cuckoo clocks, which people assume come from Switzerland, but which actually originate from the Black Forest area of Germany; so I will just say three Cs. However, in a Swiss clock shop, in which we sheltered from the rain, there were a few cuckoo clocks on the wall and shelves. The grinding of the many clocks in the shop sounded warm, but then on the hour, the cuckooing shook me out of my skin, out of the shop and back into the cold and rain. Next time I go into a clock shop, I will avoid doing so on the hour. To think there are 60-minutes in an hour and I picked three minutes from those 60, and one of them was the cuckoo minute.

Even self-catering in Geneva is expensive; but after purchasing some food for dinner and being tantalised by the competing sweaty aromas of different cheeses - displayed like works of art, we headed back to the hostel to cook. We passed in the street the fattest cat that I had ever seen. It had layers of fat hanging over its eyes, so it moved very slowly. It must have had legs, but they could not be seen under it vast bulk. Off-white, it resembled an enormous furry puffball mushroom with two triangles sticking out at one end, and a furry snake at the other.

After eating, Bearsac and I headed down the road, passing Fat Cat again - who had not moved an inch, despite water dripping from a basket of flowers above it. Maybe Fat Cat couldn't feel it through all the fur.

We spent some time relaxing in a piano bar – at least until a group of well-heeled drunken women came in and got on my nerves with their silly hyena-like laughs drowning out the tinkering piano. I now had a headache, so returned to the hostel to have quite an early night. As is common with hostels, one often shares with the opposite sex. I shared with two men, one very nice young man from New York who was studying in Scotland. The other crept in during the early hours and left after just a couple of hours' snoring, so we did not get to speak to him.

Day 2

I lay awake a few hours before getting up about 7.30ish; exploring for about ten hours in the drizzly rain made up most of our day. Despite the rain, I enjoyed taking photographs of grey. Greys really capture the scene of a beautiful wet Geneva; it was like all the colour had taken itself on holiday and given grey a chance for a beauty-sleep. People's attitude to the rain here seems so much better than ours in England; it's simply a weather condition and it doesn't stop play. People stroll through the park greeting casual passers-by and having long conversations with friends. They smile under their fancy designer umbrellas. I think they use the rain as an excuse to show off their rainproof pride and joy. I enjoyed confusing people by having Bearsac speak to them; two women huddled together, their umbrellas imtately touching as they whispered to each other, staring at us.

On my Swiss micro-scooter - purchased in London - we scooted first away from the main part of town and the tourist attractions. The park we soon found ourselves in was near-free of people. Across the road in another part of the park were caged animals and birds; the peacocks had a mini Swiss-style chalet as their shelter. They were quiet and looked bored, and paid no attention to Bearsac when he spoke to them. Stuck-up cocks!

We headed back the way we had come, re-smelling in reverse the dampness of wooden benches, wet grass and the lake. We stopped at the lake-edge so Bearsac could speak to the ducks. Not satisfied with merely speaking to them, he began to sing a song we had heard a group of students playing in the kitchen at the hostel. 'All the ducks are swimming in the water, fal la la la lall da', or words to that effect. The ducks swam over, but I think it was just because they assumed they would be fed. Guilty that the ducks had wasted time for nothing, I apologised and dragged Bearsac away, then carried on towards the main part of town.

The most popular attraction in Geneva is the *Jet d'Eau*, which is the tallest fountain in the world – well at least the height of its jet is. We learnt from a friendly local, who stopped to reply to Bearsac's greeting, that the fountain was built in 1891 and that 500 litres of water from the Lake are propelled up in the air at a height of 140 metres and at a speed of 200 km per hour. Sod's law, today it was not working! Our informer also informed us that the Lake itself is 72 km long, 310 metres deep with a volume of 89,000 billion cubic metres. I'm happy I brought my dictaphone with me to record these snippets of information; I couldn't rely on Bearsac to remember it all for me.

As we scoot into the *Jardin Anglais* (English Garden) - which was first created in 1854 – the rain intensified the smell of the many flowers and plants and almost carried us on a current of perfume into another dimension. The park is home to the National Monument, which is a statue of two ladies with their arms around each other. However, the main attraction is the flower clock, created in 1955. It has 6,500 flowers and plants, which are relevant to each season. The time it shows is the precise time – well, it is a Swiss clock!

Scooting became a little difficult as we took in the more hillsome old town with its narrow roads. I admired the square-cut cream stone architecture as I breathed in deeply the scent of wood pre-servative oil on a dark wooden building that impregnated the air. The tallest building in the Old Town is St Pierre Cathedral (St. Peter's Cathedral). Construction of the Cathedral started in 1160 and continued for centuries. Fires led to reconstructions, so it is not as it originally was. It is evidently a building of different styles, such as Gothic and Romanesque. If you look all around it, even the towers differ in style. The stained glass windows are a wonder to look at. The smell of the stone walls in the small chapel at the side was more intense and soothing that the main part of the cathedral, so held me there in contentment for an hour or so with Bearsac sitting on my lap, soaking up the peaceful atmosphere. I am not a religious person, and am a nice Jewish girl, but I love the atmosphere of churches and cathedrals. The entrance to the tower - which would have given us a view from a-high - was, by Sod's law, closed.

Out on the cobbled streets again we took more photographs of grey. Grey lends itself well to Geneva; colour – aside from stained glass – would cheapen its beauty. My eyes were opened to grey by the rain-stained sights in Geneva. Bearsac spotted a St Bernard's dog with a brandy barrel round its neck and pretended he was close to death from freezing, hoping that the dog would rescue him with brandy, just like Stan Laurel in the film 'Swiss Miss'. However, the dog turned out to be stuffed and the brandy barrel was made out of fabric and also stuffed. I sat Bearsac with him for a photograph, he didn't seem to mind.

We then roamed the town and came across a teddy bear shop, a very expensive teddy bear shop (put Bearsac to shame). The two hoity-toity, middle-aged shop assistants weren't quite sure how to react when I plunged into a neatly stacked display of chubby soft teddies, grabbing them into a group hug, oohhing and aahhhing. Their fur smelt of chocolate, which was what had drawn me to them in the first place. I think this act rather put Bearsac's nose out of joint as he told them that although they were cute, they weren't as cute as he was, and that *he* smelt like a real teddy bear.

Five cannons stand at the 'Old Arsenal', which is the head-office of the State Archives. The cannons are meant to protect the town. I wondered if this meant they get fired, but I guess not. I photographed Bearsac on one of the cannons with my Arsenal scarf wrapped around it! The building, which was originally a granary before becoming an arms depot, dates from the 17th century. The archway contains frescoes by Alexandre Cingria (1949) depicting important periods in Geneva's history.

Our return to the hostel for a combined late lunch/early dinner found a new roommate, a young woman from Thailand who lives in Sidney but had been travelling since August. Later the other roommate arrived, a young woman from Japan. We shared experiences and talked about going to the mountains next day but the weather was going to be better on the Tuesday so we thought about the Red Cross Museum instead.

Day 3

After a look around the shops with our two roommates, we came across a deserted organ music box. Four umbrellas kept it, and the two fluffy cats tethered to it, dry. One cat sat in a basket attached and the other sat on top of the music box. But where was the organ grinder? Had he gone for a cup of Swiss hot chocolate, perhaps? Mystery unsolved, we all headed to the Red Cross Museum, which was opposite the visitors' entrance of the United Nations.

By now the sun had dried up all the morning's rain and shone in a pristine blue sky. The museum was very informative, with well-designed displays. The Red Cross flag and the Muslim Red Crescent flag hung above strange looking statue men, who were gagged and blindfolded. This represented the continual world-wide violation of human rights. It is normally ten Swiss francs to get into the museum, but we had a discount of five francs as we were staying at the City Hostel. We watched a short audiovisual slideshow on a large projector screen, which opened at the end to reveal a white room, a statue of a man at table writing and display boxes with information. Printed translucent materials hung from ceiling to floor, all beautifully lit. Racks contained seven million record cards from World War One, detailing prisoners' particulars for the purpose of tracing and reuniting them with their families.

There were more display boxes, with bandages and other Red Cross items, and little rooms with artificial legs to replace legs blown off by mines. The shop had cute little teddy bears with Red Cross T-shirts; Bearsac had a few words with them, telling him who he was.

After all that, Bearsac needed a sit down and sat with three stonily silent gentlemen on a cold stone bench and got no response from them to his questions – they were stony in the literal sense.

As we left the museum, we saw beauty in the shiny wet roads; it must have rained again whilst we were in the museum. It was late afternoon, so the sun was casting long shadows. An orange glow on the distant mountains looked like someone had spread luminous marmalade on them. It made Bearsac think of Paddington Bear.

Back at the hostel we ate then went out on my micro-scooter for a couple of hours before retiring to the bedroom to discuss which mountains we would go to with the woman from Thailand. The Japanese woman was leaving the next afternoon, so she was not going to come to the mountains.

Day 4

Bearsac and I took the 7.30am train to Bern with the Thai woman, where we changed for a train to Interlaken Ost. I was surprised to see just how much people talk to each other on trains in Switzerland. People spoke quite formally to Bearsac; it was as if they didn't even notice he was a teddy bear! Silver lakes and greenery and quaint wooden houses passed by the windows of the train. It was hard to know which side to watch out of; my head must have looked like a horizontal yoyo.

Once at Interlaken Ost, we took the mountain train on the cog-wheel Jungfrau Railway. The Jungfrau Railway was constructed between 1896 and1912; it reaches a height of over 11,000 ft. Jungfraubahn is the highest railway station in Europe. We were tunneling through the inside of mountains; wow, we were inside a mountain! The smell of the inside of mountains was a cocktail of clean soot (if there is such a thing) and rock; I could almost taste this not unpleasant concoction. Train changes at different levels had us rushing for window seats, trying not to slip over. The air was wonderfully fresh and bracing.

When we reached the top of Europe we felt on top of the world as we looked out upon the snow-topped mountains below. It was freezing; I was worried Bearsac's fur would go stiff and break off. The sky, though, was so blue, like when you see holiday brochures and the photographer has used filters to make the sky appear bluer than is real. The sound of lots of husky dogs from lower down took my attention, but I could not detect its exact location as it was echoing off the mountains. I had the over-whelming urge to sing from the top of Europe and sang:

'There's only one Bear called Bearsac, there's only one Bear called Bearsac, walking along, singing a song; walk-ing in a Bearsac wonderland'.

I did get some strange looks, but who cares; my room-mate prob-ably would have joined in but I don't think she knew the words.

We visited the Ice Palace inside the mountain, where we met some polar bears who were colder than we were. Good job they didn't have central heating up there, otherwise the polar bears would have melted - they were made from ice, after all.

On the way back to Geneva we had to change at Bern, the capital of Switzerland. The woman from Thailand was staying in Bern this night so we said our goodbyes and Bearsac and I ran around Bern for an hour before catching our train back to Geneva on the very clean double-decker train. Remembering the fondue sets in the hostel's kitchen, I bought some cheese, white wine and crusty bread to make cheese fondue to share with anyone who happened to be around in the kitchen at the time. It was really a way of trying to find people to speak to by inviting them to join me. A couple from Nigeria who were living in Leeds joined me and we talked about our day and their travels around the world. I was the third adult they had met travelling with a teddy bear.

After fondue, and some slightly more nutritious food, I watched a film in the sitting room – well at least part of a film; the shrill laughter of a girl sat at the back irritated me so much that I decided to retire to the bedroom to write my notes and read. I was very thankful that the bears and I had the room to ourselves that night. As I slipped into the privacy and comfort of my tightly-made bed, I caught the scent of the dewberry shower-gel I used to wash my clothes as they dried on the radiator; it drifted me back to my 20s, when dewberry oil was all the rage. This made me think about how now I would like to travel more and see more of the world, as opposed to travelling around the UK following Gary Numan on tour, like I used to in my 20s.

Day 5

The day started out rainy. We toured the old city. By lunchtime the weather had developed into bright warm sunshine with a few fluffy white clouds. After lunch we joined three Spanish women Bearsac had chatted up the night before, who were just on their way out to go to the shops. I soon got bored of walking around shops (not really my sort of thing) and told the three women I might go for a swim in the lake and would see them later. They thought me very brave to do such a thing at this time of year. 'I'm going to swim in that there lake and there's no turning back,' I told Bearsac. On the way back to the hostel we spotted the organ with the cats again; this time the organ-grinder was present and was grinding away. The cat atop the organ appeared to sleep through the performance and the one in the side basket washed itself, oblivious to Bearsac's greetings; maybe it had been deafened over time by the organ. Perhaps Bearsac should have spoken to the organ-grinder and not the organ grinder's cat!

We returned to the hostel to get my swimming costume but I left Bearsac with Choc-Ice as I didn't know what locker facilities there would be at the lake. Half eagerly and half regretfully, I stepped into the lake, the cold hitting me straight away, like a frozen bullet in the dead of night. A couple more steps and I was up to my waist, people looking at me like I was mad, stopping only long enough to see if I would take the plunge or chicken out. Then before I could think, well at least I've had a paddle; I plunged into the freezing water screaming *froid*! (French for cold) –pronounced *frahh* as though you are freezing cold! I felt revived, excited, thrilled and more alive than ever before. I couldn't help nearly swallowing the water, which surprisingly tasted and smelt so fresh and clean. I then sat on a jetty, basking in the surprisingly warm sun and looking out at the scenes, feeling part of the town, as if I had always lived there and not yet lost sight of its beauty. The climate in Geneva is the same as in England so November is cold. I was therefore proud of myself for swimming in the freezing lake.

Rejuvenated, I returned to the hostel and took Bearsac out on my back scooting, singing 'Bearsac, Bearsac, you're my Bear Sack; you're my little teddy and you ride on my back, Bearsac, Bearsac.' I also sang:

'I love you Bearsac, 'cause you're my teddy bear, I love you Bearsac, I take you everywhere, I love you Bearsac, trust in me when I say.'

Guess the tunes they were sung to.

We scooted round to the opposite side of the lake where we found a children's playground with rope ladders and swings hung from the lake-edge trees. Children played. A brother and sister merrily playing together prompted me to photograph this scene against the lake. I then struggled into one of the tyre swings with my tri-pod and Bearsac on my back. Quite soon, the little girl asked in French if we wanted a push. We understood the word *pousser* (push) from seeing it on endless doors during our shopping expedition with the roommates, so said '*oui, s'il vous plait.*' Brother and sister pulled together in unison at the rope to control the swing. Afterwards, I pulled the rope for the little girl as she sat in it and she went so high she nearly flew into the branches, so I thought it best to slow down! We then joined them in their game of picking up – mid swing – the bark chippings that carpeted the ground of the play area.

After a while we thanked each other and I continued with Bearsac by micro-scooter around the lake, and about three miles out of Geneva, where things quieten and slow down. I felt so happy and free; it had felt so good to play with the children as a child rather than just being the adult pushing the child on the swing.

A few wooden chalets dotted a hillside, smoke puffing gently out of metal chimneys. Tired, we admired the pretty chalets from the lakeside before deciding it was time to head back to Geneva and the hostel. Scooting at rocket speed - overtaking a man on a bicycle - we took turns singing at the top of my lungs.

Stopping for a breather, we sat by the lake, taking it all in for about half an hour before scooting back to our side of the lake, where we came across the only mad person in Geneva. A large man in a large coat with large red buttons, with a large boominating voice waved his large hands in a large display of annoyance at anyone that passed him. The man kept shooing away the swans that were walking down the pavement, having just flown out of the lake, shouting in French at them and waving his arms like a windmill on speed. Daringly, I took a photograph of him but was promptly chased away. Looking back towards the man, I saw how he now cast a silhouette of a windmill. The swans - back on the water - were graceful silhouettes on the silvery expanse.

By the time we got back to the hostel, we had done about nine to ten miles on my micro-scooter and I was worn out. My tiredness, having been well earned, afforded me a nap before dinner and a share in a bottle of wine with two Japanese sisters I met whilst cooking, who thought Bearsac looked like Mr Bean's teddy bear.

Day 6 - Last day

Choc-Ice - who had been ill all week - was now well enough to come to the United Nations office with Bearsac and me. The United Nations office in Geneva is the second main UN office after the one in New York. It is located in the Palais des Nations, which was built in 1936 as the headquarters of the League of Nations. The UN was founded in 1945 after World War Two to maintain peace, develop friendly relations among nations and promote social progress, better living standards and human rights. In 1946 the UN took over the Palais des Nations as its home for working mainly on disarmament and human rights issues.

The guide took us to three different conference rooms: the first holds 900 people, the second 2000. The third is smaller than the other two but more decorative. Paintings in a large hallway have been donated by different nations and the different coloured marble for the floor is also donated, as are the monument things in the gardens, which we saw only from the window on an extremely rainy day.

I was so wet when we got back to the hostel at about 12.30pm that I was still wet five hours later when I rushed out to buy chocolates to take back home. Choc-Ice and Bearsac were under cover so stayed dry. I had packed up already, so couldn't change my clothes. Walking into the chocolate shop, I was hit by that delightful smell that takes one back to childhood and the times of melting chocolate in a bowl over a saucepan of boiling water. Warm with memories of bowl-licking, I surveyed the display of chocolate formations. There were bunnies, mice, conkers in spiky shells; but, not one to be won over by temporary beauty, I settled on a couple of ordinary but quality bars. Eating the fancy stuff would have been fine, but it was the paying for it that would have been the problem. There was no point sharing a room with strangers in a hostel and flying EasyJet if I could afford to waste money on chocolate – even if it was more perfectly formed than natural – conkers, and with fewer green spikes.

We left for the airport at about 7pm for our 9.50pm flight back to Luton. Bearsac spoke to a few people on route and a nice young man called John on the plane. It was 12.30am when we arrived back home and I called Alan, who was worried someone was in my flat when his phone displayed my home phone number, as he thought I was not coming back until Saturday. Why someone who had broken into my flat would ring my boyfriend from my phone I don't know. Aren't men strange!

United Nations - Geneva

Chapter Four

Barcelona – Spain
March 2003

Day 1 Tuesday

It was with eager anticipation and impatience that I paced the platform at Borehamwood Station, breathing the air too quickly whilst awaiting the 0528 train to Luton Airport. Bearsac spoke to a few people on the airport bus, who had never met a talking teddy bear before; he told them about his website. On the plane we sat next to two men going to Barcelona on business; we don't think the men had spoken to a teddy bear before either; must have been a refreshing change from business clients.

We exchanged a warm, dry Borehamwood and Luton for a very wet Barcelona. The airport palm trees looked out of place against the dismal grey sky, wind-strewn rain beating aggressively at their angry branches. With my hair whipping my face, we fought our way against the wind to get the train. On the escalator the woman in front of us fell head-first over her enormous suitcase. If it hadn't been for my quick reflexes, she would have been very badly hurt or worse. Luckily for all of us, I quickly grabbed the rail and, with all my strength, held us all up with my legs. The woman was not hurt but was much shaken.

I almost didn't recognise the name of the station we had to disembark at, and jumped off just as the doors were closing, nearly getting Bearsac stuck in them. Shaken, we headed for the metro. The difference between the Barcelona metro train and the London Underground tube trains was a bit too much to take in. Overwhelmed by its murkiness, unusual smells and different (though just as annoying) sounds in comparison to the tube trains, I felt a little disorientated, so sniffed Bearsac's fur for familiarity.

I find it easier to cope with annoying sounds if Bearsac or I speak over the sounds I find annoying. Bearsac greeted other passengers in Spanish, getting some animated responses along with what I guess must have been confusion. A young woman jumped out of her skin at Bearsac's greeting her and she spilt her bottled drink down herself; luckily it was just water, but she didn't look too happy about it. Four stops got us three cries of 'Mr Bean's teddy bear!', then it was time to disembark and look for the youth hostel, which was on a quiet back street near the famous Las Ramblas.

In a ten-bed room of bunk-beds, we had a top bunk enclosed by metal walls and a curtain at the entering end, and a metal platform with a locker, luckily big enough for my large rucksack and scooter. The compartment had a low ceiling so you couldn't stand up. I have always liked confined spaces, and it reminded me of sitting in my wardrobe, except it wasn't dark.

On the bunk below was a woman with a face of fury at Bearsac's greeting. She did not reply to him, just tossed her greasy hair and large nose in the air. She was dressed in a bright orange tracksuit; I was glad that Bearsac didn't suggest out loud – only teddypathically - that she had been tangoed. After dumping my rucksack in the locker we left the tangoed one alone and headed off with micro-scooter and camera to explore. We headed down a narrow street we wouldn't like to go down at night, and happened upon Las Ramblas.

Las Ramblas marks the course of the seasonal river of far-gone early times. In the dry season, the channel created by the water of the wet season used as a road. By the 14th century it was paved in recognition of its use as a link between the old town and harbour. In the 19ᵗʰ century benches and trees were added, overlooked by elegant balconied buildings. Las Ramblas now belongs to the pedestrian, with traffic forced into one lane on each side. Just over 1km long, it has lots of stalls offering flowers, colourful craftware, animals and birds. There were big birds in small cages; hens in cages not big enough to turn in; three cockerels to a slightly bigger cage and these giant pigeon-looking things. Bearsac thought they all looked very sad, apart from maybe the budgies and finches, which are normally kept in such conditions as pets.

Mercat de la Boqueria is Barcelona's main market, an orgy of fruit and vegetables bursting with vibrant round and phallic gleaming hues; of meat and fish stalls competitively vying for business. Chillies entwined in bondage, russeted red and green; cheese and pickled willy – just some of the things that could be seen. The raw smells, the merge of sonic distortions, the battling energies – my pulse raced.

Ready for lunch, bum sat upon wobbly stool at the likely best tapas bar in the market – Bar Quim. An order of fresh sardines with seductive saucy tomato and onion was rhythmically cooked. Juicy olives to munch on whilst waiting appeared in front of Bearsac while the staff fussed over him. I sat intoxicated. The sexy sofrito aromas of garlic and tomato peppered gently with paprika danced on the air. Bar Quim's simple Spanish guitar music amid the mad frenzy of the market somehow separate you from the rest of the market enough to play the objective observer, but still at the same time, you contribute to its frenzy by just being there.

Back on the Ramblas a man approached, asking about Bearsac; this man wanted to buy my beloved teddy and upped the amount of his offer with each of my rejections. I got fed up in the end and told him that Bearsac is part of my life and not a commodity. I walked off in rejection of his $200 offer. I don't know if he was Canadian or American, but it would not make any difference what form of dollar he was dealing.

We later found the 13th century Cathedral of Santa Eulalia, but decided not to photograph it that day, as the sky was grey and dull like an enormous pair of old underpants discarded by the giant man in the moon. A lady stood singing - barely covered by her small umbrella – pouring out opera in the pouring rain from her heart, swinging gaily as she sang, as the sky frowned down upon her.

Three hours trudging with wet trainers and clothes proved too much for us both. Impervious no more but deeply soaked through, we found our way easily back to the hostel, despite having changed direction many times. I peeled off my wet clothes - which proved quite hard in the confined space of our bunk-bed module - and got into the sleeping bag for a few hours' rest. There is something comforting about getting into a sleeping bag when one has sought refuge from the cold and wet but the rain still wages war against the see-through protection of a window.

8pm; Bearsac was still wet through to his stuffing when I got up to shout at the computer and email our safe arrival. I chatted awkwardly, and with as much enthusiasm as I could muster, to people in the common area; not really knowing what to say, other than to ask where they had been and what were their travel plans. A girl, maybe in her early 20s, sat poring over a map. She wore a cardigan with green threads of wool sticking out; it resembled Emu, and her long legs sprawled over the chair perfected the Emu look. I dragged Bearsac away before he had a chance to make any Emu comments, and sat and spoke to a lone female traveller. The woman, in her 40s, was from the Ukraine, had been travelling for ten months but was still on the European stretch of her world travels. In this time she had done various jobs, including, amazingly, working in a teddy bear factory in Germany. Bearsac enquired if it was Steiff, but it was just some common teddy bear factory. 'Probably not unlike the factory you were made in, Bearsac,' I told him. Our conversational companion had not made the teddies, but had worked as a cleaner there, so only really got to sweep up surplus trimmings of teddy bears.

Feeling peckish and out of things to ask or talk about now the conversation had deviated away from teddies and travel, I took Bearsac off in the hunt for food and was in bed by 10pm, worn out. The top bunk opposite us was taken by a miserable looking woman; she was about 50 and appeared to have three bellies; she may have had more but that's all we could see exposed by her cropped top with wording in German. She put a finger to her head and twisted it when Bearsac said hello to her. She was busy looking at a rather worn out map and kept turning it around, sighing deeply and flicking it. I pulled across the curtain of my cubicle, shutting out Trio-belly woman, and wrote my notes before turning off my light for the night.

The metal walls and floors of the bunk beds rattled with each person's movement and Bearsac's nose knocked against it permitting very little sleep. Someone near me was snoring for the snoring championship; my wager was between Trio-belly and the Tangoed One. Also keeping me awake was someone writing. How can a person make so much noise by simply writing? It wasn't only the frantic scribbling that grated on my nerves, but the constant clicking of the pen button during their pauses for thought. I had a good mind to get Bearsac to go stick it where the sun don't shine and get him to click, click, click away, but he was sleeping and it would have been cruel to wake him.

Day 2

A limited breakfast was included in the price of the room, but as Bearsac couldn't eat what I had taken for him, I grudgingly ate it. I, at least, was fuelled for our outing-and-abouting. The wet ground reflected the grey clouds, and the air was fragrant with that invigorating after-the-rain smell. We strolled to the harbour, making a mental note of places of interest for better weather. A gang of British youths dressed as Mods and Modettes, about 20 of them, stood eating junk food; discarded wrappings strewn around their feet and multi-mirrored scooters. Can one never escape the London Litter?

A visit to Museu d'Histora de Catalunya was interesting. We watched a documentary about Barcelona through history. The museum covers different aspects of Barcelona's history and the lifestyles of its people. I liked the displays of kitchens through different eras. I sat Bearsac at the table of a rather fetching old kitchen to take a photograph, which got a few giggles. The driver's cab bit of an old tram with a projector on top stood opposite a screen. Projected onto the screen was cine film footage of tram journeys in Catalonia, from the driver's perspective. It must have been filmed when trams were first introduced there as the people on the street - suited and booted children and tail-coated adults included - were jumping excitedly in and, at the last moment, out of the tram's path as if this was a novelty. It really felt like Bearsac and I were driving it.

It was raining when we vacated the museum so I put Bearsac under my jacket to keep him dry, leaving a couple of buttons undone so he could look out. The back streets on the far side of the harbour were free of tourists, their roads shiny and alive. In an old-fashioned grocers - which was not unlike a curiosity shop with its mismatched chandeliers and tacky knick-knacks

- I purchased some nice some crusty bread and Spanish cheese, which gave me a chance to try out some Spanish, asking the hair-netted lady for the amount I wanted and replying ' *Nada mas*' (nothing else) when asked '*Algo mas?*' We then had a long wet wander back to the hostel via an art exhibition that was opposite our hostel for the following night.

I managed to get crumbs all over the bed as I hungrily tucked into the bread and cheese, making none available for Bearsac. I cannot abide crumbs in the bed. I can be in the middle of making love and then all of a sudden feel a tiny crumb beneath me. It throws me off completely and I have to jump up and decrumb the bed there and then, much to the annoyance and obvious frustration of my boyfriend. I'm a bit like the princess in the story 'The Princess and The Pea'.

To calm and reorder myself from the stress of crumbing and decrumbing my hostel bed, I packed my rucksack. I placed each item precisely, in case I had to unpack in the dark amid sleepers, ready for checking out in the morning. Satisfied on the second attempt, I lay down, cuddling Bearsac till about 3.30pm, when I dragged him out for another walk.

Another direction, another avenue explored. All the schools were falling out; kids scattered everywhere with bright-coloured plastic Macs, pointing at Bearsac and laughing. One boy was crying so Bearsac spoke to him, introducing himself in Spanish. As the last traces of the boy's tears disappeared into the rain, he warmed up the cold with a huge and energetic smile, and his little nose wrinkled as he laughed. He waved as he was dragged off by his charge, who remained oblivious to his sudden change of mood.

We soon came to a rather interesting circular building, which, upon investigation, turned out to house an indoor market. Drab stalls offered drab, boring clothes (surely aimed at those who had given up). The clothes stalls were dotted in a ring around a centre of meat and vegetable stalls, which were mostly shut by now. However, the smell of raw flesh still evidenced a day earlier more varied in meat counters.

We walked back towards the town centre, past a school displaying paper doves in the windows for peace (anti-war). Along the back streets we got a spinach and onion pasty type thing, asking for it *caliente* (hot). I ate it hungrily, walking back to the hostel, trying not to touch the pasty itself but to eat it from the grease-proof paper, as I had not washed my hands. Would you believe I forgot to offer Bearsac some.

I was stopped by the sight of a partly demolished block of flats. It looked - from the clothes and sheets hung out to dry on the balconies – as though the remaining flats still housed occupants, even though the next-wall neighbours' flats had been demolished. The colour of each room's wall clung to the exposed side of the building, evidencing, to all who might notice, the individuality of their former occupants, but leaving no other clues. It was an unfinished story. Where had these individuals gone; what had they taken with them?

'I wonder if any teddy bears lived in the rooms,' said Bearsac, teddypathically reading my thoughts.

We got back to the hostel as the clock on a young man's baseball cap was showing only 5.46pm. – Yes, that's right, the clock on the young man's baseball cap. Now I've heard of the talking clock, but this was the walking clock!

'When you want to know the time yourself, do you take off your cap, or ask a person facing you to tell you?' enquired Bearsac of the young man. I'm not sure why, but the young man offered nothing in reply to Bearsac's not unreasonable query.

After resting for a couple of hours we went to the common area to attempt a bit of a chat with some of the other people, and to plan things to do during the rest of our stay in Barcelona. It was packed with noisy 20-somethings, as hostels so often are. We sat and people-watched for as long as I could stand the noise, and then went for a scoot with Bearsac to check out the Ramblas scene and get some night-scented air in my hair. With Bearsac strapped to my front I darted through pedestrians, stopping every so often to watch some entertainment.

The distinctive sound of Liver-birds (females from Liverpool) on a night out suddenly rode above the Ramblas rabble. One glimpse of Bearsac sitting on my hip talking to people and we were surrounded. The bride-to-be of this hen party, who were all dressed as fairies, was thrust to the middle of the pack and ordered to 'snog the bear'. And snog the bear she did. Bearsac loved it, and loved it all the more when he got stroked between his furry little legs! Satisfied, the bride-to-be and the rest of the bleached-blonde brigade headed off in search of a few more alcoholic drinks and men, no doubt. Bearsac and I bought a bottle of water and scooted our way to bed.

Day 3

We left after breakfast for our second hostel, Hostel Rambles. We had booked here for one night, then two nights somewhere else, and then back here again for the remainder of the trip. The other occupants were still in bed, so I just did basic unpacking, thankful that I had packed wisely.

At the aquarium I was cheeky and used a tall, upside-down litter-bin as a pod for my camera, as the dim lighting meant slow shutter speeds. One young man must have thought it was a cool idea, as he photographed me using the bin. Bearsac gave him one of his website cards so he could email it to us. In a glass tunnel fish, including sharks and stingrays, swam menacingly overhead. At one point Bearsac almost forgot where we were and thought he was under the ocean. He was scared when a big stingray, its gills opening and closing, got too near. He said his fur was standing on end and everything.

Little children sat cutely in a row in front of a long tank, being told about the fish that were swimming past. There was also a play area; I got stuck in straight away, crawling through glass tubes with water swirling around within the double-glazed tube. We crawled under the glass of the stingrays' open tank and even got to stroke them; we wore rubber gloves so as not to burn their cold bodies. We had to have a go in the submarine, which was cool, and although it was red, we sang 'Yellow Submarine'. We adored the little penguins, which we could see from both under and above the water; they seemed oblivious to the presence of Bearsac with his nose pushed up against the glass.

Once aquariumed out, we took to the streets and down some side road. We came to a small building, which seemed to be housing some action. It contained an indoor food market; all the stallers were dressed up. Men had dressed as women with yellow wool for hair and red spots painted on their cheeks. Both genders were dressed as nuns, and all sorts. Bearsac spoke to a dog that tangled its lead around the stool its owner was perched upon, in its excitement at meeting him. It almost pulled its rather hefty owner off the stool. Playing unaware, I bought some garlicky chickpea and spinach stew type salad and then found the beach and sat down to lunch on a log near to the sea's edge. Waves gently lapped at my feet until a big wave crashed over us, up to my knees and Bearsac's feet. We both have never moved so quickly, I can tell you.

A couple of minutes' walk along the beach found the stacked metal boxes, 'Homage to Barceloneta', by Rebecca Horn, erected in 1992; it is meant to resemble the buildings of the area. We had a little paddle and then came to a beach gym where we spoke to an old muscled man who showed us how to use the equipment. I rather think he was trying to chat me up, but I made out I didn't notice and showed more absorption in the gym equipment. After that we dodged the flower ladies, who were targeting two men, who just let the ladies take money out of their wallets.

More walking, more photos. We later headed back to the harbour side and over to the post office to peruse its décor, as we heard that it was very nice. We sat and looked at the painted walls depicting biblical scenes as footsteps echoed around us, until we gathered some energy to walk slowly back towards the hostel.

After a three-hour lie-down, we went out scooting in the dark to see the round square's fountains lit up. The round square's marble floor seemed made for scooting, but I get a little excited on my scooter and Bearsac felt as sick as a pig and had to beg me to stop. The scene in Las Ramblas was busy but not rushed. Entertainers entertained, some better than others. We stopped to watch a man singing with his Spanish guitar; listening to him for an hour or so. Bearsac bunged him a few coins afterwards, and humans around followed his lead.

After another scoot we came across a trio of young men entertaining. One was using a plastic bucket as a drum, another used a wooden speaker for his drum; a very fit looking third young man was flamenco dancing to the rhythm. Starting off slow, they built the tempo and brought the audience to a frenzy of rapid clapping, the dancer's tiny steps mesmerising all eyes upon him.

After another scoot, we grabbed some falafel with humous in small pitta. By the time I had helped myself to all the extras

– marinated carrots, olives, cabbage, couscous, tomatoes, cucumber, chickpeas and dressings – it was huge. I filled the paper bag holding the pitta too; it was a feast for three euros.

We laughed when we came across a painted sheet poster ordering 'No Weeing' on a building; I just had to photograph Bearsac in front of it. Of course, as we passed down the very alley the poster overlooked, the air was redolent of wee. I was glad I had my feast wrapped up, thus avoiding the permeation of wee spores that might still be invisibly air-borne.

Back at the hostel with our feast, we bumped onto two young men from the first hostel and had a drink with them and the people they were hanging with. The gang was going out dancing and asked us to come along. We said we would, but said we'd not stay long as I was really sleepy and had had very little sleep in the last few nights. However, by the time the gang had got their act together and had re-assembled to leave, I was ready to fall asleep there and then, so we dropped out apologetically, letting the youngsters go without the oldie and her talking teddy in tow

As it was, the hostel was very noisy and rampant with youthfulness, so we had very little sleep that night either.

Day 4

Blue sky! We got out of the metro station and asked directions to our third hostel. Simply called 'Home'; it was the best of the three. In a quiet road in the suburbs, it promised peace and quiet. It was brightly painted inside, was homely and not at all hostel-like. The roof terrace looked out over the mountains and was warm in the long awaited sunshine. After hanging our washed clothes out to dry, we headed out for the day.

We took the Metro to Espanya station, with a *t-dia* (one-day travel-card).Having climbed the stairs up to it, I sat with Bearsac by my side, his little legs sticking out over the edge of the wall, before visiting the 'Palau Nacional' (Museu Nacional d'Art de Catalunya). Built as recently as 1990, it displays Gothic art and Romanesque murals. There was also a light and airy indoor arena with a large organ, and this was being set up with tables and chairs for some function. It was rather noisy as staff were chattering and ordering each other about, scraping chairs across the floor and clanking silverware down on the tables. Nerves a-jangle, I vacated to the quieter realms of the mountain top.

At the top of the mountain we strolled around the Anella Olimpia (Olympic ring), where the 1992 Olympics were held. Onwards we walked to 'Poble Espanya', which is an old village of craft-shops and workshops on old streets and squares enclosed by a wall. It was built in 1929. Entry was seven euros per person, or 3.70 euros each for a group of 15 or more. I hit on the idea of gathering strangers together, and did so until there were 17 of us. I didn't feel guilty about this; it's not as if we were in some impoverished country.

Once inside, people were free to split up. The village was beautiful and well worth paying to enter. Various styles of colourful Spanish architecture in one area would please those into architecture. There was a tremendous atmosphere of patience, with strangers all trying not to get in the way of other people's photographs, yet waiting respectfully for their turn to take their own shots of their loved ones standing untidily with scruffy shopping bags. As I held up Bearsac against some of the buildings, cameras clicked away, married with laughter; I turned round to see maybe 20 or so people watching us, and some asked me Bearsac's name.

'I can speak for myself,' said Bearsac, 'ask *me* my name, not her.' A tangle of voices asked him his name, and Bearsac told the amassed: 'Bearsac.'

'He looks like, oh, sorry – *you* look like Mr Bean's teddy bear,' announced one young woman. Laughing seemed to suggest that others believed the same.

Manicured orange trees lined some paths, but we were not lucky enough to have any drop off into our hands as we went by. Ugly dolls in craft shops scared Bearsac, who pretended to be interested in the souvenirs so as not to notice them.

By the time we had had enough it had become overcast and was starting to get cold. We continued along the road and paid a visit to the Contemporary art Museum. Think it was free, but as seems usual with museums in Barcelona, there is no desk as you walk in. Just as well really, it was really quite boring. Maybe it was interesting, but we were too tired to be interested.

We got back on the murky metro but soon got off again to photograph Bearsac with Barcelona's Arc de la Triomf in the background. I stopped by the supermarket to get some food to cook and a bottle of red wine. I was pleased to find one of the old family favourites – Banda Azul, which is a lovely Rioja. By the time we got to the checkout, I was near destroyed by all the surrounding noise. I was then told that I should have weighed my vegetables and price-labelled them. They could not weigh it at the checkout and said I needed to go and do it. I was so exhausted by now, and annoyed and panicked by all the noise in the shop, that I simply did not have the energy to do it and queue up again. Without the vegetables it was not really worth taking the rest of the stuff; so, in a huff, I just left it and slumped behind some trolleys in a corner in exhaustion. With erratic breathing, I sat on the floor and covered my ears to shield myself from the noise. I sniffed at Bearsac's fur; I didn't have the energy to leave the shop and tackle the crowded streets. This was not allowed, security informed me. In the end – after I had explained how I was feeling through having had just five hours' sleep over the last four nights and all the walking and hill climbing - they very kindly took the vegetables themselves to weigh them and let me to the front of the queue. Will have to remember that another time! It seems such a silly system for a shop; a dishonest customer could easily just weigh a small amount, print out the label for that small amount and then add more to the bag before then sticking on the label and tying up the bag. It's not like the person on the checkout would notice the weight against the price as they passed it over the scanner.

Back at the hostel - after some well-needed rest – I cooked dinner, opened the wine and ate and drank in comfort. After dinner I spoke to some people in the sitting room before going to bed about 9.30 to peruse my travel-guide. At last I slept well, albeit just my normal four hours, but this was in one night, not four.

Day 5

The sun awoke, after me, to the second nice day of the holiday and I lay listening to two American girls, travelling together, who were sharing the room. I recorded part of their conversation. I was amused by it, but tried not to laugh; and thankfully Bearsac made no comment.

'Are you actually gonna to wear that?'

'Excuse me; do you have a problem with this particular muscle shirt?'

'Well, do you want people staring at you all day? You can see right all through it.'

'Why should I care? People all stare at me anyhow.'

'If you wear that without a bra they'll be staring at you a whole lot more than they usually do!'

'You know what? I am not having this discussion with you.'

'You will have all the men staring at you, is that what you want?'

'Whatever.'

'You know, it's clear to men you're a lesbian yet you still want to flaunt your nipples at them, what do you think they're gonna make of that? You could at least put a bra on.'

'Well hey, I don't care; I'm done on this conversation.'

Muscle Shirt Girl then exits the room to clean her teeth.

Leaving it about ten minutes before I got up, so as not to let them know I was awake listening to them, I then got dressed in the bathroom, so as not to wake the other girls in the room, just in case they had slept through the see-through muscle shirt conversation, which I sincerely hope they didn't, as they would have missed a fine story to tell their friends. This was the only hostel in which I have seen a bath; what's more, it was a roll-top bath. It would have been a bit selfish to have had a bath rather than a shower because of the amount of people staying.

I took Bearsac out for short walk in the woods on a deserted hill and got covered in green sticky balls from the plants as we took a route through the beaten foliage. Picking off the balls as I walked, we returned back the hostel and grabbed my stuff for the day's exploring of Park Guell. It was probably about an hour's walk, but we kept getting sidetracked, wondering what was down this way and that way.

We came to some shops where there were a ten-foot man and lady dressed funny and dancing; I asked the man if he would pose with Bearsac for a photograph and he was happy to oblige. Peculiar potato tube things in a coil, fried and shaken with sugar, somehow spoke to me. I had seen a photograph of them in the guide book. They tasted like fat and sugar and I wondered what had ever compelled me to buy them in the first place. Even Bearsac turned his nose up at them.

We continued onwards, now guessing our way to Park Guell, over the hills and far away. We took what we guessed would be a short cut up a mountain and came to some old men playing bowls. I sat, Bearsac on my lap, on a convenient boulder, watching the old men at play. They soon noticed Bearsac's cuteness but we declined their offer to stay and play.

At the top of the tall hill was a man picking what looked like wild asparagus; he had climbed over the fence to do so and was very ear to the edge. We downed the other side of the hill, passing a cactus plant; it was not something I had expected to see in Europe, so I was quite excited and placed Bearsac by it, carefully, to photograph him. 'Careful not to get those pricks up my bum,' said Bearsac, with concern.

After a bit more of a walk up another tall hill, we hit the swaying woods at the back of Park Guell. We were escorted by a fluffy white-haired old man out onto a terraced area rimmed with colourful curvy serpentine seating. From here a wonderful, brightly coloured toy-town-like view of the park and of Barcelona exploded into view.

Park Guell was the idea of Count Eusebi Güell, who wanted a park with a difference for the aristocrats of Barcelona. Güell thought of Antonio Gaudí as 'the man who can' when it came to designing the park uniquely enough to give his dream wings. Gaudí was maybe a man in touch with his inner child when he designed; he afforded the park lots of strange stone animal-like structures, curvy colonnades, colourful tiling and weird buildings that look like the house in Hansel and Gretel when they have eaten most of the sweets off it. Gaudi lived in a house in the park at one time; it is now a museum and contains furniture designed by the man himself.

Our descent of the terrace found it supported by elegant but powerful Doric columns; the terrace forming the roof of a court. An elegantly curving stairway leads down to Sammy the Salamander, who is covered in small colourful mosaic tiles. Sammy is not really called Sammy; that is just the name Bearsac gave him. Bearsac posed for photographs with Sammy; we had to wait for small children to get off Sammy first and Bearsac found it hard to hide his impatience. At the Porter's House I got in for the student rate of 1.50 euro without even lying about being a student; they just asked for 1.50 euro. We sat and listened to some musicians playing within the colonnades. Once they spotted Bearsac, the guitarist came up to him and serenaded him; this started the clicking of cameras and whirring of camcorders.

After a couple of hours we headed back. On approaching the hostel I spotted the two Americans on the balcony and looked to see what Muscle Shirt Girl was wearing. I smiled, wondering how many men had ogled her; thankfully Bearsac didn't yell anything out about her nipples.

After our late lunch, I lay down cuddling Bearsac until dark. But our peace and rest was shattered by gunshot type sounds, it was fireworks. Loud music joined the tortured air from the school down the road, where a party was kicking off. I hate the sound of fireworks and get worn out from it. The reason for the party and all the people we'd seen dressed up was that it was the start of carnival week. I was too tired to go out to Las Ramblas for the procession, seeing as we were now in the suburbs. Some of the others went but Bearsac and I stayed and talked to those that stayed behind. During a conversation with some of the stay-at-homes, Muscle Shirt Nipple Girl stormed amongst us, her ample breasts bouncing out of control. She was ranting, demanding to know who had sprayed perfume. Everyone apart from Bearsac was frightened into silence; he claimed to smell it too.

'I'm gonna get to the bottom of this, once I've had some air,' she seethed through her teeth as she thundered outside on her heels caked in dead skin. I stayed up till about 1.30am, having origami birds, flowers and frogs made for Bearsac and me out of newspaper by a young Korean man who lived in Japan. He had been reading a British newspaper and thought I might want to read it. I explained how I avoid Britain when I'm abroad, so he put it to better use artistically. Finally defeated by fatigue, I took our newspaper origami creatures to bed with Bearsac.

Day 6

The sun's early promise had withered away and would not be kept today. Under the indifferent overcast sky we took a walk up the wooded hill again, with our cameras this time, before heading back to breakfast on grapes. I made some dinner to take to the kitchenless but microwave-possessing Hostel Ramblas, which we were to return to on checking out of Home hostel. Shame we'd already booked, as we were going from the best of the three to the worst for the rest of the holiday. I could have cancelled and stayed at Home, but at least we'd be in the town centre where the action was.

Once we'd sorted our stuff we headed off on the metro to the river we'd seen on the map. However, the River Besòs turned out to be dominated by an ugly, highly industrial area with bare concrete walls and path running alongside its otherwise natural beauty. We made the most of it by scooting along the path with the wind in our hair and fur until the path came to an end altogether.

We walked on the grass and stones until deciding to turn back and see if we could scoot back to town. We came across a beer factory and Bearsac wanted his photograph taken outside it, so I had to brush away dust on the wall to sit him on it, and got it all up my nose. The things I have to do for my teddy bear!

It was about a three-mile scoot down industrial roads, parallel to the river, past demoralising vulgar social housing and the near shanty-style prefabs - that tourists don't get to see - to the estuary at Sant Adrià de Besòs. It was then about four miles along the beach side-walks until we got to anywhere we recognised, which was a mile from the hostel. By the time we got back for a rest we had done about eight miles on a micro-scooter.

I thought I'd make a bit more out of my travel-card and we got on the metro, getting off at random stops to see what we could see. We scooted about some more and ended up going into a church where we had been attracted by the singing and thought it would be nice to listen to a service in Spanish. I was doing all the stuff one does in a church service - all the stand up, sit down, kneeling with the rest of the congregation. On leaving, Bearsac crossed himself with holy water.

It was getting dark by the time the service had finished. We scooted back to the Ramblas and watched a Spanish rock band play before finally scooting back to the hostel to heat our dinner in the microwave.

Day 7

Out and about 8.15am through the old town and into Parc La Ciutadella, which houses the Museum de Zoologia Historia Natural. Central to the park was a nice duck pond with nice little ducks that quacked at Bearsac in delight. An ornate staircase formed a backdrop to the pond; or was the duck pond a foreground to the staircase? We then came across a huge woolly mammoth that wasn't at all woolly, called Mabel. Bearsac posed on her trunk and at her feet for photographs; she was just a statue. There were orange trees, but as with the other orange trees, we'd had no luck in the 'falling off the tree' department, and Bearsac convinced me not to climb up to pick some fruit.

We scooted to 'Sagrada Familia', which is not a cathedral, but a basilica. The building of Sagrada Familia (Temple of the Sacred Family) started in 1882, and Gaudi was made Project Designer a year later, working on it until he died in 1926. A coach of German tourists were in the way of our trying to photograph the building so we went up and talked to the teddy bears sitting in the windscreen of the coach. The driver and representative held the bears for a photograph with Bearsac. The teddies all chatted about their travels and gave each other bear hugs. After this we grabbed a snack and headed off back towards Las Ramblas again, stopping as we came to a TV crew filming the street scene. We of course took the chance to get Bearsac on screen, so he might be a Spanish TV star by now.

With Bearsac strapped to my front, we scooted round and round and round the round square, which was full of pigeons. I sat Bearsac on the marble ground so he could feed them, and they knocked him over and climbed all over him. That's gratitude for you!

At Mercat Boqueria I purchased some cheese called Mao Sec, crusty bread and a wonderfully creamy avocado, not like the watery junk we get in England. Back at the hostel we had our bread, cheese and avocado and were soon out and about again, back at Mount Juic to see what we'd missed the other day. The cable car that went from the part we were to Mount Juic doesn't run on weekdays, so we did a Jack and Jill and climbed up the hill again, though thankfully we didn't come tumbling down. There stood a statue entitled "Sardana" which was of people dancing in a ring, holding hands. I sat Bearsac in the middle for a photograph as I imagined the sculpted people singing,

'Brown bear in the ring, tra la la la la'.

Castell de Mountjuic was once a beacon tower for fishing fleets to find their way home. In the 1640 Reapers War, the beacon tower was converted into a castle fort in 30 days for fighting against the Castillian army of Felipe IV. Barcelona was starved into submission.

In 1714, after the siege of Barcelona, The Bourbons (not the biscuits) blew up the original castle and in 1759 replaced it with one that specialised in torturing Castillian political prisoners. As we sat on one of the big guns used for firing at ships, we were very happy that it didn't go off; the vibration would have blown us away. Bearsac had a go at standing sentry duty but got fed up after a few seconds; my teddy has no stamina.

Holding Bearsac's straps, I walked right around Castell and the surrounding woods, which were very peaceful with the relaxing sounds and smells of herbs and bark. We came across another old man risking his life picking asparagus, just as we had on the other hill. Passing the Castell again, the security guard photo-graphed us on the drawbridge; Bearsac was worried it might get drawn up as we stood on it; silly bear.

On the way back to our hostel we popped into the hostel we'd stayed in on our first two nights to ask if it would be OK to leave my rucksack in the lockers on our last day, which was fine. I think the man only said yes as he'd remembered Bearsac. He gave Bearsac a sweet from the Gaudi salamander bowl on the reception desk; it had clearly been refilled after Bearsac had nicked most of the sweets from it on our first night in Barcelona, which is maybe why the man remembered Bearsac and gave him a sweet.

Day 8

By midday; it was lovely and warm, so after the last few days of walking, climbing and scooting, we felt we deserved a rest and a relaxed, lazy beach day in the sun.

After about an hour of sitting looking out to sea, I decided to build a sand castle but then changed my mind, making it into a sunbathing sand teddy bear; Bearsac named it Sandy. Sandy attracted some amused smiles and questions from passers-by and got hit by a football. A nice young man from Finland, called Phillip, sat himself down and chatted for a while. He invited us back to swim at his hotel but we didn't know him and really, Bearsac and I were just happy with temporary conversation on the beach. Soon after his pleasant visit, another nice young man sat with us. He was called Lee, from Mill Hill (just down the road from where we live). What a small world!

It started turning a little chilly about 4.30pm, so I put on a long sleeved shirt and we built two small stone teddies beside Sandy, who by now had lost some of her sand as she had dried. In an hour or so the sea would have claimed her as its own and she would be no more than a memory.

We sat at the harbour, where it was a bit warmer, people-watching, then we looked around some shops and a churchyard with worn arches, beeswax candles and stuff. Back at the hostel we had dinner, and later we went out again, just a walk-about. We came to a crowd with music and waded in to see what the fuss was. A gypsy gymnast was clinging to a thin tree trunk with her green legging-covered legs wrapped around it. She was performing something very far removed from mere tree hugging! They say when we hug a tree it gives us energy and love; well that tree got its fair share too! After that nothing else could match up, so we called it a night.

Day 9

Purchased more bread and water and this time tried the soft Mao, which melted on my tongue and warmed it with its caressing flavour. I tried some strawberry slices on it, which was OK, and thought it would have been great with freshly milled black pepper. Bearsac turned his nose up at the prospect so he was glad there was no pepper-mill around.

The church bell struck ten as we set off for the Picasso museum. There were some of his paintings from a few years before his death, photographs of Picasso himself by various photographers, and there was artwork by other artists. Adorning the walls also were doodles on scraps of paper with stains on them; they looked like someone had taken them out of the bin and ironed them. Bearsac pointed out that some of the pictures looked like Mr. Bean had drawn them. I really shouldn't have been surprised at the amount of questioning as to whether he was Mr Bean's teddy bear that his comment brought our way! It took some time to move on as so many people wanted to photograph Bearsac and have their photograph taken with him to show their friends. He got kisses and paw shakes galore and it went to his head, as it usually does; my teddy bear has such an ego.

After another gallery and a church, we had a bite to eat in a bar, all without Bearsac being mobbed by fans of Mr Bean's teddy. There on the bar, sitting enticingly on a large platter, were thick slices of French bread topped generously but elegantly with various toppings: salmon mousse with dill, cream-cheese with asparagus, grilled Mediterranean vegetables, something that was like a cross between soft tofu and soft cheese, grilled fish and other delights – all with a cocktail stock sticking out at the same angle. They were a euro a-piece, the cocktail stick indicated how much you have to pay. We spoke with a couple who thought Bearsac cute and liked his baby sized boxing gloves that I had bought for him en route. They were calm in their appreciation of Bearsac, so I was able to stay for a while and relax over a glass of Rioja.

After eating, we continued to the old town and were attracted by the sound of rampant drumming. On following it, we hit upon an anti-war demo holding up traffic, and of course joined in. Photographers photographed Bearsac sitting in the road. Protesters stopped vehicles from passing, only allowing an ambulance through. Later, police in a plain white van stopped at the metal barrier that had now been erected by the protesters and one got out, moved it and then put it back where the protesters had placed it once the van had passed. This was applauded by the protesters. The police are human too, I suppose. The protesters then moved on towards the Ramblas and split up, probably to get some food. Bearsac and I sat and people-watched on a wall, saying '*Hola*' (hello) to passers-by. Bearsac danced to some nearby music and a few people gave us some euro-cents, which was rather useful.

An old man sat on the ground reading a tattered book. Beside him were two large cumbersome dogs and a box of quietly squeaky kittens with their mummy; he was trying to sell the kittens as they squirmed about in the box. Bearsac spoke to them in Spanish and the kittens just loved him to bits; well at least Bearsac told their mummy so.

Once bored with this, we went to the Turkish cake shop I had spotted the night before and got some sweet things made from ground almonds and pistachio nuts. Back at the hostel for a lie down, we found evidence of new room-mates. We had had the room to ourselves the previous night and were hoping it would the same this night. When they arrived back, one of the room-mates had a teddy bear, which they had just bought as a gift for their sister, so it wasn't yet able to speak to Bearsac. This was a shame really as we thought we had both found allies. The bear just sat in a carrier bag on top of the lockers, its ears sticking out and silent for the rest of the night, illuminated by light from the small window.

Day 10 - Last day

At 9.30am went to the market for the last time for bread. Made sandwiches for the plane then checked out of the hostel, and headed for the other hostel where we stored my rucksack until the flight. Bearsac of course took more sweets from the salamander on the desk.

We made our way to Mount Juic again and took in the peaceful-ness of the park for some time. Looked around the shops and met two dogs in a shop doorway next to a dummy dressed as a Spanish lady; they told Bearsac how cool it was to be a dog in Barcelona.

Wandering new unexplored back-roads, we heard roars from a small huddle of old people in the middle of the road. We were let to the front and saw that it was a game of bowls with silver coloured balls, like we'd seen the men on the hill playing; this must be popular here. Bearsac spoke to a few people and the woman whose house the game was being played outside of gave him a flower from her flower-box. I pinned it under his anti-war badge.

We had a late lunch of grilled hake with couscous and a green salad. I bought Bearsac a sombrero but it was soon whipped off his head by a statue artist dressed as a silver cowboy standing on a crate. Assuming the statue might try to charge me for its return, I simply whipped it back from him as Bearsac growled at him.

I got some more of the Turkish sweet things and at 6.20pm we were off to the airport. I had my hand luggage searched as a knife had shown up on the x-ray. Thankfully it was just an eating knife that I'd forgotten to hand back when I borrowed it from the hostel. They gave me it back, as it was not a danger.

The flight was delayed by two hours because the plane had to go back to England as it had faults. We were entertained for the duration of our wait by six-year-old Harry. Harry told us all about M&Ms, the sweets, who he said were his friends. He said that he went to the same school as them and everything! He told us how he only eats the ones that are not his friends and how really the sweets are as tall as he is, and that they shrink themselves to get in the tube. He collects the lids from the tubes; there are different M&M characters. It was nice to meet someone on the same wavelength! Spoke to a few other people then finally it was time to fly home. Sat next to us was a nice man called Roger, who shared with us tales of his childhood teddy.

Back at Borehamwood Bearsac was greeted to a drunken cry of
'Bearsac, you're gay.'
'In actual fact, young man, I'm a bisexual teddy bear,' replied Bearsac.
'F*** off,' was the most intelligent thing the man in his 30s could come back with. I think he felt small because I was not hurt by his gay comment.

There were no cabs for 45 minutes, so I got my scooter from my large rucksack and with that, Bearsac, my smaller rucksack and camera bag scooted carefully back home. It was just after 3am. We rang Alan, my boyfriend, to say we'd got home safe.

When we got up the next day, Bearsac had a bath; you should have seen the water. Yuck. Does this teddy get dirty or what!

**Bearing all on the beach and Bear amongst the Pigeons
- Barcelona**

Chapter Five

Sri Lanka

Day 1 - 31st December 2003

My little brother phoned one day to say he was getting married. Without even waiting to see if I would be invited, I booked a flight to Sri Lanka and waited for months for 30th December, the day I flew out. I had a window seat next to a nice young man from India studying in London, who fell asleep on my shoulder; Bearsac thought he was pretending to be asleep.

We spent three hours in transit in Doha, capital of Qatar, where we changed flights. There were lots of happy smiley faces in the departure lounge at the sight of Bearsac and Choc-Ice, with people of all ages wanting to touch them. From Doha to Colombo we had a Sri Lankan woman next to us. She didn't speak much, despite Bearsac introducing himself in *Sinhala*; think she was somewhat nervous of flying. Sri Lanka, off the South East coast of India, can be compared to a naan bread or tear-drop in shape.

I took a cab (which was really a mini-bus) to The Mount Lavinia Hotel to meet my brother David. *Tuk-tuk* drivers were pulled up on the sides of the road, slamming down playing-cards on makeshift tables. Cows lazed in the road chewing the cud; strange vehicles chugged along; colourfully clothed people and stalls punctuated the noisy and polluted street scenes. I stopped to get a sim-card loaded up with minutes I would not fully use for my unlocked mobile phone and Bearsac attracted many smiles and much pointing.

My brother's father-in-law-to-be met me at the hotel door; I didn't recognise him at first, so wondered for a second how this man knew my name. Thankfully it dawned on me who he was, so I said hello as if I had recognised him straight off.

Once with my brother, we took my stuff to my hotel before joining him, his wife-to-be Julia, their friends and Julia's family back at their hotel by the pool. Some of us went to the beach for a while; it was now very hot and I was somewhat disappointed to find the sea so warm! Had I been alone (that is, without other 'humans' known to me), I would have dumped my bags in my room and gone exploring with Bearsac immediately, for as long as my legs held out. But I was with my brother, his new family-to-be and their friends, so I was obligated to laze about by the pool or on the beach and join in with small-talk and gossip about people I didn't know. I racked my brain to think of things to say or ask in line with the subject of conversation as I could work it out, so as not to let my brother down. Not really one of my strong points. I soon withdrew into my own thoughts, making the occasional acknowledgement sounds, hopefully in the right places.

Worn out from too much sun, listening to animated chatter, lack of sleep and the long flight; I wanted an early night, but there is no rest for the wicked. It was New Year's Eve so any thoughts of catching up on lost sleep were out with 2003. Sri Lankan dancing in the ballroom with a local band followed dinner. I photographed Bearsac by the tacky 2004 ice-sculpture before it melted. A woman walked from table to table making balloon animals, swords and flowers for the children; I got her to make a teddy bear for Bearsac.

Just before midnight we all joined the pool party. On the stroke of midnight, which would have been still only 6pm in the UK, fireworks ripped through the star-studded sky and showered down upon all below, the embers falling into my hair and

Bearsac's fur but luckily going out on contact; don't know what I would have done if Bearsac had become inflamed. I hate bangers, they are so loud, but they seem to keep most people of all ages happy.

David expressed his concern that Bearsac had got a bit too in-the-face with one of Julia's friends. As I assumed would be the right thing to do, I approached her and apologised. She didn't know what I was talking about. I somehow don't think my brother had expected me to say anything to her, so when I told him I'd apologised and she hadn't a clue what I was on about, I think he felt a little silly about his comment, which was clearly not based on her reality but his. It was maybe his indirect way of saying he was embarrassed. This was maybe honestly what I suspected anyway, and that was my way of dealing with it.

The poolside party was too noisy. Once I had a chance to escape, I joined the beach party, which was quieter but more fun and with a lot more space. I danced in my own style with Bearsac at the water's edge, being joined by a few strangers. I seem to get on better with strangers somehow; they don't have any preconceptions or expectations; they just accept you as you are. They can be more comfortably attracted to your differences, rather than embarrassed by them.

David later walked Bearsac and me back to our hotel, which had a dirty floor and air conditioning that noisily used the lavatory cistern as its water source. A large spider, which I had killed earlier, had gone. Had it risen from the dead or did the hotel staff actually clean the room? As I slipped between the sheets, I prayed that they had been boil-washed in disinfectant and that they were meant to be that colour.

Day 2 - 1st January 2004

Bearsac and I walked along the rail track and beach; we turned up some road to photograph a few things that had caught my eye and ended up in a little shanty village. We came across lots of children playing in the dirt. They looked happy and healthy and crowded around asking Bearsac's name:

'*Mahgay nama* Bearsac,' he replied, to their delight. Some braved a touch of Bearsac and squealed in delight, snatching their hands away as he pretended to bite them.

We continued down a narrowing lane and soon hit upon another untouristy sight. Manky flesh-torn bones litter the quiet lane; there is one, bigger than the rest, still bearing traces of unidentified flesh; three mange-infested dogs scrap over this bone of contention. A fourth infected dog sits nearby, biting his bald and boney body, with oozing sores. Instinct turns me round 180 degrees and I head Bearsac and myself back to safer domains.

Back on the railway track we hear the approach of a train, so stand aside off the tracks, awaiting its rusty arrival. I hold up Bearsac's paw and move it from side to side, in a waving motion, as the train trundles by with smiling faces at its open windows. A skeletal cat and fat pig pass each other across the tracks after the passing of the train. Where has the pig come from and where is it going? We follow it but it soon gets herded away, I assume by its owner.

A walk to the main road, away from the hotels, sees a man with elephantiasis of the legs who sits ragged on the pavement, his long hair matted. Nearby, a stray dog of skin and bones with leaky eyes roots through rubbish by the side of the road for scraps of food. I should have been shocked, but I've seen these types of sights on TV many times, so it doesn't seem real; it is like I am on a film set or something.

We returned to my grotty hotel room to grab my swimwear and then walked over to David's hotel for the expected sunbathing by the pool. This, we were relieved to find, was now also our hotel. David had booked us into the Mount Lavina for the next three nights; it had been full, last night being New Year's Eve. I think of the man on the pavement as I walk into the spacious bedroom; the floor is clean and we have a sea view. I have a choice of which bed to take and which the bears will have. I wonder if the man's bed is the ground, or does he have somewhere of comfort, or at least of safety to sleep?

After too much sunbathing I decide to go into town. I test out my Sinhala, asking in Sinhala if there is a bus from here to Colombo, and am pointed to the correct bus-stop. Chugging along Colombo's main road, we near collide with a bus turning out of it into a junction. Traffic fumes pour in through the window; I cover my nose and mouth with the sleeve of my shirt, pulling my arm up inside to allow for more material to shield me. Amid the Sri Lankans on the other crowded bus is sat another lone western woman, her mouth and nose covered by a scarf. Our eyes meet on this near-collision and lock; we smile a knowing smile of recognition, dealing with the polluted scene. I know she is smiling as her eyes wrinkle above the top of her cheeks and the scarf moves upwards. We draw away suddenly, but at the same time, almost as if in slow motion, like when you ride the Waltzer at the fairground and your eyes lock with a spectator and you watch them get smaller as you are pulled sharply away.

At the end of the route the bus stops abruptly, in the puff of smoke emitting from the bus in front. The doors fling open sharply. Everyone tries to leave as one mass, like some huge bubblegum chewing monster has gobbled us all up and discarded us within the bubblegum, arms and legs thrusting and wreathing in no control of their destiny. I am somewhere amid this mass, clinging tightly hold of Bearsac, praying he does not get accidentally ripped away from me by the mass of churning bodies.

The reason I am going to Colombo is to look for an evening bag for Julia's hen night. I can't have my little brother dying of a heart attack over his concern about what he assumes Julia's friends and mum will think of me if I don't have a cool handbag. As far as I'm concerned, I have the coolest handbag in the world, Bearsac.

There are no bags I like, and certainly none as cool as would have been brotherly prescribed, so I get a train back to Mount Lavina. Bearsac and I both try a spot of train hanging; that is, holding onto the handrail and hanging outside the train, standing on the footholds (when it is going slow, of course). This thrilling way of travelling is safer than the bus we'd got into Colombo. Sri Lankans are crazy drivers; it's every man for himself, as if the four-minute warning has been sounded. So travelling on the roads in Colombo can be terrifying.

On the train people smiled at Bearsac but were annoyed by the men singing. We had learnt a bit of Sinhala and recognised the words for 'woman' 'night' 'beautiful' and 'good'. The mind boggles, but maybe only a little bit. The smallest of the men progressed onto his fourth bottle of beer in ten minutes; did he have hollow legs? Another of the group, a man not unlike a hippo, spluttered his way through a McDonalds as he chocked their song of clear filth.

After a quick swim I dressed for the hen-night and left Bearsac with Choc-Ice. Bearsac wasn't allowed on the hen-night, being a boy, but he said that he didn't want to go anyway. Still left without a handbag, I improvised. I had one of those purses that contain a small nylon shopping bag when turned inside out. I bunched it up about three inches from the top and tied around it, into a bow, a gold piece of ribbon that I had packed in my rucksack last minute in case I needed it for any random reason. I thought writing 'Prada' on it might be going a little over the top; but at least the brown bag matched my brown silk trousers and the light gold ribbon matched my top. Coordinated, I went to meet the girls.

The hen-night was calm as hen-nights go and I was glad to get my tired body into bed rather than carry on after the restaurant and stripper to meet the stag party and spend the whole night in a noisy casino.

Day 3

I woke just before 4am feeling somewhat ill and was sick about 5am into the bin. Yuk. I think I had accidentally drunk someone else's drink, which was the same as mine but had melted ice in it, instead of my own without ice. One should be careful of ice in case it is made from unpurified water. Choc and Bearsac nursed me until I got up at 8am for breakfast. I consumed several helpings of fuzzy-tasting fish curry, earthy steamed vegetables, refreshing grilled tomatoes and creamy scrambled eggs (the second best ever, after my mum's). Bearsac and I shared two types of *kesel* (bananas), a fat yellow and a fat red one. The red one felt like it had soft seeds down the middle and I slid my tongue along from end to end, loosening the middle from the rest of it, and smacked at the pulp with my lips.

Bored of looking at the swimming pool from the same unspoken spot, and as I was the first person by the pool, I decided to sit in a different area to look out onto the beach and sea instead. Later, when the others came out to take their usual spot, my brother came over to me in concern, enquiring into my reason for sitting in my new spot alone. He used a tone of voice one should not use with someone older.

Firstly - I was the first one out, so why did he not ask the others why they had not joined me? (Not that I expected them to. Nor did I have any problem with any of them, they are all nice people).

Secondly – What, I beg, is so strange about wanting a beach and sea view rather than a two or three-day old pool view?

Thirdly – What is so strange about wanting to have some quiet time with one's own thoughts rather than overhear gossip about people I don't know and about which celebrity is on which diet or going out with what other celebrity; not to mention conversations on which washing powder people use and the sparkling white merits of their choices.

For a break, we checked Bearsac's website; there was a message from Alan asking where I was; he'd not yet heard news of my safe arrival. I emailed him, grabbed some food and then we headed back to the pool, and then a beach walk taking us to sunset. Back in the room I checked out Sri Lankan TV - very corny.

I dined on the beach, sharing with Bearsac my lagoon crab with ginger sauce, which was too nice to describe in English.

'Bohoma Rasay,' I called out three times (very tasty). It both zinged and comforted my taste buds at the same time. In the hotel lobby I sipped a lime-soda whilst listening to the pianist to unwind before retiring to our room to sit on the balcony and look out over the sea. The moonlight danced on the rippled sea to the music of the waves, lapping the shoreline; distant laughter filled in the gaps and spices swam across the night air, mingling with the floaty aroma of exotic flowers. The bed had been made for the second time that day; on the pillow was a beautiful flower with such a strong and beautiful aroma, which served as a sleep aid. It seemed to help me, but the bears complained my snoring kept them awake most of the night!

This didn't occur to me until some time after the holiday, but I think I was meant to eat with my brother and Julia this night, as there had been a missed call on my hotel room phone and David had said to me, when I saw him the following day, that he had waited for me. I guess I needed direct information that he had intended for me to join him and Julia for dinner each night, except the night he spent with his new in-laws. I am so used to my own company, I forget that other people assume as the 'norm' that you will all do things together without saying so.

Day 4 - Wedding Day

The morning saw a walk and pool and beach swim, the afternoon and evening was what we were here for - my little brother's wedding. Everyone looked beautiful as they drew together in the lobby and Bearsac looked very dapper in his plum velvet suit and bow-tie. Down the stairs came Julia on her dad's arm; she looked beautiful in her pink sari. The bride and groom were greeted by an elephant that needed to relieve itself of the contents of its bladder. Calmly they stood, piss gushing by their feet, as they smilied at the camera. Things moved on from there as he set about proving he was a male elephant by developing a fifth leg at the back, if you know what I mean! Drummers and dancers, who seemed to be high on drugs, shook their bodies in frenzied fashion all the way to the wedding stand.

The ceremony was orchestrated in a whisper and we didn't know at which point they had become husband and wife. One bit we recognised was the stamping of the glass by the groom, a Jewish custom; the few Jewish guests shouted 'Mazel Tov'!

I felt more like a guest than the only relative of the groom, and wasn't sure if I was meant to be in the photographs, or if I would be asked. I was asked to be in a couple, but got the feeling it was almost forgotten.

A disco followed the beautiful dinner. Sri Lankan food is similar to Indian but this was fresher. For some reason, I was surprised to find I was on the head table with the bride and groom and the bride's family. I had been looking for my name on the other tables when I was told I was on the top table. I got a little upset as I thought of my parents not being there for David's big day, as they have passed away. Maybe it was just as well they weren't there; I wouldn't have wanted to see my mum feel she was playing second fiddle grandmother, nor to see them both feel just like other guests. That is how they would have felt, even if they had not been made to.

I was not sure if I was meant to make a speech or not; no-one had involved me in any organising and I didn't know if I was allowed or expected to make one. However, it was nice to be there and see my little brother on his big day - not that weddings ever seem to be about the groom as much as the bride.

Day 5

I checked out of Mount Lavinia Hotel. I had planned to move on today but decided to stay for elephants on the beach and the river trip through the mangroves the next day. The elephants on the beach turned out to be just one, and it walked for about one minute, so we didn't bother; there would be a better chance elsewhere. I got a simple apartment for 500 rupees (about £3). I didn't mind sharing it with the army of ants that were marching around the kitchen units; I wasn't planning on doing any cooking and I didn't think that they would march up my legs as I slept.

The room had its own sun terrace and the neighbour's king palm tree was within reach of the young yogi called Nano, who showed me the room and risked life and limb to pick one of the king coconuts to let us sample its delights. There was so much juice inside. Nano said he could come the next day and teach me the correct way to do yoga on the communal roof terrace. I think he was a 'higher karma in the next life seeker' (a person that genuinely gives of themselves freely, for the hope of a better karma in the next life). There are, apparently, a lot in Sri Lanka and India. As much as I wanted to learn yoga properly, and had been told via a medium that I would be shown properly, I thought I had better not as I didn't know him and didn't want a strange man doing weird things with his body in front of me. In the west we are not meant to open ourselves to strangers in case they are not safe. I feel that this gets in the way of new horizons, but I thought I should play safe anyway.

The day was again spent walking around the quiet areas then lazing by pool and on the beach, not much else to do in Mount Lavinia, and I was bored of it; holiday resorts are not my thrill. Had dinner at The Golden Mile, which sits on stilts on the beach. Jason, David's mate, and his girlfriend Helena joined Bearsac and me towards the end. I enjoyed speaking to Helena; we talked about life and not people, diets or washing powder.

Bearsac and I were at the Golden Mile for over three hours and the waiters had forgotten that I had eaten there and I had to ask for my bill about four times; don't know if they'd lost it or had just not made one out. Bearsac said I should just leave without paying but I told him off for suggesting such a thing. The 522 rupees was quite a bit to lose for them but only just over £3 for me, and it had been a nice meal. If it had been some rip off place in the UK being so slack with the bill, it maybe would have been different. The *tuk-tuk* driver quoted 200 rupees to take us all back to our hotels, which we laughed at. We offered 70 rupees, finally agreeing on 100, and he dropped Bearsac and me off first. The driver apparently still tried to charge Jason and Helena more at the end than agreed! Alan phoned, waking me at 3am; he was in the pub, it was only 9pm.

Day 6

Bearsac and I joined David, Julia and her friends for the Mangroves and river trip in Bentota. The water-dwelling mangroves, with the twisted roots rising above the water, looked like a jungle to a small teddy like Bearsac! There were small crocodiles and lizards, chameleons and all manner of colourful birds; it was so nice to see them in the wild. I was surprised not to see frogs or toads; despite Sri Lanka being rather small it is home to more than 2% of the world's toad and frog varieties.

We sheltered for a while under the mangroves so that those who participated could share a few joints, before heading to a gem shop, where we saw gems being cut and polished. Bentota is renowned for gems. Water sports followed this but not for Bearsac and me; we just watched. Luckily the annoying noise of the speeding water-jet engines didn't put me off my lunch of seer and roast potatoes, which I shared with Bearsac. The sand on the beach at Bentota was like talc, almost as white but just as soft. I took a few photographs whilst the others swam and, after returning back to Mount Lavinia, tried the Angler for dinner, which was a bit of a disappointment as the prawn curry I'd ordered medium-hot came very mild, though the prawns were wonderfully fresh.

Bearsac and I went to pick up my large rucksack (later than David had requested), which was in his room for security and found, by chance, that there was a birthday party for one of Julia's friends, which everyone else (including David's friends Jason and Helena, who I bumped into on the way to David's room) had been invited to. David seemed quite put out when his mad sister turned up at the door. Why it appeared an issue for him I don't know; I doubt that his apparent fears of what Julia's friends thought of me were based on reality, and they would have no consequences for me anyway, even if they were. I stayed an uncomfortable polite while, and then David walked the bears and me, rucksack on back, to my apartment and the bears and I sat on the terrace in much needed peaceful contemplation.

Day 7

I hadn't slept at all due to the sound of the very shaky fan, which I'd had to have on full blast due to the sweltering heat of the night. I lay for some time in the early daylight, watching the fan spin round and round before I got up.

We left Mount Lavinia at last, for Kandy via a few hours in Colombo Town, where we lunched at the Galle Face Hotel after a stroll on Galle Face Green, where people play cricket at the weekends. The Galle Face Hotel was mentioned in my Sinhala course book a few times, so Bearsac begged me for us to stay there. That was out of my budget, so we just ate on the veranda served by white-suited waiters, being fanned by the sea breeze.

I took a waving Bearsac in a *tuk-tuk* to visit Colombo's largest Buddhist temple before getting the 3.35pm train to Peradeniya, which is eight miles from Kandy. The journey was spectacular and is something you do for its own sake. The train passed through changing scenery offering an experience to the eyes: flowering plants and shrubs; far-reaching open expanses of greenery; hills and valleys; colourful sari-ed ladies amid the green of tea plantations; terraced rice fields, rusty, tin-roofed shanty homes, children merrily at play; people washing their clothes in the open, and much more, both beautiful and sad.

Various vendors paced the train, up and down, calling out their wares in a repetitive, escalating tone; I soon learnt which food was about to re-enter the carriage by their cries. I did more train hanging with Bearsac, during the slow bits; some of the passengers do this the whole journey.

In Sri Lanka it is considered bad manners to blow one's nose in public; so we sat on the train amid an orchestra of sniffing. A man sitting opposite us turned his head to the open window, pressed down one nostril with a finger and shot snot out from his other nostril. Thankfully it did not get blown into my face or onto Bearsac. I assume, considering the dislike of nose blowing, that this is quite the normal way to rid oneself of snot in Sri Lanka.

The two bears and I were picked up at the station for the Blue Haven Guest House in Kandy. Our *tuk-tuk* tootled through a small village, with lots of people walking in the road in its path. I was able, by now, to tell Tamils from Sinhalese; Muslims were more visibly different and easier to recognise. I perceived an uneasy tension in the air between the three different groups, especially the Tamils and Sinhalese, who have had civil war and unrest since 1983. I asked the driver about this and he told me in a seemingly unbiased, matter-of-fact way about the past troubles, explaining that in the current climate of rest there is now tolerance but with underlying tension.

Near the top of a woody hill, the guesthouse was shaded from direct sun. My room was basic, clean and had a pink mosquito net over the bed, which calmed Bearsac and Choc-Ice; they were worried there might be teddy bear eating mosquitoes. There was a terrace just outside, and also upstairs where a welcome drink awaited my consumption. Kandy is cooler than Mount Lavinia but still warm enough for shorts. We relaxed on the terrace, catching up on my holiday notes. A tree on fire in the far distance had now being extinguished, much to the relief of another guest; his concern must have been for those nearby or for the environment, as it was too far to cause us any worries.

A flicker in the corner of my eye and a scampering and scuffling sound distracted my attention from the still smoking tree. I turned, just in time, to see a monkey steal a hat that had been left on a table nearby, but I was left a little disappointed that the monkey didn't see fit to put the hat on its head. Bearsac and Choc-Ice were very excited and called out for the monkey to put the hat on. The monkey soon disappeared from sight and the two bears settled down again.

Kandy was originally known as Senkadagala pura after a hermit called Senkada helped out the king, who thus named the town after him. It was the capital of Sri Lanka until the British got hold of it in 1815. Some Sinhalese Sri Lankans call Kandy *Mahanuwara*, which means the 'Great City'. But the name Kandy was derived from the Word *Kanda*, which means mountain.

The family of the guesthouse were lovely; one of the daughters had lots of teddy bears and brought them out to party with Choc-Ice and Bearsac. We all had a photograph taken together. One of the other guests gave the mother some tapestry patterns in German, which resulted in her bringing out her tapestry handiwork, so our teddy bears' picnic turned into a crafts party too!

During the night spooky noises from outside enticed Bearsac, Choc-Ice and me to venture out onto the terrace. Screeching, moaning, groans and cock-a-doodle-doos in the moonlight were what we found: all the ingredients for a restful night. No, wait, surely that must be wrong! Have these creatures got nothing better to do at night than sit in trees doing impressions of each other?

Day 8

Having not slept, yet not being tired, we again ventured outside. It was now about 5am and we'd been intrigued to find out what these new sounds were. It was praying; Buddhists were praying. They were joined about 5.30 by Muslims praying from the Muslim part, so we were told by the only other person up. The rhythms were different but together were harmonic as they intertwined; it was nice to sit and listen to against the backdrop of creatures. Animals and humans now competed for vocal dominance of the dark. I guess it must be annoying to some people who don't pray and don't want to be woken early, as the praying was amplified over speakers.

Before breakfast I went for a walk with Bearsac to explore in the safe daylight the surroundings that held the strange sounds of the night. We met the cutest puppy you could ever wish to meet. He was sitting in the middle of the sun-streaked road in the shallow trench formed by tyres of - no doubt - a large heavy vehicle. He was a little timid to say the least. I sat cross-legged on the ground with Bearsac on my lap and we watched the little puppy with affection as it soaked up the sun in its trench. I was a little worried about leaving it there, as it was so small and might get run over; the dry mud-track of a road probably got used just a few times a day, but I thought it best to take the puppy to safety. Assuming it came from the nearest house, about 20 metres up the hill, I took it there.

Voracious barking alerted the house dwellers to the presence of a stranger; the dogs were loose, so I was very happy when a woman came out of the large house. I held up the puppy and said '*Barlla*' (dog) – I didn't know the word for puppy. I pointed to the road with puppy in both hands, to indicate that it had been sitting there, then saying the same in English. The woman understood, if not the words, then the actions. She shook her head in that peculiar combination of side to side and circular movement which I knew to mean yes. I handed the puppy to her and she spoke gently to it, stroking it behind its ears. As one of the big dogs trotted over, I could see it was a parent. The woman spoke to the dog and it sat obediently just behind her left side.

The woman asked 'Country?' I replied that I was from England and she said 'Princess Diana, sad.' She then pointed at Bearsac and said, smiling, 'Mr Bean teddy.' Bearsac pointed to me and said 'Debra's teddy', and then said '*Mahgay nama* Bearsac', to which the woman laughed, balanced the puppy in the crook of one arm and offered the hand of the other for shaking,. laughing again when Bearsac bit her. She said in English 'good Sinhala.' A child's voice called out from the house; we said our goodbyes in Sinhala and she thanked me. Woman, puppy in hand, dog at heel, walked back to the house and Bearsac and I turned back down the hill with a smile - well, at least I smiled; Bearsac doesn't have a mouth but his heart was smiling.

The distant mountains cried out to be photographed but as it was still not quite light enough to use small apertures - without getting camera shake with the slow shutter speed - I tried to take the photographs on self-timer to get less shutter blur. I had not used the camera's self-timer for a long time, and accidentally opened the camera instead; what a stupid woman. I quickly shut it so maybe only three to seven shots would be fogged.

I had had so many eggs in the last week and don't eat meat, so I opted for the offer of a Sri Lankan breakfast that the family were having. It contained lots of rice with chilli eggplant, chilli potatoes, tomato and onion, daal and popadom.

At 9am our driver took us to Sri *'Dalada Maligawa'*, known worldwide as the Temple of the Tooth. Revered as the most holy place in Sri Lanka by it's Buddhist majority, this is where, reputedly, lies a tooth of the Buddha. It was very beautiful (the temple that is, not the tooth - we didn't see the tooth). Before we entered, we were grabbed by touts and prompted to walk under an elephant's trunk and body three times; this one luckily only had four legs! It wasn't lucky for the pushy touts, as I didn't give them the 100 rupees they then suddenly demanded.

I made my way with Bearsac around the temple in a clockwise direction, in the way that I'd learnt from my research. The gleaming white of the exterior was echoed in the interior; rich colourful fabrics, wall paintings and golden relics adorned the alcoves, nooks and crannies; sweet spiciness graced my olfactory system, and dust danced in streams of sunlight in the few areas it was permitted to enter.

It was interesting watching the many pilgrims offer flowers (which had been washed in the fountains outside) to Buddha. I saw a woman touch a flower left by another; she then put her hands together as if offering the flower herself, but without picking it up; this, I noticed, was done by other pilgrims too. The scent of flowers filled the temple, hopefully aiding the meditations of the many people, children included, who sat on the cold stone floor with their eyes closed.

Since 1774, in August or July, celebrations are held for the festival of the *Perahera*, during which decorated elephants, humans with masks and dancers party in the street all night by torchlight. We exited the temple to find lots of monkeys in its yard; they were curious, if a bit scared of Bearsac and backed off or scuttled away as soon as Bearsac spoke to them. One monkey remained where it had been, a little further away, as it considered Bearsac, its head cocked to one side, cock in hand, fidgeting.

The temple is by a lake; but it might not be appropriate to say it that way. Rather, it would be more appropriate to say the lake is by the temple. Made in 1807, Kandy Lake was constructed by flooding the rice fields that lay there before. The last king of Kandy (Sri Wickrama Rajasinghe) had erected around the lake the *Walakulu* (clouds) wall. This pretty white wall extends just half way around the lake. The wall was not completed because the king lost the war and was no longer leader of the City.

A short but pleasant drive took us to the Botanic Gardens (300 rupees). At 147 acres, it is home to over 3000 varieties of plants, which pour their scents into the air, offering visitors an olfactory sensation to build memories upon. Memories formed by sound were on offer too, as we heard strange squeaky sounds from the trees; it turned out to be bats. Hundreds of large bats hung from the trees and some flew around showing off their wingspan; I'd always assumed bats to be nocturnal. The foreigners were the people without umbrellas; the Sri Lankans were prepared in the event of bat droppings raining down upon those brave enough to walk beneath the trees. The Sri Lankans smiled at Bearsac as I covered his head and we strode under the trees to the other side where the trees stopped. By some miracle, we came out unpooed upon and decided we wanted to go and paddle in the longest river in Sri Lanka.

At 335 km the Mahaweli River is a long one for sure. Our driver took us down the not too safe stairway, made out of tyres in the mud. There were a few people washing clothes, and themselves but they didn't seem to mind some strange woman and her talking teddy bear sharing their bath.

Next stop was Pinnawela Elephant Orphanage in Kegalla, which is situated between the central hills and lower country. Established in 1975 by the Sri Lankan Wildlife Department, the orphanage is home to about 60 elephants that have been abandoned or orphaned. Mostly open area, the elephants can roam around the 24 acres. After the feeding we followed the procession of elephants across the road to the river where they bathe; this we found a lot nicer to see than the feeding, where they were tethered and on concrete. It was great to see the elephants spray water from their trunks and roll over in the river. Bearsac wanted to join them, but I managed to convince him it would not be safe as he might get accidentally rolled upon or drowned.

Since 1984 over 20 elephants have been born here. Pinnawela has the world's greatest amount of elephants in captivity; but they are not confined to a tiny enclosure like in a zoo. The famous three-legged elephant, Sama, was there and she seemed pleased to meet Bearsac. It is thought that her leg was blown off by a landmine but this is unclear. Attempts had been made to equip Sama with an artificial leg, but she rejected all attempts, banging the offending feature until it was off. Maybe Sama doesn't want to be normalised, made to fit in with what humans think will be best. Good on you, Sama, be a proud three-legged elephant!

On the way back to the guesthouse I got the driver to stop so I could photograph a cow sitting nonchalantly in the road. I felt awkward asking as I felt I didn't have the authority to ask, even though I was paying. Once back at the guesthouse I took Bearsac for a walk into the village; I bought some sweets because I could not find any pens. The children in Sri Lanka ask for money, pens and sweets from the tourists (though money just gets taken by their parents - and maybe not for food). We walked along the rail track, coming across a hen and dog that passed each other in opposite directions, neither creature looking at the other. On the way back to the guesthouse, three children ran to us, as they'd seen the brown paper bag which spelt sweets.

We returned sweetless to our room to see how Choc-Ice was and to put more film in my camera. Bearsac told Choc-Ice all about our day as I sat on the terrace to read in the peaceful setting, taking a photograph of the rainbow spanning the mountains and woods. Family and guests all gathered on the terraces and watched the sunset; orange flickers painting the sky. Other than sunset comments I had a quiet evening, not having to make small-talk with anyone.

Day 9

The Blue Haven had a family of frogs and a turtle accommodating two small ponds. The two bears chatted to them for a while until it was time to leave the guesthouse and move on. The first port of call for the day was a batik factory; it was interesting to see the process. Made over days or a month, each colour is a separate layer; tremendous work goes into them. The work conditions looked comfortable, the happy, contented-looking women had comfy-looking armchairs and footstools, well spaced out in the clean, cool room. One does wonder, though, if that is just a front hiding a sweat-house at the back.

The intensity of smells at an herb and spice garden floated me along the winding path. I rubbed some of the extracts of aloe vera onto my skin. Bearsac and Choc-Ice joined me in the delights, or not, of sniffing at the aromas of nutmeg, cocoa, and other plants and their bearings. Nutmeg grows in shells like conkers with spikes on, and opens when ripe. I had a face massage with aloe vera and sandalwood ointment. Pleasant was my visit to the spice garden, even though it was clear its main purpose is as an open-air trade-show of hair and skin products.

Eroded by time and man were the steps up to one of the listed tourist must-sees, 'Dambulla Rock Temple', which turned out to be my favourite; Bearsac's so far was meeting Sama. The walls-cum-ceilings of the caves are painted with depictions of Buddha and his life. There are also painted carvings; the intensity and subtleness of colour just as one would expect it. Bearsac sniffed at the Buddha's decorated feet; I was just so glad he didn't say that they smelt. Lots of monkeys around that were scared but fascinated by Bearsac entertained the humans with their contra-dictory curious but timid reactions to him. Bearsac had become a real hit in Sri Lanka.

Dambulla dates back from the 1st Century BC, and has five main caves, which are built at the base of a 150m-high rock. It took ten minutes to climb up rather than the half hour we were advised. On the way back down, a man approached me carrying a wooden box with beautiful carvings. He challenged me to try to open the secret box. I took a quick look, turning it, and to his amazement, opened it with ease. His face was a picture when, following me trying to sell it to me, I took it back off him, placed a sweet in it, closed the lid, and gave it back to him.

On the way to the Sacred City of Anuradhapura, we stopped to sample some mangoes from a roadside wooden stall. They were like nothing we'd tasted before, the insanely beautiful taste and perfume almost took me off my feet. '*Bohoma rasay.*' (very tasty). How could we ever eat another mango in England again?

Anuradhapura is one of the ancient capitals of Sri Lanka; its ruins and intact buildings are spread over lots of sights, so it was not quite what I was expecting, I was expecting it to be more like Pompeii in Italy. There were bigger monkeys here; they were also scared of Bearsac and edged away from him as he greeted them.

Bearsac spoke to the oldest tree in the world. The scared Bodhi tree was grown from a cutting of the Bodhi tree in India, under which Buddha gained enlightenment. Buddha's tree burnt down long ago. The cutting, planted in 288 BC, makes the tree grown from it in Anuradhapura the oldest living human planted tree in history. Its view was somewhat spoilt by the railings that protect it; which was maybe a shame for the many pilgrims who had travelled from all over Sri Lanka to see it and offer flowers. A man came to me and said he'd seen me yesterday in Kandy, he remembered me because of Bearsac!

The guesthouse that was home to us that night was a timbered building, well at least on the outside; the interior walls were regular walls coated so thickly in eggshell paint that runs were highly visible. Geckos, in an assortment of colours, ran up and down the shiny surface of the walls of the hallway; I was disappointed not to have any as room-mates.

Dinner was an assortment of spiced vegetables and rice, and rather tasty. Darkness and strange sounds surrounded the guesthouse as I sat with Bearsac and Choc-Ice on the porch, letting dinner relax in my tummy. Choc-Ice was a little scared, but Bearsac took it all in his stride. My driver sat on the other side of the porch and played a card game with the guesthouse owner and two friends; glasses of Arrack aided their concentration. The game was punctuated by much shouting of what I recognised to be numbers; the volume of shouting grew with the volume of Arrack consumed. My driver brought me over a glass of Arrack, which is made from distilled coconut flowers. I asked the name of the game and he told me it was 'Three Nought Four' and is popular in Sri Lanka. He went back to the raucous game for half an hour before turning in to the separate building at the side of the garden, which is his home each time he stays.

The card players all now dispersed, I sat with the bears on the porch for a further hour or so, listening to the rhythm of the night, which was orchestrated by much variety of wildlife.

Day 10

It started to rain warmly whilst we waited on the porch for breakfast, watching the monkeys that had been joyously jumping between the trees. Suddenly, not so playful, they took cover.

It was still raining when we arrived at Sigiriya Rock, and it was going to be a long climb. It wasn't that long, about 20 or 30 minutes; but I didn't want Bearsac to get wet, so I put him in a large plastic bag, which I also had my camera and trainers in. I went up barefoot rather than get my trainers wet; the texture of the weathered stairs cut into the rock and worn smooth by footsteps of time made me feel grounded and at one with my surroundings.

Our climb to the top of the rock rewarded us with the view of the jungle. The greens, luminous from the ground, were almost lost in the mist but not quite; they danced a green dance of intertwining shades as the mist hovered over. Beautiful below and peaceful on top; it even stopped raining for Bearsac to come out of the bag. I paddled in the pool, laughing at the monkeys who appeared to watch this in surprise. Bearsac and I spoke to a Buddhist monk; he didn't have any sweeties for Bearsac unfortunately, despite Bearsac asking in Sinhala.

Sigiriya Rock stands 200m out of the jungle and is said to have been transformed in about 500 AD by King Kassapa into a fortress that became his safe haven, as he became a little bit of a scaredy cat for his life. The king's palace, 'The Heaven Castle', remains today only in its foundations. Frescoes, centuries old, depicting pretty Sigiriya maidens, adorn the face of the rock. Bearsac – being a bit of a lad – was intrigued by the bare-breastedness of the maidens rather than by any historic or artistic value. That teddy bear can be so embarrassing at times.

We went next to Habarana Elephant Safari, where we rode an elephant called Samani; Choc-Ice joined us for this. The water we passed through had lots of elephant poo floating in it; Choc-Ice nearly fell in! We had bananas to feed to Samani and when we said his name he reached up his trunk for them. We were given a certificate with each of our names on as evidence of our brave act.

The sites of the ancient city of Polonnaruwa were spread about, but we were quickly transported between them by car. Polonnaruwa was the second capital of Sri Lanka after the destruction of Anuradhapura in 993. The present capital is Colombo.

Bearsac said hi to the Reclining Buddha but was greeted by a stony silence. You should not have your back to the Buddha (though I don't think that applies to teddy bears, so I took a photograph of Bearsac in front of it). At another of the sites a group of monkeys lay on their backs sunbathing; they looked most human side by side. I had my digital camera wrapped up in a large leaf to keep it dry; this attracted the attention of two very large monkeys, who tried to grab it from me, seeing food! I tugged it from them and they showed off their very sharp-looking teeth. I showed them Bearsac, having noticed earlier how the monkeys were scared of him, and they shot off like bullets.

At a wood carving factory, our next stop, we were shown the different types of wood available in Sri Lanka. Loving the smell and feel of wood, I went round sniffing and stroking it. We were eagerly directed to the array of beautiful furniture, wooden animals and stilt fishermen, made by master craftsmen and probably sold by master salesmen. There was no way we were buying any though, it was not exactly cheap.

We arrived at The Giritale Hotel, where I headed for the swimming pool. People seem to think it's mad to swim when it's raining but the rain is wet like the water! There was a wedding party and the photographer wanted to take photographs of me, while other Sri Lankan men wanted their photograph taken with me saying to me '*Bohoma Lahsahneh*' (very beautiful). Maybe they were *ahn-dhah* (blind)!

The scenery, though, was indeed *Bohoma Lahsahneh*. Our room overlooked the Giritale Tank, a large man-made lake built by some of the old kings' men. As it got dark, Bearsac and I watched monkeys chasing around, and mongoose. Bats swarmed out of the cave beneath us. Two of the staff came over as one wanted Bearsac to speak in Sinhala to the other. Bearsac was more than happy to oblige, but spoilt it at the end by biting, as he so often does. The now four assembled staff said that the other guests didn't speak to them and it was nice that I and my teddy bear did; and they respected that we had spoken in their language. It got me thinking, as I sat listening to the flapping of bats and scampering of monkeys and mongoose; how I don't get this unwritten rule whereby we have a place in life's hierarchy, and we are meant to magically know our rank and stick to it. I think everyone is equal but that we each play different roles in different aspects of life. I thought about how in previous jobs I had got into trouble for treating everyone equally, in that I treated the management as equals rather than superiors, and failed to recognise the 'assumed' ranking within my peer group – based on what, I have no idea.

Back at my room, I couldn't get my key in the lock, so I had to go to reception to get them to try. The man at the desk asked me about the elephant; I thought he was asking if I knew the word for elephant in Sinhala as I had spoken in Sinhala earlier that evening, so I said *'Ahlilah'*. But what he meant was: where is the elephant key fob? It turned out that I still had the key to the guesthouse we'd stayed at the previous night and had been trying to get in with that!

Choc-Ice didn't join Bearsac and me for cocktails, so Bearsac and I shared a Giritale Queen, which consists of Arrack (the distilled coconut flower drink), pineapple juice, Cointreau and coconut milk. We removed the soppy pink umbrella before diving in. By now we were not only speaking in Sinhala but also thinking in it. *'Bohoma Rasay,'* we both thought together.

During dinner, three men playing instruments serenaded Bearsac. After dinner, on the terrace we spoke to a couple from Holland and their driver. Our driver came to say goodnight and I gave him the key from the guesthouse, as he would be back there next week.

On returning to our room for the night, we had another door incident. This time, right key but wrong door! Good job the key didn't work, or else we'd have ended up in someone else's bed! Back in the room, and after my shower, the two bears enquired whom I had been speaking to in the shower; it was a pink gecko called Gayle.

Twice during the early hours, reception staff came to my room as they said the phone had rung from there. I had not phoned. The young man spoke very little English and my Sinhala was far, far less. When I mentioned it on checking out, they said there was a fault on the line. I suspect, however, that the young man working the night-shift had really taken it upon himself to assume that a woman alone in a hotel room had maybe wanted some late-night room-service from him.

Day 11

We left beautiful Giritale for Nuwara Eliya. At around 2000 metres above sea-level and carpeted by lush tea plantations, the hills of Nuwara Eliya are the main producers of tea in Sri Lanka. We passed some of the swirling green plantations before arriving at Aluvihara Cave Temple, where the Sri Lankans laughed at Bearsac and wanted to take him home. The cave temple - its walls adorned with images portraying the life of Buddha - was the result of a landslide. A monk wrote my and Bearsac's names for us in Sinhala on some parchment paper he made in front of us from a dried strip of ola leaf. We checked with our driver and he confirmed what the writing said. However, the lettering is not so much a direct translation, but the ordering of Sinhala characters in relation to the sound of the names in English.

At a tea factory, all the staff thought Choc-Ice and Bearsac cute; they were permitted by their supervisor to take time out and crowd around and stroke the bears. Choc-Ice, being bigger and older, got more of a fuss made of him than Bearsac, which rather put Bearsac's nose out of joint.

We learnt about the process that the leaves go through, and about the different teas. Five kilos of fresh leaves, dried at 80 degrees, make one kilo of tea. . The best is BOP (Broken Orange Peking) and BOPF (Broken Orange Peking Fine). The finer shredded the leaves, the stronger the tea. The strong tea is drunk with milk and the weaker without. I bought some of the BOPF as most people I know have tea with milk; I don't drink tea. I bought Bearsac a new friend called 'Tea'; she is a tea-picker souvenir teddy.

It was a long slippery walk down the hill to the waterfall next. The spray speckled my glasses as it splashed off the rocks. We found out afterwards that there are lots of leeches in the water, so it is a good job we didn't fall in.

My driver dropped the now three bears and me off at the Grovesnor Hotel, which is built in a colonial style. I bought him a bottle of Arrack to say thank you. Bearsac and I got talking to some other people: a young man, originally from Sri Lanka but who had lived most of his life in New Zealand, and a couple and their driver. The driver and couple said it would be OK to go with them the following day, as they were going to Ella and I had no plans.

I took a walk into town to find Internet services; what I found was very slow so I just did a bit of emailing and limited research. Later, I dined with the young man from New Zealand, and we spoke of our travels in Sri Lanka. He went to bed early that night as he had to rise very early to get to Adams Peak, which is best climbed during the small hours of the morning in order to reach the top for sunrise. Maybe I should have joined him – not in bed, I mean, but to Adams Peak! However, I don't think my bad knees would have stood a task as arduous as all that climbing; and besides, I had now planned to go to Ella with the couple.

Day 12

Left Nuwara Eliya for Ella with the couple, the driver dropping us at the station so we could do the beautiful train journey. He picked us all up at the other end. The rain that fell for the most part of the journey did not disturb the views too much. Ella is quite cool in temperature and is lush and green. A quiet little village on the east side of a mountain range dotted with a few shops, houses and guesthouses, there is a lot to see if you like walking and exploring: Ella Falls, Ravana Ella Falls, Ella Gap, 'Little' Adams Peak and other places where there is magnificent scenery. You could just go there, though, to get away from the hubble of the more touristy parts of Sri Lanka.

The wooden inn - which was a large hut with four or five rooms in a row - was simple and reasonably clean, and cost 1000 rupees a night (about £6). I met up with the couple and their driver and we all ate dinner in a pub full of local Sri Lankans. I recognised the numbered cries of the card game 'Three Nought Four' being played in a corner of the pub; I was not surprised to see that a few bottles of Arrack accompanied the cards on the table.

Thankfully the driver and the couple escorted me back to my inn; there were no street lights and no confirmed path back. As in other villages in which we had so far stayed, strange noises outside my room kept me awake all night, so I met no sleep.

Day 13

Our unpaved path to the train station at 6.30am was dimly lit, and the softness of the squishy substance I had just walked in worried me somewhat. Having managed to scrape some sort of animal poo off of my shoe, we got the 6.55am train to Colombo. 1st class at 500 rupees was not available, so for 154 rupees I got 2nd. This was 91p for a nine-hour journey! I was thinking of sitting in 3rd class, even though I had a ticket for 2nd, as a group of British lager-louts on a cricket tour were standing by us on the platform and I didn't fancy the prospect of a nine-hour journey with them. Luckily there were a few 2nd class carriages. The school children we shared the carriage with at the start of the journey looked so cute in their white uniforms, the older kids in ties and the younger with bowties. They giggled and pointed at old Choc-Ice and Bearsac. Bearsac was again upset that Choc-Ice received more attention than he.

Once at Colombo we went into Railtours tour place for suggestions of where to stay. The only place available in our price range was the YWCA, at 1066 rupees. Nice enough building as you walk in, colonial style. It was an experience, to say the best. The hostel had staunch rules: in and doors locked at 9pm, in bed at 10pm! The devout Christian woman on the reception outside our makeshift room with two beds – one with a mattress with a large hole in it - guarded the place more fiercely than the randy dog that kept trying to grab my leg!

As I was talking to a young man I'd seen at the guesthouse in Kandy, the woman asked me if I had a boyfriend. When I said I have been with him over eight years, she asked if we have sex! She then went on to lecture both me and the young man about premarital sex, once she realised we had stayed in the same guesthouse in Kandy. What was she expecting!

To keep some semblance of order, I went to stow my rucksack in the wardrobe. I opened the door and was greeted by a spider; I'm sure it winked at me. It was enormous, big enough to shag a tennis ball, maybe. Normally OK with spiders, I was paranoid it would be poisonous and so quickly stomped my rucksack down upon it, stopping it dead in its tracks. Two legs stuck to the bottom of my rucksack and I had to scrape them off with tissue, feeling rather cruel and guilty.

Due to poor drainage, I was instructed that I should stand in a bucket when using the shower, and pour the water down the lavatory; I nearly fell over from laughing! My laughing must have got Tommy the dog excited, as when I came out he was near wetting himself as he tried again to grab my leg.

'*Kæri Barlla!*' I yelled, (sperm dog). By the time I was back in the room, my feet were dirty and I had to use bottled water and tissues to clean them before putting my shoes on. We wouldn't stay here again, but were glad we did just once as it was an experience we won't forget and will make us laugh when we recall it.

Colombo at night is quite scary, so Bearsac and I didn't venture too far in search of dinner. The only place clean-looking enough to eat at was noisy and brightly lit, so we ate quickly and returned back to the YWCA well before the curfew.

The reception woman left about 1am and, like a naughty boarding school kid, I ventured disobediently out into the reception hall-cum–living room. With a dim, low-lying florescent tube on the wall at one end of the room, it was rather spooky. The old furniture, gong and pictures on the walls and the creaky floor took me back to my school days when the girls' dorm would sneak down to the hall with the gong and bang it, then run back to bed before the nuns came for us! I didn't bang this gong though, I was too scared that the woman might return and tie me up with the randy dog! I found sheets of Christmas carols and sat on the rug with Bearsac, singing them softly whilst pretending the rug was a magic carpet flying over Sri Lanka. Bearsac claimed he felt a warm rush of air through his fur like we were really there, then I lost my imagination when Bearsac farted and we plummeted back to earth and the eerie YWCA room with an auric bump. We were singing 'Silent Night' when, at 2am, the clock struck up that exact song; this sent us running back to bed! At 3 and 4 o'clock it played 'Twinkle Twinkle Little Star'; we know, as we didn't sleep at all that night, just like the previous one.

Colombo has a population of nearly one million. It is the commercial Capital of Sri Lanka, and keeps up with modern developments while preserving its old world charms. There are lots of Buddhist temples, Hindu temples, Mosques and old churches; night-time entertainment includes karaoke bars, and discos.

Day 14

After breakfast, which was not much to talk of, we packed up and headed to the Qatar Airlines office close by, to confirm our return on the 15th. We left my large rucksack at Railtours and looked around the shops and market. Housed in a dirty little hovel, wooden planks offered narrow paving from the mud. Stalls tightly packed together availed little passing space; yet a little old man, all ribs and dirty dhoti, darted through the confined spaces, large wicker basket atop his aged head. His red bananas, the abundance of yellows, oranges, and greens brightened the greying wooden stalls, which looked mostly to be in much need of repair.

With my shoes now covered in mud and possibly worse, we departed the market and took my camera films in for developing. I bought some Arrack from Cargills (which is the oldest department store in Sri Lanka, built in 1845), and some plastic Sinhala letters to practise with. I also got some children's learning books with pictures of animals and objects with the names in Sinhala from a market stall. I nearly did the whole transaction in Sinhala and then walked down the main street in Colombo Fort with all the traders trying to sell to me, and *tuk-tuk* drivers touting; and I didn't use a word of English as I turned them down and agreed Bearsac was a beautiful baby or teddy bear!

The Colombo Fort area is one huge cloud of pollution; buses

gridlock the road, each puff their contribution into the air filled with overwhelming sounds, too many to count. Bus conductors hang from their buses shouting their bus's destination and main stops, constant beeping of car and bus horns, street vendors yelling. Not knowing whether to put my hands over my nose or my ears, I manage, just, to co-ordinate myself into the relative quiet of Railtours. I have a sit down and talk to the reps inside and thank them for looking after Choc-Ice for me. Grabbing said teddy bear and my rucksack, we get a train to Negombo.

Took a *tuk-tuk* to the Golden Star Hotel; dumped bag on bed, got hot body into bikini and dived in the pool, leaving Bearsac and Choc-Ice to kill mosquitoes. The hotel staff were all very friendly, especially the male staff. I had to pretend I was married when, at 3am, I went to the poolside to cool down and get some air. I was asked chat-up questions by both a man who appeared to be sleeping rough, and a member of staff who was skiving on the sun loungers in his white uniform, whom the rough sleeper seemed to know. I fibbed that my husband's snoring had driven me out of the bedroom, hiding my unringed hand under my bum as I lay on a sun longer. They concentrated their questioning on my impressions of Sri Lanka after that.

Day 15

Had breakfast of the best poached eggs I have ever tasted, after expressing my annoyance that there was only a banana and croissant as a vegetarian option, and trying to leave for a paid breakfast elsewhere. . It's discrimination of vegetarians, I pointed out – but then I do work for a campaigning organisation!

Bearsac lazed by the pool as I swam. We later walked the beach where we met a local family; the father asked me to take a photograph of their son and we noted their address to send it to.

At 2.30pm we got a local bus to Colombo, 30 rupees. At the House of Fashion, I got a Sri Lankan outfit and then rushed to get our photographs before the shop shut. On the way back by public bus, we met a Sri Lankan man who wrote our names in Sinhala, and a British couple who were staying down the road from our hotel, so we shared a *tuk-tuk* with them and headed for the pool as soon as we got back. Bearsac and I had dinner in the same place as the previous night as it was so nice. I shared with Bearsac chilli and lime seafood and vegetable fried rice, but we couldn't decide if we liked it more than the tuna steak of the night before. I received lots of compliments as I walked back to the hotel in my Sri Lankan outfit, and we wound down our last night at the poolside bar with a couple of Arrack cocktails.

Day 16 – Last day

The *tuk-tuk* driver, who had taken us to the hotel and whom we had booked to pick us up at 6am, let us drive the *tuk-tuk* on the way to the airport. On the second part of the flight, from Doha to Heathrow, I drank too much alcohol (flying triples the alcoholic effect) and was sick a few times. The flight attendants moved people so I could lie down, and Choc and Bearsac looked after me. My boyfriend Alan was to meet us in arrivals but was late as the tube was stuck for 20 minutes. Welcome back to England!

Elephant orphanage – Sri Lanka

Chapter Six

Amsterdam – Holland
1st Trip

Day 1 - Saturday 20 March 2004

I know why they have windmills in Holland; it's because of the gale that nearly took us off our feet as we walked down the road in Amsterdam to where Alan, Bearsac, Choc-Ice and I were booked in to stay. I actually got blown past the door and Bearsac was whipped about rather roughly.

Our accommodation, The Amstel Inn, was on the edge of the pretty Amstel River. The couple that owned or ran the place were pleasant but we didn't see much of them. The room, although nice, did not have a shower as we'd expected, so the couple said the next day that we could stay in their new place in the town centre at no extra charge.

Choc-Ice slept whilst Bearsac, Alan and I went out to hunt down some food and have a look around. In reality, Alan had put his foot down at Choc-Ice coming out with us (he is quite a big bear), but he knew better than to insist Bearsac stayed with Choc-Ice.

I like to think that my teddy bear is innocent and that the sex museum would be therefore a bit of an eye-opener for him - but really he is not at all innocent. The ground floor exhibits were somewhat disappointing, but upstairs was more interesting. Many aspects of erotica are covered by different media in the museum. Bearsac and I just had to sit on a large penis chair. It suddenly started vibrating and I jumped in shock, almost hitting the ceiling. Having got over the unexpected, I sat down on it again, finding it more comfortable now, knowing about its vi-brations. Graphic photographs of humans with animals grabbed Bearsac's attention, but it wasn't my sort of thing at all.

This was followed by a visit to a coffee house. The distinctive, fresh herby smell of skunk hit us as soon as we opened the door. A lovely tabby cat sat contentedly on the counter, all mellow like; but as soon as he saw Bearsac he became very alert and excited, as if he had been on catnip. Alan smoked some of their finest but, neither puff nor coffee being my cup of tea, I just allowed myself to be used as a medium of communication for Bearsac to the cat. There didn't seem to be anyone drinking cof-fee in the coffeehouse, which was good for me as the smell of it gives me a headache and can sometimes make me panicky. Back outside, the whipping wind was so aggravating - especially over the 'Skinny Bridge' - so Alan wanted to go back quite early. Think he was missing Choc-Ice really.

The Skinny Bridge (Magere brug) is one of the most famous bridges in Amsterdam. The Internet tells me it's claimed that the Skinny Bridge was named after the Mager Sisters (*mager* is Dutch for skinny). These two rich sisters lived on opposite sides of each other along the river. It is claimed that they had the wooden bridge built to make it easier to get to each other's homes. However, realists state that it gets its name because the original bridge used to be so narrow that it was hard for two people to walk past each other. When more boats and barges started using the river, a wider bridge replaced the narrow bridge in 1871. Although the word 'skinny' no longer really applied, it stuck and does so to this day.

The name 'Amsterdam' is said to derive from '*Amstelledamme*', which means 'dam across the river'. Amsterdam is also said to have been rescued from the water. By the way, 'New York' in the

USA was once called 'New Amsterdam'; it was renamed New York in 1664, when captured by the English.

We didn't venture out during the evening as Alan was so worn out from the day. Luckily for me, the Inn was no smoking; but for poor Alan this meant standing out on the doorstep in the wind, a little strange in Amsterdam.

Day 2

The entrance of the Anne Frank museum is just like any other; we made our payment at a modern-looking counter and did not really consider the immediate surroundings.. It was seeing and touching the bookshelf that was the reality check of where we were. It was strange climbing up the very narrow, steep creaky stairs to what turned out to be quite a spacious hideaway – mind you, not so spacious for eight people when a growing girl shares a bedroom with a male stranger and her older sister shares with the parents.

Alan got split up from Bearsac and me upstairs; we were in different parts of the slow moving line of people traipsing through the rooms. When we were reunited, Alan told me that I had done the same things he had done, even though he could see that I had not seen him do them. We had both turned on a tap over the kitchen sink, and we'd both felt the surface of the kitchen units; no one else had touched a thing, he said. We both felt that this exploration, by touch, somehow brought us closer to the fact that Anne and the others had lived here for real and it was not just a horrible tale frozen in a museum. I have a habit of sniffing at things, even if they are not expected to have any smell, so I sniffed the walls at one stage, but I think Alan missed that one!

For those of you, if any, who don't know who Anne Frank was, or her story, I will try to explain.

Anne Frank was a German-Jewish girl living in Holland who, with her family, ran away to live in hiding in Amsterdam during the Second World War. Anne's dad, Otto, was Managing Director of a company that had its premises in the building where the secret annexe was. Over some months, the annexe was prepared and furnished with the family's furniture as a hideaway; they took residence on 6th July 1942. A large bookcase was erected to cover the doorway to the annexe.

Anne is famous for the diary she kept, which starts on 12th June 1942 on her 13th birthday. In it, she talks of her feelings about herself, her family, friends and boyfriend Peter. She sometimes mentions her inner struggle against the imprisonment of hiding and of war; but the resilience of childhood, and a child's ability to lead a normal life whatever the predicament, shines through in Anne's very eloquent writing about the usual teenage feelings towards everyday life.

The last entry in the diary is on 1st August 1944; on 4th August, having been betrayed, the family were arrested when SS officers and detectives stormed into the no longer secret annexe and took them away to a prison. On 8th August 1944, they were taken to Westerbork transit camp, before being transferred to Auschwitz concentration camp and finally to Bergen-Belsen, where Anne died in March 1945. Had she survived a few weeks more, she would have seen the day, April 15th 1945, when British Army soldiers gave the survivors back their freedom from the camp and the horrors they had faced for what must have seemed like an eternity.

Of the eight secret annexe inhabitants, only Otto Frank survived. When he returned to the annexe, he was given Anne's diary, which he published in 1947. Threatened with destruction, the building with the annexe was bought by Amsterdam residents. They started a foundation called The Anne Frank House Organisation and the house was opened as a museum in 1960.

After the time spent at the museum - which was made emotional more by our sensual exploration than by the knowledge gleaned from the video and information adorning the walls - we strolled along the canals, trying in earnest to avoid getting run over by old worn-out bicycles. Bicycles are everywhere in Amsterdam and are mostly old. Many bikes are not padlocked and mostly all look the same. It's not hard to wrongly assume that they are there on a 'use as required and leave for next person' basis, as they don't seem to get nicked and there are always piles of them every few metres. So if you were to take the nearest bike and leave it at your destination, there would always be another one for your use if that one was not there when you left!

Alan was moaning as his feet were hurting from his old cowboy boots - poor thing – so we didn't stay out too long. Had lunch in a tapas bar, sharing various yummies, and then took a quick look around the shops before returning to room for a rest. As promised, the woman took us to the new place in the town centre; it was better, with en-suite shower / lavatory and had a hob and fridge. It was right opposite a coffee house and next to a café that baked its own croissants.

We checked out our neighbourhood and a couple of bars; Bearsac keeping a low profile, only speaking to a couple that noticed his cuteness – much to Alan's embarrassment. I know bicycles get everywhere in Amsterdam, but riding one inside a bar is going a bit too far. The rather stoned man was soon asked to leave, but not before riding over someone's toes and knocking over a drink. Within another half hour, it was my turn to moan as it got too loud for me to cope with and we called it a night.

Back in the room we lay listening to people outside; Alan thought that Dutch people speaking English sound American; Bearsac suggested that maybe they watch a lot of American satellite TV. Alan even answered Bearsac; I hoped that this would be the beginning of a beautiful friendship between them.

Day 3

Alan managed a bit more walking today. We went back to the Anne Frank museum shop to get a book for his mum and then looked around the shops at all the marijuana paraphernalia. Was not much going on in Dam Square, just some twats dressed up like pillocks. It is said that 'all roads lead to Dam Square', which is bang in the middle of Amsterdam. The Royal Palace, the War Memorial and the Nieuwe Kerk are housed here, where greedy fat pigeons peck about and poo all over the joint.

We thought it would be nice to do the boat trip on the canals, and with Bearsac in his plastic yellow sailor coat, he was dressed the part. We passed the Mayor's gaff; Bearsac swore he saw a face peering through the window and a hand wave at him. We also went past the clock tower, called 'Crazy Jack' because it always tells the wrong time. There are 165 canals in Amsterdam; Bearsac said he wanted to take a paddle boat down all of them, but there was no way Alan and I were going to do that, even if we had the time, which we didn't.

Later that night we tried the coffee house opposite our room, which I think might be the oldest one, but which still only dates from 1985. It was from another coffee house that we got some space cake. For about 30 minutes after eating it I was fine, but then suddenly I started getting what I will call an 'allergic reaction'. I became high and giggly and was in fits of laughter over silly things. The dark brown coffee pot on a shelf became a monk's head. Alan's coat on the coat stand beside the shelf formed the monk's body and the arm of his jacket was the monk's arm. I knew it wasn't really a monk but it looked so real. I went over to it to explain to Alan exactly where the monk's head and body were; I thought I had spent just a minute explaining this, but Alan informed me later that I spent 20 minutes going on about the monk! Later, making love, I was a jockey and Alan the horse. The gap between the two halves of the bed became the racetrack as I galloped down the track, climaxing at the finish line into a simultaneous implosion and explosion as everything burst into bright light.

This high mood slowly evolved into a darkly reflective mood. Alan seemed to start distorting his face, making it go in and out. He swore he wasn't doing anything with his face and although I knew he wasn't, it really looked distorted. Random images from my life flashed by: for example, the time I buried a step in a sandpit with sand; and when the spoke from the buckle in a pair of Clarke's school shoes poked into my foot. Although it didn't hurt me, I will always remember it. (Anyone born in the UK before the mid 1970s will remember those shoes from Clarke's; they were brown, round-toed with small holes in the upper of the shoe and a strap going over the top of the foot.) I have had that 'spoke in the foot' memory often come back to me in random images that flash through my mind as I drift off to sleep. Images and scenes that I told myself, at the time of their occurrence, I would remember all my life, but thought no more of, were vividly recalled in those random flashes in Amsterdam.

When the room appeared to be caving in, and Alan could not convince me otherwise, I became hysterical. He tried to calm me down by giving me Choc-Ice to cuddle but I didn't want Choc-Ice anywhere near me, and the same with Bearsac. When

I grew worse Alan wanted to get help, but didn't want to leave me. I soon burned myself out and started calming down. I finally drifted calmly off to sleep around 5.30am, according to Alan, and woke up later to the smell of chocolate croissants. The monk had regressed to its former form of coffee pot, and Alan's coat and everything else was ordinary once more. Needless to say, it was an experience I will not forget too soon.

Day - Last day

After almost getting run over by a tram that shot past, missing us by inches, we had a look at the small flower market and popped into a little shop where we recognised a Liverpool / Irish accent. The young lady running the shop was born in England and had English parents, but had lived in Amsterdam most of her life and her boyfriend was Irish, so she had a jumble of accents. She was very nice and chatty, we would have probably seen a bit more of Amsterdam if we'd gone in on our first day, I'm sure.

The flight back was as quick as coming, about 45 minutes' air-time. But the funny bit was we departed at 1320 and arrived at Luton at 1330! Bearsac said he was a bit upset he didn't tip furry toe through the tulips, but in all he had a good time, as did the rest of us.

Canal trip - Amsterdam

Chapter Seven

Amsterdam
2nd trip

24th July 2004

Just a day trip this time, but it was a long day, much to Alan's annoyance, as we had to get up at 2.30am to get ready for our 6.30am flight. Alan moaned and groaned all day long, all over the gaff; so the day was not as good as it could have been. Bearsac and I wanted to go to the Van Gogh museum; but it was out of the question with moany Al in tow.

We looked around a few sex shops, but Bearsac claimed there was nothing a hip teddy bear like him hadn't seen before. Still, he was toying with the idea of buying some furry bondage items to keep his lady *Tea* under control! Further into the red-light district, a decorative open-air urinal on the street took my interest – a work of art almost. I wanted to photograph it but Alan convinced me it would not be a good idea, as it was in use by a very large man!

After losing count of the number of fluorescent painted bicycles we saw, we had a break and a snack in Danizig. Home-baked bread, still warm, and some *Rijpenaar* (old Dutch cheese). The cheese sure did taste old – not in a mouldy sense, just that it had a real dry and mature taste to it; real yummy yum yum, as Bearsac exclaimed, rather too loudly for Alan and the people sat nearby, but fine for the staff.

We later had another snack in a Spanish style tapas bar, where we had eaten on our first trip to Amsterdam. Spicy olives, plump sardines with sun-dried tomatoes, red peppers stuffed with rice and pine nuts, and a complimentary bowl of pistachio nuts with the drinks. This time we spent a little longer sitting watching people pass the window: a man with clogs, beer belly spilling over his tracksuit bottoms and McDonalds spilling from his mouth (must have been British); some stag groups and, for some reason, lots of people wearing yellow. One little girl noticed Bearsac sitting in the window when she was having her laces tied by her mother. With snot dribbling from her nose, she waved back at him and wiped her nose on her sleeve before being dragged off. This was the only child I had seen walking in Amsterdam all day. I don't think I had even seen a child walking in the four days we were last here; they all get carried on their parents' bicycles.

The purchase of lots of duty free items at the airport persuaded Alan it was worth the trek afterall.

Bicycle with teddy seat - Amsterdam

Chapter Eight

Hungary, Croatia and Slovenia
September 2004

Day 1 - 18th September 2004 - fly to Budapest

Out of the six teddy bears Bearsac and I met at Luton Airport, only two were with children. You'll probably call me biased, but I think Bearsac was by far cuter than any of them. It makes a change from Bearsac thinking that himself, though.

The plane had a leak, so we had to wait for a replacement, which took a while to fuel, and so got off late. On the bus into the city, people didn't seem to know how to take Bearsac; not a smile was cracked between the many people bumping along on it. I wondered if this was the face of things to come for Bearsac in Budapest. If so, would my darling little teddy bear's huge ego take it?

The Red Bus 2 Hostel was in what must once have been quite a grand apartment block; traces of its former glory echoed in the lobby and stairway. A small hostel, it was clean, with pay Internet. We shared a mixed room with five others. Two of them were Brazilian identical twin sisters; one loved Bearsac and the other took an instant dislike to him. Both Bearsac and I were unable to tell them apart until we got either a smile or a death look.

The quiet inside the hostel contrasted with the street outside, where Hungarian football hooligans aggressively bated each other. I was warned, by an impossibly thin, green-haired room-mate, that the ladies' shower was subject to flooding if used too long. I used it for too long. Green-hair spoke a lot in her sleep but in Spanish, so I couldn't make it out. Bearsac snuggled up to me, whispering that he could feel the nasty twin sending vibrations of hate toward him. Silly little bear!

Day 2

It was the dirty 1015 westbound train that took us to Zagreb in Croatia. We'd booked the train the night before. The journey was over six hours. We sat in a compartment with a respectable looking young family, as the other carriages were full of drunken chain-smokers, or were empty, which worried us, in case one of the drunks came in. The family took a shine to Bearsac and the kid sang to him and showed him drawings he had done. Our stay in the compartment was short lived, though; this was just as well as the child was asking Bearsac if he knew what his drawing was of, and Bearsac was clueless as to the subject of the child's proudly presented scribble. The ticket-man came and said something about going down the train.

We went further down the train, with cigarette smoke clinging internally to me as I held my breath against the stench, and found another compartment with a family. However, not two minutes later a drunken man pulled the door back with a bang. He coughed out a chimney of smoke and spluttered smoky drunken fumes. As he gasped for breath, he took a draw on his dying fag and fell into the cubicle, setting off the baby crying. Thankfully, his friend was behind him and scooped him up and dragged him off, apologising in Hungarian.

Ticket-man came again; we had not gone down far enough for Zagreb, so decided it best to go to the front. We came to locked doors - which I assumed were just stuck - so got off the train at the next stop to try and get on further down from outside. Panic set in as no doors opened and we mad-dashed it back to the door where we'd got off, fighting with the weird mechanism in blind panic that we would be left on the platform! We got back on and were informed by an amused passenger that the carriages we'd tried to board was the sleeper carriages, and we were fine for Zagreb in the one we were in! I sank heavily into the dusty seat and let out a sigh, relief riding stronger than a need to cover my nose and mouth from the cloud of dust slowly rising to my head.

We passed what I thought to be a couple of lakes and I inquired from a young man the name of one of the lakes. He informed me, with a smile, that it was a pond. We found this to be true an hour later when we started the long, long run passing Lake Balaton! Lake Balaton is the biggest lake in Central Europe; it is 77 kilometres long and its width ranges from four to 14 kilometres.

A Turkish man in his 50s shared the compartment I was now in. He tried to chat me up, leading with his bushy Magnum moustache, which made me want to puke. I tend to look at people's mouths when they speak, so I avoided looking at him altogether. He noticed and said:

'You 'fraid moustache; moustache harmless.'

He even had a name for it, like it was an entity in its own right. I don't remember the name, as I was blocking out the foulness of it from my mind. It was like the stereotypical scene from a film where the slimy, medallion-wearing moustache-man is unaware of how unattractive he is to women, and thinks he's God's gift, assuming any disinterest in him is down to the woman being shy or afraid, and not down to the foulness of his moustache and his sliminess.

Thankfully, Slimy Moustache Man got off a couple of stops later. A woman who was also in the compartment, but had until now been silent, voiced her relief at the departure of Moustache Man and his hairy entity. We laughed at this recognition of shared feelings between women of two different nationalities (she was Croatian).

At 1435 the train stopped at Gyekenyes (on the border of Hungary and Croatia) to split the train. A herd of passport control officials boarded the train; a young official entered our compartment, trying in earnest to look serious when looking at and stamping Bearsac's passport, though I did detect a hint of a smile. The train started going backwards, which was a bit disconcerting, but we got to Zagreb at 1611 as due.

It was Sunday, and we could not get my travellers' cheques changed anywhere, so used a cash-point after being assisted by two Aussies, who had the exchange rate in their guide. The rate was 12.25 kuna to £1. The Aussies also told me which trams to get to my hostel: numbers four, seven, 11, 12 and 13. Tickets cost eight kuna on the tram, but were cheaper if you bought them from a news-stall.

It was a relief, after the long journey, to get to the hostel and find that my room-mates were all out, leaving us a chance for a peaceful rest. Our later hunt for food was not too successful, but we did get a barbecued corn on the cob whilst exploring the ground market, which was mostly old ladies selling jumble on towels on the ground. Sadly for Bearsac, there were no teddy bears being sold that he could speak to, so he just spoke to a few humans instead; they didn't quite know how to react and just looked silently at him.

In a wine bar we sipped smooth Croatian red wine. A rather drunk man leaving the bar with his dog was trying and trying to shut the door; it had been shut to protect me from the cold night air finding its way into the conservatory, where I was sitting out of the smoke-filled bar with Bearsac on my knee. The man was being tugged forward by his enormous and rather smelly dog, but he tried and tried until he succeeded in his polite attempt! I don't think too many people in Britain would make such a polite effort, even sober. Croatian Big Brother was on the telly as we paid and left. We would have stayed to watch it but that part of the bar was very smoky. It was on in the sitting room at the hostel when we arrived back anyway – not that I understood a word.

We were joined in the sitting-room by a young Nigerian man, who jumped out of his skin when Bearsac greeted him, but laughed deeply when the realisation hit him that Bearsac was just a teddy bear and not a monkey, as he said he thought he was. I enjoyed listening to him recall his travels, until he started slagging off Dutch people for some reason, referring to them by some urban dictionary of derogatory terms. What happened to him in Holland? I wondered, but didn't encourage him by asking. Did he assume that I, by my mere presence in the same room as him, would share his opinion?

Bearsac and I sought refuge in the kitchen until we realised the Spanish men in there were slagging off Pakistanis and homosexuals. What was going on? Had I checked into the International Bigots' Conference or something? I went to read on my bed with Bearsac sitting on my tummy.

Day 3

At 7.34am we left the hostel for the day breakfastless, to do a walking tour of the Old City. The Old City tour started in Ban Josip Jelacic Square, which is surrounded by buildings of different styles. The square houses a fountain, which in turn houses a watering hole and communal bath for pigeons. Whilst we were there an old lady approached the fountain. A clatter of wings shattered the peace as most of the pigeons flew away before she got anywhere near, even though they had stayed put when Bearsac and I walked around the fountain. The woman walked round one way, then the other way, looking for coins that had missed the fountain. An old man told us that the woman came every day at the same time and did this walking around the fountain each way, looking for coins. He said that the pigeons didn't like her and flew away when she came. The old woman seemed pretty harmless, but who knows, to pigeons she might be the devil in disguise!

The fountain is a few steps away from the original spring well, which is thought, partly, to have given the city of Zagreb its name. Ban Josip Square, named after army general Ban Jelacic, has existed since the 17th century. A statue of Ban Jelacic on a horse was removed in 1947; it was hidden from the Communists in a gallery in the cellar. In 1990 it was returned back to the square when Croatia regained independence. The square seemed to be a hangout point for the youth of Zagreb and a people-watching spot for adults. We sat watching people watch people for a while over an ice-cream.

Another noteworthy item on the Old City tour is the statue of the famous Croatian writer, August Senoa. It is brass, I think, and he leans against an advertising pillar, taking a little break. If we'd had a KitKat, I'm quite sure Bearsac would have offered him some.

I like to absorb the energy of busy markets, at least when I am not stressed out or buying anything. This particular market is known as the Belly of Zagreb; if this is the case, then Zagreb is vegetarian; at least on the surface. Old ladies in colourful scarves confidently demand the best vegetables by pointing, and shunning inferior items with a shake of their hands. I bought baby-sized corn on the cobs that had kernels in various shades of yellow, orange, brown and red – more as a souvenir than to cook. (It was only some weeks later, once back home, that I located the source of my moth infestation; the pretty corn on the cobs had been playing host to moth eggs. I then remembered that spirit had passed on a message to me via a medium a few weeks before my holiday, saying that I would bring moths back in my rucksack.)

Anyway, under the market square is the meat market, which is the unrestful grave of dead mutilated animals; it reeked of carnage. I could have done with wearing a pair of welly boots, but we didn't hang around; we were chased out by the raw stench.

There were originally four formal entrances to the city, but only one of them remains. Kamen vrata (Stone Gate) was last reconstructed in 1760. The gate suffered, according to legend, a great fire, which burnt up all the wooden parts but left out, in its hunger, the painting of Mary and little Jesus. The painting was found amongst the ashes without damage. People come to worship the painting, housed in the gate, which has a tiny chapel. In 1931 a golden crown was added to the painting – a bit like gilding the lily, if you ask me, and an insult to the original artist. Nearby, in Nun's Street, we found ourselves walking behind a nun, which we took as good luck.

In St Marks Square is St Marks Church, which is probably not such a surprise. We didn't enter, but admired the pretty, multi-coloured roof tiles, which have shields representing the coat of arms of the Kingdom of Croatia. Entering St. Ciril i Metod Street we found, at number eight, the stone head believed by legend to represent Matija Gubec, the leader of the peasant uprising. Word has it that he was executed on the square, but historians have not yet agreed this to be the case. Intellectual historians are an unagreeable lot!

At Lotrscak Tower, every noon for the last 100-odd years, a cannon is fired, giving people a chance to set their watches. We were there at the wrong time, but seeing as we both had no time-telling instruments anyway, it was not such a missed opportunity. Near Lotrscak Tower is the funicular railway, which was built in 1891. This, or the stairs beside it, takes you down to the lower town where, after a turn, we found ourselves back where we'd started our tour in Ban J. Jelacic Square.

We had lunch in a quiet Croatian restaurant decorated with fake columns and loud murals. We had the non-smoking room to ourselves; the smoking room was quite full. The mushroom and buckwheat soup with plenty of parsley was thick, creamy and pleasing on the palate. However, my walnut pie - although filling - was rather bland with a greasy sauce. At least the side vegetables were fresh and *al dente*. With me fooded up and Bearsac sweeted up (the waiter had given him a few sweets), we then did the newer city.

The new town, or 'newer' town wasn't, so interesting and noteworthy but there were some nice old buildings to admire and find out about. We were both too tired by now to bother doing all the newer town tour, so we returned to the hostel worn out. We chilled out sitting in the garden after having washed my clothes and later joined some of the other backpackers, who photographed Bearsac with each other until it was too cold to stay outside, I was quite relieved when it turned colder, as it was then a convenient chance to get away from the young group and have some dinner in the kitchen and talk one-to-one to an older person. I haven't a clue what 20-somethings are chatting about these days; it makes me feel rather old. Not that I had much idea when I myself was in my 20s.

Day 4

The 0755 train headed out to Ljubljana, edging us away from the busking male nuns that were being moved on by police. Bearsac greeted a woman in our compartment, who voiced her disapproval at my travelling alone.

'Women should not travel without companion, it is not like lady and is scared.'

'It can be scary sometimes and anywhere can be dangerous, but what a sad existence we would live if we never did anything due to it being a little bit scary.' I replied.

'Tut tut tut,' she tutted.

I wasn't in the mood, so found another compartment where Bearsac and I learnt a few words of Slovenian from a Slovenian lady. Got Bearsac's passport stamped again by a bemused passport official.

Pulling into Ljubljana, it looked ugly by comparison to the scenic Slovenia we'd seen so far. However, on inspection of the town centre, Ljubljana proved to be a beautiful capital city with that Eastern European, unpretentious weather-touched elegance merged with careful restorations.

There were no hostels available so we booked into the most affordable hotel, Park Hotel, which was rather drab but had a good view of the drunks outside who were spreadeagled on two benches with beer cans scattered around. I handwashed my underwear and Bearsac's T-shirt; relaxing as my aching hands were soothed in the warm water. I was taken, for a moment, back to childhood. I pulled the plug out and placed my hand over the plughole, enjoying, as I used to, the sensation of the light suckage. I love that gurgle burped up as the last of the water run downs the pipe, all the stronger for having been held back from its flow.

After writing up my travel notes, we took a walk around town, stopping at the side of the market to eat grilled sardines with potato, and tomato salad drenched in garlic. Bearsac shared our bread with a friendly sparrow that was hopping around on the table; it even took bread from Bearsac's paw. As we ate, we watched the small busy market stallers selling their colourful wares and picked up a few more Slovenian words.

Bearsac got a few smiles and giggles at his greetings as we strolled along the river and the back streets to Ljubljanski Grad (Ljubljana Castle) on top of the hill, 78 metres above the city; where we climbed the tower and admired the scenic panoramic views of Ljubljana with its red-tiled roofs and the surrounding green hills and mountains. A young couple took a shine to Bearsac and they shared their thoughts with him of what they had seen so far. They then posed with Bearsac, who had told them how famous he was.

We excitedly took the mini train back down to town and had Italian ice-cream whilst strolling down the river and people-watching from the Triple Bridge. This bridge has not always been a triple bridge, it now has three parts to it – one for traffic and two either side for walking – but it was originally just in one part. Using his newly acquired Slovenian, Bearsac greeted more people, getting a slightly more animated response than he had in Croatia and Hungary.

The pedestrian trafficlights in Ljubljana have a countdown in seconds for when the next green man will appear, which is quite useful. Crossing the road in this town is taken very seriously. I received many looks of horror and shocked gasps whenever I crossed where there was no crossing, or if I crossed the road before the green man appeared. If you have ever wondered what jaywalking is, then the last two examples are it, and we later found out it is illegal in Croatia and taken seriously if caught by the police. Thankfully, we managed to keep ourselves out of jail.

After a break at the hotel, we went to find somewhere to email Alan and got some food. Sitting outside eating, I was chatted up, rather feebly, by some slimy man. I was more interested in my food and as this slowly dawned on him, he remembered some prior engagement and bid us goodbye. We wandered around for a while, darkness making its presence felt, and took breathers every so often to sit and scene-watch. The Triple Bridge is beautiful lit up, but the area was a bit noisy, so we found a quiet wine bar. Bearsac drank most of my red Slovenian wine as we sat in quiet contemplation and wound down for the night.

Cold from having just got out of the shower, I shot into bed. I cuddled Bearsac, feeling slightly naughty for cuddling my teddy bear naked! Once warm, I sat by the window, watching drug deals being made and dogs being walked.

My night's sleep was interrupted by a loud shrill ringing tone. I thought at first it was the fire alarm and grabbed Bearsac as I shot out of bed. The noise we were rudely awoken by was in fact the telephone. It was after 2am; and it was Alan. He was in a panic as he had misunderstood my very rushed email, which said I was going to Bled. He only thought I was bleeding!

Day 5 - Bled

We took the 8am bus about 55km from Ljubljana to Bled in north-western Slovenia. Taking just over one hour, it passed teddered fields[2] and quaint houses with bright coloured wooden shutters. The bus suddenly slowed and high pitched shouting filled the air. An old woman in a buggy was driving it in the middle of the road and was no doubt swearing as she was being waved aside by the car driver behind her, who was gesturing at her to get onto the pavement. I don't know what it means, and I doubt it's polite, but she was thrusting her palm upwards at 90 degrees to the road at the man in the car as she shouted at him and carried on in her tiny buggy, which was barely big enough to support her rather generous body.

We were picked up and taken to The Jakelj Hostel; a pretty house with wooden shutters set at the bottom of mountains and hills in Zirovnica in the quiet country. Tall sunflowers nodded at us as we took a look around the large garden; Bearsac was a little miffed that they didn't reply to his greetings. Although our bedroom was a five-bed room, there was just one person to share with, a nice young lady called Tina. The 15-bed hostel was run by the lovely Jakelj family. Momma and Poppa - as they were known - looked after you like you were their own. Bearsac was treated like a baby; normally he complains if I treat him like a baby, but here he just loved all the attention.

We were shuttled down to Bled, a few miles away, and first went to Bled Castle, perched 130 metres on a cliff rising out of the trees like a phoenix from the fire. Silence filled us both as we looked out over Lake Bled. The lake from here looked so tranquil against the backdrop of mountains and forest. We took the more dangerous route back down from the castle to next take a boat ride (normally 2000 sit, but Bearsac bartered it down to 1000 sit as the boat was near full) to the small island in the lake, and the church. There are 99 steps leading to the Church

2   Teddered fields have had the hay laid out to dry by a machine called a tedder.

148

of the Assumption, and, during weddings, it is customary for the groom to carry his silent bride up them.

The church has a wishing bell, dating from 1534. We tried and tried to ring the bell three times to make a wish, but it wouldn't ring. One lady got it to ring and passed the rope to me so we could do it, and we finally got it to ring three times. Hope it still counts.

After a quick walk around the small island - looking at trout in the turquoise water - we took the boat back to the village and strolled around aimlessly before spending nearly two hours sitting in a church, occasionally disturbed by tourists taking a quick look. There is not much to do in Bled if you're not going to partake in water sports.

We were picked up at 7pm along with some others staying at the hostel. That evening, we all sat up talking over drinks; Bearsac sipped away my cherry brandy whilst I wasn't looking. After a few hours, the situation arose where no-one wanted to be the first to go to bed but we were all desperate to do so. I was too tired to play games and made the first move, and that was the cue for everyone else to turn in. What a peaceful sleep I had cuddling Bearsac.

Day 6

The Jakeljs had remembered that my eggs needed to be more healthily poached and not fried, so it was a good start to the day. After much thanking and much kissing of Bearsac from the three female Jakeljs, Poppa dropped us off at the local train station, where we got a train back to Ljubljana. We spent a bit more time in Ljubljana before getting our return train to Zagreb. For ease and convenience we thought about staying at the Omladinski

Hostel, which was slated by so many people on-line, as we wanted to be in the town centre and it was the only affordable place without tramming it. We also wanted to judge it for ourselves, so we could at least say from experience if it was as bad as made out; it felt almost like an adventure.

We walked into the dismal reception area, took one look at the receptionist's intensely miserable face (she did not even greet us) and turned on our heels and walked out! A face so miserable I have never seen; she could win awards for having the face of misery itself. We left the sour-faced crab to wallow in her misery. I bought some food to cook, some wine to drink and thence the tram to the hostel we'd stayed at before. Luckily, they had a bed.

We roomed with three French people but spent most of the evening talking politics to an American man and disagreeing over Israeli occupation with an Israeli woman in the kitchen. At least tonight the hostel was not full of rowdy 20-somethings. From then on the Israeli woman tried her feeble best to upset me by whispering deliberately loudly to her friend that I was crazy and the bear was 'like a rat'. She seemed rather wound up that I wasn't upset, and made herself feel better by concluding to her friend that I was in blissful unawareness of what she was saying.. Had she been of any consequence, I would have told her it was more a case of blissful 'couldn't give a shitness'!

Day 7

Rain greeted us as we left the hostel and I'd left Bearsac's raincoat at home. Have you ever got stuck in a tram jam? Well, we have. Don't know what was going down, but there were 20 or so trams in stationary convoy and we were at its back. We saw that the front tram contained the driver and two officials by the driver's cabin by the time we'd walked down, so continued walking in the rain but took shelter in a department store before catching our train back to Budapest. It took the whole seven-hour journey for my trainers to dry as the heater kept going off. Did they stink! The heater was quite useful for drying off Bearsac's fur and stuffing. It's a hard life for a teddy bear when the silly human responsible for its well-being leaves its yellow plastic rain-mac at home. We had the cubicle to ourselves for most of the journey, apart from a short visit by some man who eyed me up and left when he realised we didn't speak the same language.

Trudging with small but heavy rucksack, we thankfully soon found the Aboriginal Hostel, where I made some dinner and ate it watching an Austin Powers film in Hungarian – beats watching it in English. The hostel, if you haven't guessed by its name, has an Australian theme. The doors are painted in aboriginal style and there are boomerangs and didgeridoos adorning the walls. It is in an apartment, is quiet and reasonably clean; and Internet use is free. One room does not have four walls, but three walls and curtain; this was the room we were in but it was still quiet. There are 18 beds in this hostel.

Day 8

Left the hostel at 8am to explore, using the Chain Bridge - which was the first permanent link of Buda and Pest - to cross the Danube. The Danube River divides Budapest into Buda and Pest. Pest is on the Eastern side of the Danube and Buda the Western.

We first went to Buda Palace on Castle Hill, reaching it on foot as the Siklo - a 19th century funicular - only goes a very short distance so was not worth the tourist-based fee. Near the foot of the Siklo is a monument called "Kilometre Zero"; from this zero-shaped monument all distances from Budapest are measured. The hill shows off a great view of the Danube and Parliament from its summit. The palace was the home of Hungarian kings for many years. The palace and its defence system were built in the 13th century, following the Mongolian invasion. Destroyed and rebuilt many times, it is thought of as symbolizing Hungary itself.

The Fisherman's Bastian was heaving with tourists so we just had a quick look. I'm not too keen on crowds of people moving around and getting in the way, wearing inane frozen smiles on their faces while waiting for some pratt to take a photograph of them. Built in 1905, the Fisherman's Bastion was named after the guild of fishermen whose responsibility it was to defend this stretch of wall from enemy attack in the Middle Ages. Seven turrets represent the Magyar tribes, who once populated the country. We then checked out some colourful shops and small galleries before going to the history museum, which covers two millennia of history.

After the museum we came across a brass statue of a horse. A queue of students were climbing up and stroking the horse's male bits. The brass was greened and blackened with age but the much-stroked male parts were shiny. We learnt from one of the students that it is meant to be lucky to stoke this part of the horse, so up I climbed and we took our share of good luck; maybe going a little overboard. After having touched the horse's bits, I had to find somewhere to wash my hands – not because I had touched the horse's genitals, but because of the brass smell which offended my nostrils even at arm's length from my nose.

We left Castle Hill for Margaret Island, in the middle of the Danube. Margaret Island is a large park connected to both sides of the Danube by two bridges, one at each end. Entering from the Margaret Bridge end, we watched the performing fountain while taking a rest; it performs to classical music. Nearby was the Centenary Monument (designed by István Kiss, 1972). It was erected on the hundredth anniversary of the union of Pest and Buda. The only road on the island permits buses, but no other traffic; this lends itself nicely to the purpose of the island – peace, quiet and relaxation. The trees are hundreds of years old and are filled with birds chirping merrily away. Flowers sing out their scents to the buzzing bees, which are no bother to humans or teddy bears.

Through the bustling and petrol fumed streets we tracked down the Hungarian Wine Society. I perused the various bottles and asked a few questions. I think - because I had expressed my relief at finding the place after much searching, and because of the questions I asked and terms used – that the man in the shop assumed I was more knowledgeable on wine than I am, and let me sample some expensive Hungarian red wine called 'Gere Attila, Kopar', which is now my favourite; but at over £20 per bottle, we just settled for the taster. I would hate to think how much it would be in the UK. I think the man was a bit annoyed that I didn't purchase any. I bet he had never had a teddy bear sample the wines before in there.

We arrived back at the hostel at 6.30pm for our first food of the day, with a rather humble bottle of Bulls Blood. The name Bulls Blood, or 'Bikaver' in Hungarian, refers to the story that tells of when, in the 16th century, the town of Eger was set upon by the Turkish army. The Hungarians fiercely fought back; so fiercely that when the Turkish invaders saw them drinking red wine that stained their beards red, they assumed the ferocity was gained by drinking the blood of bulls.

Day 9

Out just after 6am, we walked to the Gellert Baths early, leaving the rest of the day for other stuff. As I pampered myself, Bearsac sat locked in the changing cabin envisaging the marathon exploring we would no doubt be doing once we were out. More like a cathedral than baths, the art nouveau décor was a blur of colours without my glasses. I couldn't make out the patterns of the mosaic floor tiles nor the painted ceilings, but the colours seemed to move and swirl like when looking through a bottle and turning it; and the splashing of swimmers echoed off the walls.

Bearsac and I set upon Gellert Hill the hard way, taking short cuts. Bearsac hates it when I take short cuts as it always involves some sort of danger; or at least he'd have it said that way. We sat taking in the views for a while; layers of different architecture that must have taken many years to morph into the tapestry of eras before our eyes. We headed back down and looked around the shops, where Bearsac was pointed out by shop assistants. We perused a synagogue in the old Jewish quarter. We took lunch and a glass of wine in an old inn; its lead-paned windows and wonky looking arched door had attracted my eye. It appeared to be family run and a woman who I guessed to be the Gran or Great Gran (as there was a younger looking old lady) pointed out Bearsac to the middle-aged man behind the bar. It was the young woman in her 30s who took our order and first spoke to Bearsac. I don't know what she was saying, but she gestured to ask if she could take Bearsac over to the two older ladies, and I permitted this with an upward waft of my hand toward them. The elder of the clan cupped her hands under Bearsac's chin and blew kisses at him; the second in age patted his head. The middle-aged man then took his turn at petting and placed Bearsac on his shoulder like a parrot. He did a little dance, to which the ladies all clapped a rhythm known to them as a group. I got Bearsac back and a pat on the head myself from Great Gran.

My paprika fish soup was pleasing and was accompanied with lots of bread. Known as *the Bouillabaisse of Hungary*; this soup is unfussy but tasty. Hundreds of years ago, fishermen cooked it over campfires on river embankments. Neither Bearsac nor I could work out what fish it contained, but there were at least three different types. Our exit of the inn was graced with waves and kissing sounds towards Bearsac from the two older ladies, and back out on the streets we walked some more.

Whilst sat on a bench watching people walk by, we were joined by an old Hungarian Jewish man. He spoke to us in Hungarian despite us saying we didn't speak it. After some time he asked if we spoke German; we said no but I thought he might know some Yiddish so said, 'I am *meshuggeneh*' (crazy). He laughed and spoke Yiddish. This was the most we were able to exchange in words – not that I speak Yiddish, but I do know more words in it than in the other two languages. I mimed 'exhausted' as I said '*oysgemitchet*', in explanation of my sitting on the bench. Pointing at my half-eaten pastry, he said '*Fress*' (which means to eat – especially between meals). The man gestured for us to wait there and dashed off into the flats behind, returning soon with three teddy bears, two old and one new. We assumed, by his obvious love for them, that they were his. Bearsac kissed them all and the man was over the moon, saying '*haimisher*' (friendly). After another ten minutes I indicated 'walking' with my fingers. . I said '*sholem aleichem*', and Bearsac and I continued our exploration, thankful that I'd revised some Yiddish phrases from a small book I have at home in case I ever come across any old Jewish people.

Back at the hostel, over dinner we watched Tom & Jerry and The Flintstones in Hungarian. The Flintstones music was different and rather strange, but Hungarian seems to suit Fred and Barney.

About 9pm we took an after-dinner stroll along the Danube to see it in its glory at night, and the view from both the Pest and Buda sides. Whilst we sat watching the moon, an old lady with headscarf, apron and Wellington boots limped slowly past, with a very heavy-looking bucket in one hand. I don't know what she was doing or where she was going with it in the dark; we thought of asking her if she wanted help but got the feeling she would refuse any offer and would feel insulted. I don't think she would understand why an offer of help was being made and we think the people walking past her, turning back and looking at her, would have had the same thoughts as us. What does an old lady do at night with a heavy bucket? Where does she go and why? These questions were perhaps better left a mystery and were my last thoughts as sleepy head hit comfy pillow.

Day 10 – Last day

Climbed up Gellert Hill again soon after 6am; as if yesterday's visit wasn't enough. It was freezing. I meditated, with Bearsac sitting on my lap, whilst the hill was still free of tourists and dog walkers. We visited the cave church (Sziklatemplom), which was real groovy with calming soft interior cave walls. It is a cave of chapels, established in the 1930s by the Pauline order, which is the only order native to Hungary. Founded in1256, it was ended in 1773 by Josef II. It was re-established 150 years later; the monks of the order were confessors to Hungarian Kings. In the 1950s the Communists, who then blocked up the chapels, jailed the monks of the Sziklatemplom. The cave and its chapels were only re-opened in 1989.

Wandering around the winding streets, Bearsac waved at passers-by; older people seemed to get it and nodded their admiration, but not the younger ones. One young woman nearly fell off her bicycle after letting out a squeal when Bearsac greeted her as she cycled past. Straightening her hat, she rode off into the road, maybe feeling it was somewhat safer than the pavement.

At 11.30am we left the hostel for the airport, where we met a few people in the queue and on the plane. We sat next to a woman that was a bit kinky; she wanted to spank Bearsac for looking in her bag! A young man sitting in front of her asked her if they could swap seats as he wanted to speak to Bearsac, but he was quite lost for words for most of his visit to our row. Bearsac often has that effect on people but it could have been me scaring him off; I have that effect on people too!

I was halted by customs for having 2400 cigarettes for Alan, instead of 200. I thought the old rule of 200, which had been upped to lots more, applied to Hungary, but it doesn't. The young official let me off when Bearsac charmed our way out of trouble. Alan came to meet us at the airport and when we got home he wouldn't let me cuddle Choc-Ice, as he wanted to. I desperately needed to re-energise by hugging Choc-Ice, but had to go without until Alan was sitting in front of his dinner and I ran into my bedroom and grabbed my chance, sinking my nose into his head and inhaling.

The next day, as usual after any trip away, I washed out the fumes of travel from my beloved teddy bear and put him out on the balcony to dry in the sun, and later sniffed at the 'teddy bear fur in the sun' smell I have loved since childhood.

On the whole people in Hungary, Croatia and Slovenia had mixed reactions to Bearsac, less animated than anywhere else (apart from the Inn in Budapest and the hostel in Bled). Some people smiled and laughed, but a lot simply looked puzzled.. In Croatia, the pre-teenage girls in full make-up expertly exuded boredom out of every pore and stuck their little noses in the air as though they thought they were too sophisticated to react!

In all three countries, I found that the folk are quietly friendly, if approached first, and although not cold, they don't seem as warm on first meeting as people I have met in other countries (again, apart from the Inn in Budapest and the hostel in Bled).

I still wonder what the old lady in Wellington boots was carrying in her heavy bucket.

Fountain of the Pigeon Devil-Woman of Zagreb and Bearsac looking out over Lake Bled

Budapest Tunnel

Chapter Nine

Amsterdam
3rd trip

Day 1 - Saturday 10 September 2005

To help relieve a friend of his fear of flying, we chose to take a third trip to Amsterdam as it is a short flight. The only thing was that he chickened out before getting the train at Borehamwood Station. He had no need to worry, as the flight was fine.

We got bus 22 from Centraal Station to Camping Zeeburg, which is a camp-site about a 20-minute ride from the centre of Amsterdam. Bearsac and I stayed in a hut with a bunk bed. Thanks to my friend not coming, Bearsac and I each had our own bed; Bearsac took the top bunk whilst I was in the bottom. The hut was basic and reasonably clean, although I moaned about the bottom of my feet getting covered in dust from the floor.

If you are the sort of person or teddy bear that likes to swing cats, I would advise against staying in the huts for one to two people, as the poor cat would get splattered up the wall! Still, for cheap accommodation without having to share, or stay in a tent, it serves its purpose well. The basic showers and lavatories are clean. There is also a small laundry and sinks for hand-washing clothes. There is a nice cafe/bar with three computers for pay Internet. The thing that is real cool about the camp-site is the small animal farm with goats, a brown sheep; hens and a turkey. They apparently roam around the camp-site amongst the tents when not in the enclosure. There were also a couple of families of ducks with cute ducklings that sucked up the rain and condensation from the tents in the morning.

Bearsac said hi to a few people, who looked a little stoned. We checked our emails before taking some Dutch cheese and some wine to sit on the grass by the water's edge, sipping and nibbling as the sun danced on the water to the music of goats mæhhhing in the background. The camp-site is in a reasonably quiet area, apart from ducks quacking and coots cooting just outside our hut. If you are ever to stay there and are unlucky, as we were, you might have three male twats in the next cabin giggling most of the night like teenage girls on the other side of the thin walls.

Day 2

At 7.15am we went to find the camp-site's animal farm and said hello to the animals. We also followed the ducklings around the tents, and filmed them scrambling over empty Heineken cans outside one of the tents. Mother duck must have got a bit paranoid as she waddled over to me at great speed and pecked at my feet.

In Flevo Park, Bearsac spoke to some of the joggers, got screamed at by a heron and chased by a swan. What with being chased by mother duck earlier on, it is easy to get the idea that birds in Amsterdam have attitude. Onwards through the falling leaves, September smells filled the air; the changing seasons mingling. The underworld of the stairs to the park sticks out like a sore thumb amid the otherwise unspoilt nature reserve. Lager cans and bottles lay strewn about the deserted, graffitied skate ramps. Some of the artwork could be in a gallery, but it has been dissed by less talented graffiti vandals, tagging over it in their scrawl.

Bearsac was eager to move onwards to the town centre, so we headed for tram 14. The tram broke down and we were stuck for ages. Still, it gave Bearsac a chance to sit in the driver's seat for a photograph. At Dam Square it looked like something was being set up in the square for later, so I made a mental note to come back.

We came upon Volendammer Vishahandel haring shop and shared a lovely fresh raw herring roll with mild pickled onion and gherkins in wholemeal with poppy seeds; it was, in Bearsac's usual eating words, yummy yum yum. The haring shop is on one of the alleys between the main road leading from Dam Sq. to the station and the main shopping pedestrian street and is near the Dam Square end. The herring fuelled us for more walking and we then returned to Dam Square to see what was happening. There was a homelessness festival organised by Z Magazine, which is the equivalent to The Big Issue in England. A band was playing, rather too loudly for my ears. There were information stands and a food tent feeding the homeless. We sat and watched for a while before more walking. We came by a parrot in a cage in a flat above a shop; the window was open with the cage in its openness. The parrot was the loudest and most talkative parrot I have ever had the pleasure to come across. Bearsac tried to teach it to say 'Bearsac' and 'bearsac.com' but it didn't even try. Who knows, maybe it remembered later and drove its owner and passers-by mad repeating his name forever more.

Two of our hours were spent at the History of Amsterdam Museum. Here we learnt about how Amsterdam was rescued from the sea by being drained by diking. We learnt about the city's development from early to present day, and the population rise. There was a set-up of an old pub, in which Bearsac tried to get a drink from the bar by lying under a beer tap. However, nothing came out; you can't get the service these days even if you try to serve yourself.

We left the museum and walked about some more and came upon a small art gallery that had an artist's sales event or something.

We didn't know if it was a public event or invited guests only, but no-one asked to see an invitation and we got a glass of wine as we admired the art and spoke to a few people. I should at least name the place in payment for my wine. It was Galarie Mokem at number 334 on the corner of either Oude Zijds Voorburgwal, Centrum or some other road.

We did more walking around, taking photographs of bikes ridden by adults with babies, small kids and dogs strapped on in various fashions. We had more herring too, this time from a street stand; it was not as good as from the earlier shop but still good enough to have Bearsac yummy yum yumming all over the place, drawing strange looks and laughter from nearby strangers.

A popular fast food joint in Amsterdam is Febo. As well as buying from the counter, you can self-serve from coin slot glass cabinets that are constantly replenished. Junk food is not something we favour, but we wanted to try it for the experience, though didn't, as there was only meat available. We photographed and videoed other people going for it, though.

We took a well-needed break for a beer in a Dutch pub, 'Cafe Otten', where we were warmly welcomed. Bearsac even had his own small glass of beer with a straw. He had a fuss made of him by people, especially as we were leaving, when a group of men sang a song to him in football fan style. It was well cool; but then, he's such a cool dude teddy bear.

We came across a young man doing a stunt of juggling. Amongst the items he juggled were: a very large knife; a flamed torch and a yellowing green apple, of which he took three bites whilst juggling with the lethal weapons – all on top of a free-standing ladder. Bearsac yelled out to him, ' You could have used a fresher apple!' We bunged a euro into his hat at the end, not the –four to ten euro he joked about people putting in. Still, I'm sure he must have made enough to get very, very hung-over the next morning.

In the red light district, Bearsac spoke to a lovely young lady who was standing in a doorway with a crowd of men around her. She had in her hand a black leather whip. Bearsac asked her to whip him with it; laughing, she obliged. Happy, Bearsac thanked and kissed her. We were then followed by a dog that Bearsac had spoken to, but managed to shake it off at the main road by crossing. We were back at Camping Zeeburg and in bed by 11pm to the sounds, again, of ducks quacking, coots cooting and twats giggling.

Day 3

A tabby cat sat on the seat of a motorbike parked outside a caravan in the warm morning sun. It meowed at Bearsac as we passed, and we stopped to greet it. We got a train from Central Station to Zaanse Schans, where windmills and pretty green painted wooden buildings laze along the River Zaan. As well as the windmills there were workshops. At the Klompenmakerij Woodenshoe Workshop, the clogs we bought were still fresh and still moist. The Catharina Hoeve Cheese Workshop was, not surprisingly, cheesy smelling. Shelves displayed rows of Gouda. Bearsac and I sampled some decent Gouda (not like the stuff Holland exports to UK supermarkets). The two women dressed as maids on the samples counter gave Bearsac some sweets too.

The costume museum was closed so we missed out there. We met the nice owner of a toy and wooded puppet shop and he had a look at Bearsac's website on his laptop. After strolling around for a couple of hours we got the train back to Amsterdam, had a short walk about and then returned about 6pm to the camp-site and were in bed by 7.30pm as we were both worn out. The water birds and twats were at it again but we slept well on the comfy bed.

Getting up again at 1am, I took Bearsac to the tabled area with some wine and got talking to a couple in their 60s from Austria, the man with a cool handlebar moustache. They were touring Europe in their caravan and were nearing the end of a year's travel. They related to me that they had been on their honeymoon in France and ended up buying the caravan on impulse; they had then returned home and put their house up for rent before setting off on their current travels. I can never imagine being in that position in my life, but wouldn't it be wonderful to be free and not have to worry about finding a new home when you return.

Day 4 - Last day

We left the camp-site about 10.30am, and had some more herring at Volendammer Vishahandel haring shop. This time I ate the Dutch way, suspending the fish above tilted back head and lowering it into open mouth.

At the airport I got a bottle of Drysack sherry, which doesn't seem to be sold any more in the UK, and a bottle of Boomsma Jeneva (Dutch Gin), which is the colour of whisky. On the plane the man seated next to us gave Bearsac a chewing gum and Bearsac gave him his card.

Bearsac Sipping Dutch Beer in Amsterdam and standing in someone else's shoe

Chapter Ten

Berlin – Germany
May 2006

Day 1 - May 9th 2006

Within one minute of leaving the plane at Shonenfeld Airport, I was sneezing. It seemed that everyone in Berlin was sneezing.

'It's hay-fever,' I was told when I yelled at myself, between sneezing bouts:

'Why am I sneezing?' But I don't get hay fever, or at least not in England. Not to be left out of sneezing, Bearsac started sneezing too; a teddy bear sneezing was not something I think Berliners had experienced before, and they didn't quite know how to take it.

Standing rather proudly at over 6ft, outside a café, was a brightly coloured fibreglass teddy bear. I sat Bearsac on Mr Giant Teddy and took photographs; so did other people! A young German woman in a green tailored dress told Bearsac that the United Buddy Bears had been painted by artists from 120 different countries.

'The Buddy Bears say,' she continued, "We must live together in harmony and peace"'.

At one stage they were altogether in a park, but we must have come too late to Berlin to see that. We thanked the young woman, bid farewell to Mr Giant Teddy and continued to our hostel.

Bearsac's wife *Tea*, and daughter *Teasac*, had accompanied us too, so we had a real family day. First we took a short stroll down the river Spree to the The Pergamon Museum to see the

Pergamon Altar. The Pergamon Altar was originally built in the 2nd century BC, in the Ancient Greek city of Pergamon. A German archaeological team, lead by Carl Humann, shipped the Pergamon Altar out of the Ottoman Empire from its original excavation site and reconstructed it in the Museum in Berlin in the 19th century. The Museum also houses other monumental structures such as the Market Gate of Miletus and the Ishtar Gate from Babylon. It's weird having these huge ancient external structures inside a building in a country not renowned for being ancient.

In Friedrichstrasse train station/shopping mall, we met smaller United Buddy Bears representing different world cup teams. We spent more time strolling around taking photographs of lots of random things, and Bearsac greeted people and had his photograph taken by both tourists and Berliners. Dogs, it appeared, just wanted to eat Bearsac. A pack of four out-of-control dogs, being ill-managed by one small woman, suddenly spotted him and vowed to be the first to *get the bear*. I held Bearsac aloft, as high above my head as I could, while the woman fell over her mutts in her bid to control the unruly canines. Thankfully none were tall enough to get Bearsac, even whilst standing on two legs and stretching their wet noses. Their owner managed to untangle their legs from around my body and now, set free, I moved away, taking Bearsac to safety.

The safety, though, was short lived. A sharp yapping alerted us to a ratty looking runt of a dog that now had Bearsac in its sights. What the little rat lacked in strength, it made up for in energy and acrobatic ability. On its lead it performed somersaults, high jumps and what looked like a canine version of the quickstep; was this dog trying to impress its way into Bearsac's heart in order to get him into its mouth? Its sharp and rapid yapping assaulted my ears. Throwing my hands over my ears, I barked a big dog bark at it, and it cried off around the other side of its owner, who picked it up and walked off muttering in angry German, shaking her head and kissing the little rat. I kissed Bearsac in the same fashion, wiggling my bum in mockery, as she had done, and we continued on. Tea and Teasac had been in my bag all through this, so were hopefully unaware of Bearsac's ordeal.

Bearsac pointed out a few buildings with war-scarred walls. I don't know if it's the right thing to say but the marks gave character to the buildings; history etched into the walls. A refreshing paddle in the stepped fountain on the green of Museumsinsel (Museum Island) overlooked by The Berlin Dom was well needed, and the fountain sprayed us in a refreshing manner. I held Bearsac carefully by his straps so he could dip his feet into the water; this earned us a few odd looks. A little kid, also paddling in the fountain, fell over whilst she pointed at Bearsac and laughed! She started crying, but luckily she was okay and her mum was with her.

A TV crew were filming a young human couple messing about on a bed on the pavement. For some reason best known to themselves, the film crew declined Bearsac's offer to let them film him and Tea on the bed. Across the road we got some herring and some freshly-squeezed orange juice and sat taking in the scene in the Hackescher Markt by the statue of the two socialist philosophers, Karl Marx and Friedrich Engels.

Thanks to Bearsac asking, we obtained some free Red Bull from Red Bull promoters when I spotted the Red Bull car near the Red Bull model aeroplane. They weren't yet giving it out then, but I remembered this from London, so Bearsac asked if they had any free and we got one.

Nearby were the ruins of Berlin Castle, which stood from 1443 until 1950, and now bore only the cellars. It was badly hit by bombing on 3rd February 1945 during World War Two. At Peugeot Avenue, cool cars were on display; there was even a teddy bear-sized car, which the teddy family sat in for a photograph.

We *bummeled* down Unter den Linden. This is a boulevard of linden trees (lime trees). The name '*Unter den Linden*', means Under the Lime Trees. Berliners would '*bummel*' down the streets of Berlin. To '*bummel*' means to cruise the streets. German born Hollywood actress and singer Marlene Dietrich, (Berlin's 'Blue Angel') refined the art of bummelling when she sang her songs. Even as the Nazis were chopping them down, she kept singing, 'As long as the old trees still bloom on *Unter den Linden*, Berlin will stay Berlin.' Her signature song was 'Falling in Love Again'.

Our brummelling took us to Pariser Platz to the 'Brandenburger Tor' (Brandenburg Gate), which is the last remaining gate through which one used to enter Berlin. The gate, standing 65ft high, 213ft wide and 36ft thick, has served many purposes over the years but I'm not going to go on. We wandered into Tiergarten Park where the bell tower tolled to us musically as we strolled down the riverside sharing ice-cream.

The Reichstag (Parliament Building) queue was so long and noisy that we didn't bother at this time, but we got to go in when we returned at 10pm after I'd cooked us all a well-needed dinner back at the hostel. The Reichstag's dome is made of glass with a spiral walkway to the top; it gives excellent views of the city. You also get to look down on the politicians for a change, whilst they are working in the basement in the conference hall. After the Reichstag we headed back to the hostel. A fox came running down the pavement right in front of us; it was the equivalent of a fox running down Oxford Street. It was too quick for me to get my camera out, as on seeing us, it skidded and ran away around a corner down along the River Spree. Back at hostel and in bed at 11.30pm; worn out.

Day 2

Just one other person shared our eight-bed dorm room last night, so we slept OK apart from the large wattage light outside the window that lit up when anyone was outside putting away their bicycles. Just before dawn I was woken by a purring sound, and the feeling of something lightly pressing down on me. I opened my eyes to a cat. There it sat on me, curled up, purring away contently. I was told that the woman who had the bed before me had stayed for a week and had been feeding the cat, and that it had been coming in through the open window to sleep on her. The hostel worker said that the woman had even named it and it was simply called 'Pussy'. I thought it strange that Pussy didn't realise the human it sat on smelt different. I was glad that it hadn't ripped up Bearsac, Tea or Teasac. I didn't get Pussy sitting on top of me the following morning, which Bearsac was quite upset about, as he wanted to sit there talking and playing with the cat.

We took a stroll around the hostel area, taking time out for quiet contemplation, in a graveyard surrounded by trees full of bird-song. It was like the 'Secret Garden' with its flourishing flowers and ivy and many undisturbed birds gaily hopping about in search of juicy worms. Bearsac sat next to me on the bench, the morning air heavy with the warmth of honeysuckle and the buzz of busy bees. The traffic sounds were way off in the distance and the world felt at peace. I could have sat there all day but had to get back to the hostel for breakfast before meeting the guide for the walking tour of Berlin.

The tour picks up people from the hostels and then sets out from Brandenburg Gate for four hours on foot, with a 25-minute break. The tour guide, Jesse, was brilliant; he really knew his stuff and made it very interesting. Jesse told us so much about the sights and about Berlin. If you are ever in Berlin and staying in a hostel, do this free tour. The guides don't get paid, but of course they get tips, so they make the effort to make it good.

The history of the German Mark is really interesting. Jesse gave us Mark notes to look at, a one-Mark note and a 10,000,000-Mark note, and others in between. They were printed only on one side as they were worth less than the ink on them. During 1923, inflation rose by so much and so quickly that workers were paid twice a day with sacks of Mark notes. They would chuck their sacks of money out of factory windows so their wives could rush to buy food before it escalated in price by the end of the day. I followed this subject up on the Internet and found that a loaf of bread that cost 20,000 Marks in the morning cost 5,000,000 by that night, and that the price of a meal in a restaurant rose as one ate it (bet that caused a lot of indigestion!) When economic collapse finally came on November 15th, it took 4.2 trillion German Marks to buy a single American Dollar. These days, it takes about 1.51 German Marks to buy one US Dollar. (Yes, I know they use the euro now).

We learnt about how, on 27th February 1933, a young Dutch communist, Marinus van der Lubbe, was said to have burnt down the Reichstag, shouting "Protest!" With a fire torch in his hand, he said this was a signal for revolution. When Hitler and Hermann Göring were shown Marinus van der Lubbe, Göring declared the fire was set by the Communists and had the party leaders arrested. Hitler took advantage and declared a state of emergency. It allowed him to transform Germany from a democracy into a dictatorship. We were next taken to The Holocaust Memorial, which consists of 2,751 concrete pillars.

From there we were taken to Hitler's Bunker, or at least to the spot where it used to be. Flats and a car park for the flats are now built on top. It used to have several bedrooms and a conference room. It is where Hitler shot himself to death. The cool thing about the area now is that the flats are very ugly (the last building phase of the Communist era), and the inferior patch of grass is where locals take their dogs to poo. Some people come out of their way on the anniversary of Hitler's suicide to have their dogs poo on it. (How Bearsac wished he could really poo!)

Next was the Berlin Wall. The wall stood from 1961 to 1989. It was erected by the East German Government along the border between East and West Berlin, and later extended along the entire border between East Germany and West Germany. It was erected to prevent East Berliners commuting to the West at a time of growing tension between East and West. Only small sections of the wall remain. Road bricks put into the road and pavement follow the line of where the wall once stood.

Jessie takes us on a little further to Checkpoint Charlie, which became a symbol of the Cold War, representing the separation of East and West and - for the East Germans - a gateway to freedom. The real checkpoint was torn down when the wall was knocked down. However, it was rebuilt as a tourist attraction. Cafe Adler is just by Checkpoint Charlie. The cafe used to be a hangout for spies and cold war journalists. Also, famous movie stars such as Sean Connery and Liza Minelli used to come here while researching their roles, as it was the closest they could get to East Berlin at the time.

A break for lunch, and then onward we all trek. Gendarmenmarkt Square is surrounded by French and German Cathedrals and a concert hall; in its centre is a statue of Germany's famous poet Friedrich Schiller. A statue stands in the Square, in front of the concert hall; the conductors line their backs to the statue during concerts. From there we walked to another square, 'Bebelplatz', which was once the site of Nazi book-burning. The Nazi burnt books written by Jews, Communists and those that opposed them. Nearby is a statue of Friedrich Wilhelms, a Prussian army captain. From here we paid a quick visit to a statue of Mary and Jesus, which is housed in a small building with a round hole in the roof that lets the sun shine down upon it. I was more interested in watching the dust swirl in the stream of sunlight.

As we headed towards Museum Island we saw the very tall Berlin Fernsehturm (better known as TV tower). Completed in 1969, it stood 365 metres high. However, after the installation of a new antenna in the 1990s, the height is now 368 metres.

It was intended as a symbol of the permanence of East Berlin and the German Democratic Republic.

However, it is considered to be the Communist finger-up to the West in reaction to ongoing suppression of church institutions in East Germany. It is also known as the 'Pope's Revenge' because of the large cross that appears on the ball bit in certain sunlight. This was not the intention of the builders and it is seen as a big joke against them.

We didn't get to see this phenomenon because it had been decorated to look like a football for the World Cup.

Jesse told us lots more interesting stuff on the top of the steps of The Altes Museum on Museumsinsel, where the tour concluded. The Altes Museum, constructed by Karl Friedrich Schinkel in 1830, was the first museum built on the island and three other buildings up to 1930 followed it. I only had about 16 euros left and had to get a travel-card and water for that day and the next, which was our last, so I was sad to be able to give only two and a half euros to the excellent guide. Bearsac bid everyone goodbye after having a few photographs taken by them, and off we went.

We paid a quick visit to the History Museum, perusing a photographic exhibition of all the world cups, but other than that there was nothing to see. On the way to get our travel-card we came by a giant teddy bear outside a shop; Bearsac and he spoke a little in German as I sat Bearsac on his arm. Berlin has a bear much like it on its Coats of Arms.

In the travel shop we greeted, in German, the man at the desk nearest to us. Bearsac started to ask in English for advice on the best travel-card to get. However, a pair of muscular arms with manicured hands planted themselves, and the person attached to them, onto the desk in front of the man's face. With an exalted sense of its own status, the head attached to the arms demanded:

'Vhot it is you vhant?'

I had a vision of my travel-card being perforated with Enigma punch holes. With much huffing and puffing, which seemed to shout 'the inconvenience these people put me to!', the commandant went about the arduous task of equipping me with a travel-card, exuding an air of authority that no doubt kept the poor man I had first spoken to clearly in the place she deemed him fit for. I caught his eye and gave him what I hoped he would recognise as a supportive smile, to which he nodded his understanding with a wink. I managed to hold back my laughter until I got outside, clutching my travel-card tightly in case the commandant came after me to demand it back for having laughed. Bearsac had been stunned into silence in the shop, poor bear, but this was maybe just as well.

Back to the hostel for dinner and change for the Gary Numan

concert we were here to see. Outside in the queue Bearsac and I spoke to other Numanoids. I was expecting to see some British fans, but I was the only one as far as I could make out. I am well known among the British Numanoids. However, it was nice to meet the German fans who were quieter, less cliquey and not as obsessed with Gary as the British fans. Bearsac was accepted as no less a Numanoid than any human and had his photograph taken with quite a few people.

The concert was at a club considered very cool; why, I couldn't see. But the concert was fab - as Numan concerts normally are - and Gary spoke to Bearsac, saying 'Hi there' as he waved at him where Bearsac stood on the stage in front of him. The lager-enslimed floor and annoying music after the gig was too much for me and my sensory overload, even with my earplugs in; so rather than wait for Gary to come out and get an updated photograph of him with Bearsac, we called it a night and headed back to the hostel. There will be other times to get an updated photograph of Bearsac and the godfather of Electro rock.

Day 3 – Last day - Potsdam

Taking a surprisingly quiet train south-west of Berlin, we did a day trip to the pretty Potsdam. Just 25% of the area is built upon, the rest being open land or water. There are 20 lakes and rivers in Potsdam, including the River Havel, which we crossed to Nikolai Kirche, having spent some time sitting on the grass on Freundschafts-insel (Friendship Island), where Bearsac spoke to a group of students and got happily molested by two of the young ladies who took a fancy to him. Nikolai Kirche, a gothic hall church, was built in two stages between 1307 and 1488. Its two towers date from 1500 and have different spires, one rebuilt in 1617. It has been fired, seen Prussian occupation and two world wars, but is restored beautifully.

Potsdam's beautiful buildings, parks, woods and waterways, wild with birdsong, are a welcome retreat from the noise and madness that is embraced by nearby Berlin. We spent some peaceful time in Neuer Garten Park, where we found Schloss Cecilenhof (Cecilienhof Palace), which was, erected between 1914 and 1917 for Crown Prince Wilhelm and his wife Cecilie von Mecklenburg-Schwerin.

The architect, Paul Schultze-Naumburg, was inspired by the English Tudor style. From 17th July to 2nd August 1945, the Potsdam Conference negotiations between the victorious Allies of World War Two were held here. The Cecilienhof is the last palace built by the Hohenzollern dynasty. We strolled around aimlessly, taking time out to sit every so often to take things in at Neuter Garten with its beautiful tree-lined lake. We met some nice people and dogs on our walk and had a pleasant ride on a tram back to the station.

Back in Berlin I picked up my rucksack for our flight home. What a great view we had of Germany, Amsterdam, South-East England and London, all lit up from the plane. Got home soon after midnight, and Bearsac and family told all the other teddies about what a great time we'd all had.

Brandenburg Gate - Berlin

Chapter Eleven

Poland
June 2006

Day 1 - 28th June 2006 - Krakow

Just two people stood before Bearsac and me in the check-in queue at Luton Airport, a couple; but this didn't mean we were seen as quickly as I would have expected. We and the rest of the queue waiting behind us were subjected to a petty argument that erupted between the couple, just because the woman's luggage was too heavy. She sobbed red-faced,

'I have never been so embarrassed in my life innit' as she opened up her pink Burberry bag to give her partner some of its contents to put into his bag to make the weight limit. He shouted at her for being embarrassing and she wailed back at him inaudibly. Not too clued up on unwritten social rules, I'm not sure what is embarrassing about having a bag too heavy, or removing its contents; what did she have in there? I was more impatient than empathetic with them and their circus act. Just hoped they weren't off on their honeymoon!

On the plane we sat next to a young man from Poland who had been working in the UK for the past two years and was going home for a week to see his family. He was the only person brave enough to sit next to someone with a talking teddy bear. What's wrong with talking to my teddy bear anyway? There are people who talk to their cars, some even swear at them; at least Bearsac has a face, even if it's stuffed with fibre. Bearsac is usually great for getting empty seats next to me on flights where the seats are not designated, but it didn't put this man off; I think he found it a pleasure to talk to a teddy bear.

A wave of heat hit me full in the face as we got off the plane; I'd not expected it to be quite so hot. The train station, where we head to from the airport, was hardly a station; there was nowhere to buy a ticket, just a platform with a bus-type shelter that provided no shelter from the sun's intense glare. I wanted to change into my shorts but there was nowhere to change without anyone seeing, and I didn't fancy the prospect of getting arrested. I noticed a hen on the tracks pecking away, Bearsac shouted at it to get off the line as it would get run over, but it paid no attention and continued pecking away. Thankfully it soon walked under the fence to the field opposite with other hens.

The terrain between the airport and town centre was quite flat and green with odd buildings dotted around. Fields were tended as their produce filled wooden carts and old-looking vehicles that looked like they would conk out five minutes down the road. Getting nearer to the town centre, buildings became more abundant, as did people walking about and dogs pooing - trust Bearsac to notice that and point it out to me!

I photographed Bearsac in front of various things that caught my eye, like a flowerbed that looked like a rabbit's face with two fir trees forming its ears. We followed the decorative paving to the street that led into the square and crossed it, trying not to step in horse poo from the horse and carriage that nearly ran into us.

It was Wednesday, and on Wednesdays free fruit is laid out at Mama's Hostel so we scoffed a fix of healthy food and got off to a healthy start. The person asleep in the bunk above mine stank to high heaven of BO; I prayed that they would shower when they awoke from their no doubt fetid pit.

Our first stroll around found us *Wawel*, consisting of a castle, cathedral and other buildings set upon a hill overlooking Krakow and the River Wisla, which, at 678 miles, is the longest river in Poland. It starts in Barania Gora in southern Poland and empties itself into the Baltic Sea. Wawel is where the earliest settlements in Krakow began, some 50 000 years ago. We strolled about the old town with its pretty buildings and sat in Rynek Glowny - a lovely medieval square – people-watching before looking around Sukiennice (cloth hall), which comprises various market stalls selling traditional Polish crafts. Bearsac spoke to some wooden puppets, which really confused the puppet seller; maybe his puppets couldn't speak! However, I found I was wrong when a French tourist laughed and spoke to Bearsac; the puppet seller sort of got it then and made one of the puppets speak to Bearsac. As we left the puppet seller, he was making one of the puppets speak to the others, so I think we started of a trend.

After browsing round an art gallery full of blurred paintings of Krakow, I checked out the food in a grocers shop, buying some Polish food to take back to the hostel to cook. Bearsac got called Mr Bean's teddy bear twice in the shop. As I ate, I was soon aware that 'BO person' was amongst us in the lounge, as I could suddenly smell them; I hadn't seen the person in the bedroom because they were under the bed covers. Following my nose told me it was likely that BO person was the tall woman with the dirty hat, reading chick-fic, who was with two men. When I was later sorting my clothes in the bedroom, the woman entered and climbed awkwardly up to the bunk above mine I smiled at my correct identification of the stinker.

Night time creates a different scene and rhythm. Things warmed up and we chilled out with a Polish beer, sitting on the Adam Mickiewicz monument in Rynek Glowny, watching it all unfold. People started filling the square-side bars in evening-wear rather than day-wear, skate boarders showed off their stunts and couples of all ages strolled hand in hand. Bearsac was a little scared walking around the quieter streets in the dark, as long shadows were menacingly cast by the street lamps; he was later calmed when he recognised we were nearer to the hostel as I took us both back to go to bed.

During the night there appeared to be a momentary lull in the noise outside; then suddenly the quiet gave way to torrential rain, the heaviest rain I had ever heard, which broke into a thunderstorm. We were worried it would carry on all the following day and spoil our visit to Auschwitz. Krakow is the noisiest city centre I have ever tried to sleep in; needless to say we didn't sleep at all as the hostel was just off the main square. The nightlife was happening right outside our open window. That got quiet enough by 4am to hear the rain, thunder and toll of the church bell each hour. Each hour some prat kept bugling the same military type tune after the bell tolled.

Day 2

After not sleeping at all due to the nightlife outside our window, church bells tolling and prats bugling, we left the hostel at about 6.30am. We had a little walk about in the now light rain before getting the 7.20am minibus to Oswiecim (the original Polish name for the town of Auschwitz). I It cost seven zol, which is about £1.74, for a one and a half-hour journey through the countryside.

Can't really describe my feelings walking around Auschwitz, but I found it hard to connect emotionally to the terrors that took place there; such can sometimes be the case with some Aspies. The large metal gates at the entrance with wording arched over them reminded me of the gates of Anfield, home of Liverpool Football Club (Booooo!). However, there was nothing sporting about the place these gates were entrance to. The dingy gas chamber didn't really hit home to me the evils that had taken place within its walls, as some people had said it would. In some buildings there were drawings by the imprisoned, still visible on walls. In an exhibition was a large photograph that struck me. This photograph was of a woman before and after Auschwitz. She was so thin afterwards that she had to hold herself up by grasping the bedrails with a nurse standing protectively behind her for the photograph. Torn skin hung from her emaciated legs.

The exhibitions were so well presented; the sound effects of heart beats, trains on tracks and walking on gravel all attempted to add to the emotion of the theme. But it's not something that any sense of atmosphere can capture; it cannot get anywhere near the sense of the suffering that took place – not that I would ever want to know what it was really like. I questioned myself as to whether I should feel bad for my state of nonchalance about being in this place of mass death and torture. I looked, matter-of-factly for my grandfather's name in the book of names of those who died there, but did not see him.

The bus journey through various villages on the return to Krakow was a pleasant one. I picked up a few more Polish words, guessing their meaning as they were repeated each time a passenger requested that the driver let them get off, and whilst they were getting off. When we came near to the end of the route and I saw something I wanted to photograph, I repeated the words that other people had said when asking to get off, and the driver stopped for me. I didn't know the meaning of any of the words but safely assumed that they meant something like 'Can you let me off' rather than 'Your mother is a whore and your cat is flea-ridden!'

In the square an event was taking place; children dressed in traditional folk-costumes danced on stage, and many sat on colourful cushions on the ground gossiping whilst awaiting their turn to take to the stage. Bearsac approached a two-legged pantomime horse that had a long-haired, bearded man sticking out of its back, wearing a wizard style hat. The horse spoke good English and told Bearsac the story being enacted up on the stage; then he trotted around in the next act.

Back at the hostel I washed my Bearsac T-shirt and hung it to dry in the window, praying it wouldn't blow away. After a rest and then Bearsac being chatted up by a group of young ladies from Ireland, we went for a night stroll. We came by lots of street entertainment: musicians, brass band, street dancers spinning on their heads and backs. We met a curly blonde furred teddy bear that did not have a name and his owner, who did - Patricia. When we came by a one-man band busker with a clown puppet playing the cymbals. I asked if I could put Bearsac on his knee next to the puppet for a photograph. Bearsac, the puppet and busker had a bit of a singsong.

Swathed in a cloak of night air, we took a walk through the tree-lined paths, finding our way to a bar playing live Polish music. On entering, I trip on a step and am greeted by the sound of rapturous applause as I bump into an air-kicking, dancing and singing man dressed in traditional folk-costume, and nearly send him flying into the accordion player. Steadying himself, he grabs my hand and raises it into the air, with Bearsac still grasped in it, and dances me around him to the further delight of cheering, beer-swigging locals. I kick my legs up in imitation of his but am completely overwhelmed by this unexpected greeting; a moment ago I was walking down a quiet, tree-lined path and was just a little curious as to what was going on in the bar from where the music came.

Mr Folk Dancer kissed my hand on completion of the song and finally let me go, not having paid any attention to Bearsac. I gave him a little curtsy and subtly wiped his wetness from the back of my hand as I sat at the one remaining empty stool at the bar and ordered a Polish beer.

Now it was Bearsac's time to get the attention he always craves. The barmaid picked him up, making him dance in the air to the music. Locals turn to face the bar, pointing their clapping hands at her and Bearsac; I wondered if I would ever get my beer and my bear but after a minute or so, got both. As the tempo of the music softened, the atmosphere subdued and I was greeted in Polish by a group of people nearby. I explained I spoke no Polish and when they discovered I was from England, two of them said together, 'Manchester United.' Bearsac replied 'No, Arsenal', to which the taller of the men replied, 'Thierry Henry.' A woman within the group then said 'Mr Bean', pointing to Bearsac, then said, 'Mr Bean teddy.'

Things calmed down from there on and I sat and drank my beer watching others drink theirs. The people and atmosphere I met in this bar enriched my evening and created a memory I will treasure for a long time.

Day 3 - Wieliczka Salt Mines then Czestochowa

It's not much after 8am, but it's humid and hot; windows of buildings reflect the sun and appear to dance in the distance as we take a walk before meeting our coach. We had booked a tour of Wieliczka Salt Mines, about a half-hour bus ride from Krakow. We learnt that in medieval times the mines were one of the world's most profitable industrial establishments and salt was the commercial equivalent of today's oil, so was very valuable. An old king of Poland once owned the mines; there is a salt statue of him, which I sat Bearsac on for a photograph. The statues, walls, roofs, floors in parts are carved decoratively from salt that was evaporated sea centuries and centuries ago. Salt formations still seep through, forming cauliflower-looking formations on the walls and ceilings.

Starting at 64 metres deep, the tour takes you through caverns, churches and three underground ponds. Statues carved from salt greet you as you pass. Wieliczka is the oldest working mine in Europe open to tourists. Salt has been mined there for as long as 700 years. It was in the 13th century that mining for salt began. It is said that when the Hungarian princess, Princess Kinga, was to marry the sovereign of Krakow, she wanted to bring a valuable present for him. As the people of Poland had everything other than salt, Princess Kinga asked her father for a salt mine as a dowry. She chucked her ring of Kinga into a salt mine in Hungary and went to Wieliczka in Poland. When she told miners to dig a pit, they found salt and enclosed in the first bit of salt was the ring of Kinga. Or so the legend goes. 'That's a load of baloney!' blurted Bearsac.

In a cathedral carved from salt, even the chandeliers are made of salt. The magnificent stairway transported us down to the lower floor where we could see in more detail the walls showing carvings of biblical scenes, expertly carved into the walls, which I sniffed and found cold on the tip of my nose. Weddings can be booked here; I would hate to think how much that would cost.

Part way through our tour we heard Irish accents yelling 'Bearsac!' We looked around to see the Irish girls from the hostel with another tour group. Bearsac was pleased at the attention and had already told people in our group that he was a famous teddy bear, so he was very happy that he now had proof of his boast if any had doubted him.

The route ends 135m below ground level. Only one lift shaft was working so tourists had to use the same lift as the miners; this was bad in that we had to wait over half an hour to get the lift but great as we saw the miners and got to go in the tiny cage shafts that take nine people shoulder to shoulder and zip up really quick.

The train from Krakow to Czestochowa took about three hours and cost 28.38 Zt, about £4.76. Scenes of traditional rural villages and farms added interest to the train journey. We shared our cabin with a nice lady called Dominika and a mother and son who Bearsac spoke to, passing the time.

There is not too much to see in Czestochowa other than its main attraction, 'The Black Madonna'. Our cheap hotel was 'Hotel Polonia'. Hideous sun-faded paintings attempted to brighten the dark hallways. The bedroom was bright but with chintzy pink nylon bedspreads and flowered wallpaper. Looking beyond the years of neglect, Hotel Polonia may have been quite nice in the dark past; but now it was in need of calling in Bob the Builder. Still, it served its purpose of a secure roof over the head and we had a room on our own, so slept well after our visit to see the Black Madonna.

The home of the Black Madonna since August 1382, Jasna Góra Monastery is known as Bright Mountain. In 1430, it was invaded and a looter struck the painting twice with his sword. It is claimed that before he could strike it a third time, he collapsed to the ground and died. The sword cuts are still visible on the painting and look like scars. Talks of spontaneous healings have been doing the rounds for centuries and as a result, many people make pilgrimage to the portrait. I thought the Black Madonna was painted to be black, but it was in fact centuries of candle soot that discoloured it and made it appear that the Madonna was black, and this is why it had came to be called the Black Madonna. Word has it that the Black Madonna is made from a piece of wood from a table used by the Virgin Mary in Nazareth. Thankfully, Bearsac didn't call this baloney.

We hoped to spend some quiet contemplation time in the church but entered to find wall-to-wall pilgrims standing in awe, staring at the portrait. It took some time to get a good view ourselves and once we got to the main section where the portrait was, a service had started. We sat on the floor like some of the others and were given a small stool to sit on by a nice man.

We were soon prompted to the front by the old ladies sitting nearby and had a great view. It was 8.45pm when we had entered and was 1.30am when we left at break time. It was weird, as it never seemed appropriate to leave during the service since we were at the front. We had only intended to stay a short while. It was great though, as it was spiritual rather than religious to us. Young priests in full gown sat on the floor gently playing guitars and singing. Because I only understood about four words (as it was all in Polish), I was able to just enjoy the rhythm of the singing and speaking and not take it as a religious thing.

One of the young, good looking priests walked amongst the congregation. When he placed his hands on each person head, they took his hands and kissed them. I was feeling awkward as I was worried about his hands not being clean. Part awkwardly and part unsuitably willing, I kissed his hands, as I had seen the others do. I felt like Madonna in her 'Like a Prayer' video where, scantily clad, for a church setting, she rapturously dances in abandon in the church whilst a secondary clip shows her kissing Jesus as though she is Mary Magdalene. I couldn't look at the priest afterwards! I left energised but I was glad to get to bed at about 2am though, and so was Bearsac.

Day 4 - Warsaw

It was some time from checking out until our train was due; so we strolled about and sat in a sorry little square watching the locals going about their business. A man walked past with a metal barrel of cooking oil on a shopping bag trolley frame minus the bag. A wheel got stuck in a crack and the barrel fell off but thankfully didn't get damaged and leak its contents all over the ground. We left the sorry little square and collected my rucksack from the hotel reception to go and catch our train.

On the train from Czestochowa to Warsaw we got chatting to a young Polish man from Warsaw who had also gone to Czestochowa to see the Black Madonna. He was perfectly happy talking to a teddy bear and madwoman. He told us of his teddy when he was a kid and how he used to take it everywhere and how its worn limbs were pulled about and ripped by his older brother. It upset Bearsac to hear of such things, so the man told Bearsac how his teddy had been restuffed and mended by his grandmother and made to look strong and proud again, but how, once mended, it wasn't the same bear he had loved. I looked at Bearsac's balding general sagginess and understood exactly.

The Oki Doki Hostel in Warsaw was cool; Bearsac wanted the bed over the doorway of our five-bed bedroom. I had a bit of difficulty climbing up and down in the dark. I made some dinner and used the free Internet before spending some time talking to people in the sitting room.

At the monument of the unknown soldier, Bearsac waved and spoke to the soldiers on guard; they could not reply but were

189

holding off smiles. A local young man escorted us to where he pointed out the old town. We thanked him in Polish and went on our way exploring. A group of male students with hats on and a flag were singing in Polish as they passed Sigismund's Column and through the streets. For a while we followed them to see what they were up to but when they turned out of the old town we left them to it.

We spent time at an outdoor photographic exhibition and also paid a visit to a small art gallery with paintings of Warsaw. Enticing food smells led us around for a bit longer until we decided to return to the hostel and see who was about to talk to, in order to find out what was worth doing the next day. We met a couple who lived in West London and a young man they were chatting to and I took Bearsac's photograph with them. The woman had wanted to bring her cuddly toy but had left it at home as her other half would be embarrassed; we were disappointed at this as it would have been great for Bearsac and her cuddly toy to have met. I'm so glad I don't have to suffer from other people's concern over what they think other people will think of them if the person they are with has a cuddly toy. Travelling alone means I can do just as I please.

Day 5

Warsaw's beauty is confined mostly to the old town and parks; on the whole it is quite an ugly town. We walked around the old town before it got too busy and went in search of the place where we had been recommended to eat by the man on the train the day before, 'Samsone's', a Jewish Polish restaurant; but it was not yet open. We sat in a small square, watching people sit and stroll around and watched a little sparrow having a good nose around for crumbs. Returned to the hostel to get my sunscreen on the way to go to Lazienki Park where the Chopin monument lives.

One of the others staying at the hostel said there was classical music in the park by the Chopin Monument in the afternoon and also spoke of a Russian market on the other side of the river, so as we still had lots of time, we checked the market out first. Strolling down the river to cross at the bridge time slowed down to lazy pace as clouds floated on the silent water, mirroring that which lazed above in the deep blue sky. Trees let slip their green auric fields and rippled with the slow current.

Couldn't see what was Russian about the market; it seemed that the stalls either sold fake CDs, sandals and over-white trainers or dirty second-hand tools. The market was set on the stairs leading to an amphitheatre, desolate, apart from the weeds growing between the stepped concrete fixings, which showed signs of previous seating. Had I had the energy, I would have run down to the football pitch in the middle and got away from all the people walking too slowly around the market stalls, which were far too close together on the crumbling steps. Having to finish what I had started, I carried on around the stadium until I recognised the first stall of trainers, which looked much like any of the others except for an overfed dog lying under the ramshackle stall, looking bored to death.

Due to blisters on my feet and having to sit in the shade to escape the heat, it took us ages to get to the park. We still managed to catch some of the music and we met one of the pianists, Waldemar Wojtal, who is famous in Poland. I photographed him holding Bearsac for Bearsac's website. In another area of the park were peacocks and peahens in trees and walking about. Bearsac spoke to one of the peacocks for a while but it was scared off by a group of children in yellow T-shirts who tried to circle it.

The peacocks' calls were driving me insane, overloading me and disorientating me, so we escaped back to the quieter part of the park by the Chopin Monument and had soothing ice-cream.

It is easy in Warsaw to get confused about which of the public lavatories are designated for men and women. A triangle denotes it is for men and a circle for women; this is what we overheard a tour-guide explain to his English tour group gathered near us. It was just a shame he didn't go on to explain why this was; when Bearsac asked him why, he didn't reply but just stared at me as if I'd asked a ridiculous question to which the answer was obvious. So the exact reason will remain a mystery for me.

My tired, blistered feet managed to get us back to the hostel; we had no idea which tram or bus went by it. We had dinner and a lie-down for a couple of hours before going to the sitting room to talk to people. Here me met a young man from Japan and a young woman from Hong Kong (whose toy monkey was asleep in her room), and another young man from Argentina. I took Bearsac off to bed around 11.30pm; it was so hot in the bedroom so it was hard to sleep, but at least there weren't any smelly people sharing the room.

Day 6 – Last day

Our last day in Poland was another day spent roaming around Warsaw. I got some bison grass vodka for Alan. This, I had heard from a Polish friend of mine, was a luxury vodka infused with bison grass native to the Bialowieza Forest, home of the European bison. W. Somerset Maugham said, 'Drinking Zubrovka is as delightful as listening to music in the moonlight.' I also got some honey vodka for myself. I still had enough money left over to have some proper Polish food, and ice-creams for walkabouts and sitting in the small square.

The Polish restaurant we went to was called Pierogarnia. Although just near the old town, most tourists miss Pierogarnia as it is on a side road and the menu outside is all in Polish. I think they might intend it that way, but they were friendly anyway. Pierogarnia is located in a in a tenement house in Bednarska Street and has a *pierogi* (Polish ravioli type dumpling) hanging outside. The fare is traditional Polish and they have lots of varieties of *pierogi*. Our meal, including a cold soup of red cabbage and cream or yoghurt with parsley, two different *pierogi* and vegetables with *Podpiwek* (a Polish soft drink that tastes a bit like beer, not lager), altogether cost 16.5 zloty, which was about £3. It was all very tasty and the restaurant had a nice rustic peasant look. You order at the counter and then pick up your tray when it's ready, so this is no posh restaurant but caters for locals that like good home style cooking in an unpretentious setting.

Fuelled, we continued our walkabouts, speaking to people, including two policemen in a buggy with whom I photographed Bearsac. A TV crew were filming, interviewing a suited man. I stuck Bearsac's head over his shoulder as we went past; so I hope that he got on Polish TV. When we got back to the hostel to collect my bags for the airport, there was filming for a documentary about the hostel taking place, so Bearsac and I got filmed for that; Bearsac insisted on it.

Flight back to Luton went ok and we got home just before midnight. Bearsac was pleased to see Choc-Ice and the rest of the gang, and to tell them of our trip and all the ladies that fancied him.

Wawel Clock-tower - Krakow

Chapter Twelve

Japan
July 2006

Day 1 - 19th July 2006 - Flight Day

My excitement at Bearsac being greeted by noisy, battery-operated walking toy animals in Hamley's at Heathrow Airport overrode any sensory overload they might have given me had I been stressed out or concentrating. Bearsac spoke to them all, telling them how cool and famous he was; but they just continued to walk around and bump into things, paying absolutely no attention to him.

The flight was not direct to Tokyo but had a change at Malpensa near Milan in Italy. The flight from Malpensa to Narita was long and we watched three films and a documentary on our tiny personal screen, which didn't overload me like the personal screen a few years ago on a flight to the USA. The good thing about ordering a veggie meal (or any special meal) is you get yours before everyone else. I got extra sweets for Bearsac; the good thing is I get to eat them as, being a teddy bear, Bearsac doesn't really eat. I did though do the usual sound effects that accompany my pretence that he is eating by saying 'yum yum yum yum' in a voice slightly higher than my usual. Boredom got the better of both Bearsac and me and we both pawed over my out-folded map for the umpteenth time during the journey, colouring routes in fluorescent pink and orange.

Day 2

It was – about 10.30am (Japan is eight hours ahead of the UK) when we arrived at Narita Airport near Tokyo. Two nice police officers on the wonderfully clean train wanted to see Bearsac's passport and had a bit of a chuckle. I got the overwhelming urge to swing from the ceiling bars of the train; needless to say, I followed up on my urge, much to Bearsac's embarrassment. To make out he wasn't embarrassed he had a bit of swing too, or at least I tied him by his straps and put one of his arms through a handle suspended from the ceiling; all this was, of course, after the police had gone.

The immediate part of town round Tokyo Hostel was not too interesting at night so we just walked about buying a selection of sushi with various toppings, including large orange salmon eggs, raw tuna and some raw white fish, as well as a Japanese health drink like yakult, and a Japanese creamy set dessert – well, too much healthy food is not healthy without a bit of unhealthiness! I am glad I don't have the Aspie trait of being a faddy eater.

Most of the afternoon had been spent looking for a bank to get money exchanged; some banks stop exchanging at 2pm and we were ten minutes late. Luckily I had changed £40 before we left the UK so we had some for the first night.

The area of Tokyo the hostel was in was ram-packed with mashed up bicycles and for a moment I thought I was in Amsterdam and started greeting people in Dutch rather than Japanese; even Bearsac did too, which caused even more looks that I guessed, from the context, spelt confusion. The area was also packed with a web of overhead cables; which I seem to find myself photographing in any country I see them. I guess a lot of people would find this really sad, but I love the character it gives a place. I was also intrigued by the drinks vending machines in the streets, with their colourful displays of dummy drinks bottles, both of western and Japanese chilled beverages.

The hostel itself was small and clean with free Internet and a lion under the pool table. Bearsac was a bit worried that the lion might eat him, but his mind was put at rest when I picked it up to give it a hug, showing Bearsac it was a cuddly toy like him. In the kitchen / sitting-room we met a nice Japanese woman in her 50s, wrestling with a large water melon; she spoke little English, but understood Bearsac introducing himself in Japanese and gave us a large slice of water melon to share. The woman kept coming over and stroking Bearsac and bowed her head at him on exiting the room.

Day 3

My night's sleep had been disturbed by the bright light being turned on by inconsiderate westerners sharing the room. Still, I took great care not to disturb the other inhabitants as I crept out in the dark at 4.30am. I always organise my stuff so I can creep out in the dark as quietly as possible; shame it doesn't occur to others when sharing a room. Being an Aspie, I'm supposed to be the one that does not think of the effects of my actions on others, but I have learnt these things manually and so just give it more deliberate, conscious thought.

I exchanged my JR voucher for a JR pass and Bearsac and I got the next train to Kobe. It was our first time on a bullet train and it was fast and noisy. The Japanese train stations were murder for my sensory overload and the trains have very irritating, stupid noises and music coming from their PA systems. The platform was a frenzy of repetitive, high pitched noises, constant loud PA announcements and lots of people rushing about in a blur; it all set me off panicking. It was like everything that moved did so faster but in slow motion, and anything that was still, blurred. My mouth dried and I had difficulty controlling my breathing. I needed water but it took a while before I was able to direct my feet to move from the spot to which I was frozen. I remembered a paper bag I had in my pocket, which I had thankfully forgotten to throw away when passing a bin; I used it to breathe into and control my breathing, like I had seen someone do one time. It soon helped, along with cuddling Bearsac and smelling his fur.

The train was an array of annoying noises, but worst were the sounds coming from a teenage girl interacting with a pesky pokemon and emitting - from her orangey pink lip-sticked lips - the odd 'oooooo' or 'arrrrahhh' as the various sounds alerted her to computerised success or failure.

It was too early to check-in at the Kobe Guesthouse (which is more of a hostel, as you share rooms). Luckily a delivery man arrived at the same time so I was checked-in as the door was opened for him. I had to do all the shoe palaver, which consists of taking off your shoes on one part of the floor and putting on slippers on another part, without touching the floor with your feet. When entering a tatami matted bedroom one should take off slippers, putting them on again as you leave the bedroom and change to bathroom shoes without touching the floor before entering the bathroom. On leaving the bathroom one must change back to slippers from bathroom shoes. There were no kitchen facilities, just a fridge on each floor, and water. This was maybe just as well, considering the part shoes would play in it.

We went out to explore Kobe, spending time at the harbour. Giving in to my urge, I rolled up my trousers and paddled in the ground fountain with a demented duck that wouldn't stop quacking. I then climbed over the railings to paddle in the sea on the rocks. The sea looked almost black; I had to hold some in one of my hands to show Bearsac is was in fact regular water, colourless colour. I suddenly realised I had lost my Japan book and did a quick backtrack to the places I had taken photos of Bearsac and found it just where lots of people had been. If it had been in the UK, it would have been whipped up by someone straight away. Aspies can tend to be absent-minded, so I'll blame Aspieness.

We had a tremendous view of the city from the 24th floor of Kobe City Hall. We looked out over Rokko Island, which is a man-made island. Small sections of the city were reflected in the mirrored windows of skyscrapers; it looked like people were walking on the sides of the buildings and Bearsac played a game of seeing how quickly he could find the people on the actual street. As we exited the building, excited voices in front of us commented 'Mr Bean's teddy bear'. A group of about five suited women bowed and giggled; Bearsac waved and bowed at them, and they giggled and bowed all the more.

Street cleaners in Kobe tended to be all old people, barely able to stand up straight; it made me wonder what the retirement age is in Japan. Bearsac greeted one of them as she grinned at him from her beautifully wrinkled mouth, devoid of teeth. She waved at him, then continued to sweep away at nothing, with a large willow besom broom on the clean pavement. Wearing a green sun bonnet, she reminded me of the Ingles girls in 'The Little House on The Prairie'.

Two Japanese businessmen – who where fascinated by Bearsac's ability to speak (even though they knew it was me) - escorted us back to the station to get the monorail train over to Rokko Island. We didn't spend too long there, there was not much to do; it was just cool to be on a man-made island. It is quite big so it's hard to tell you are really on an island. Rokko is Kobe's second artificial island and is reclaimed land. It was constructed between 1973 and 1992. It is oblong and measures 3.4km by 2km and covers an area of 5.80km². There was a church with a grass-covered sloped roof, I think it was part of a university. It sloped from the ground to the cross at the top but was fenced off, so Bearsac could not drag me up it.

The Great Hanshin Earthquake left the island one of the hardest hit areas in Kobe. On Tuesday, January 17th 1995, at 5.46 am (local time), an earthquake of magnitude 7.2 struck the Kobe region of south-central Japan. There is a section of ruined street with caved-in paving and lampposts, which has been turned into a monument to the people who were affected by the earthquake.

The longest suspension bridge in the world is the Akashi Kaikyo Bridge. It was opened on April 5th, 1998, and had taken ten years to build. Our guest-house, which was a few minutes' walk from the bridge, was very basic but it was nice to be in just a two-bedded room. We shared with a nice Japanese lady and spent the night speaking in broken English and very broken Japanese, drawing pictures and using our own sign language.

Day 4

Not too far from Kobe was our destination for a day trip, Himeji Castle, which is one of the oldest surviving structures from me-dieval Japan. It is not how people in the West would imagine a castle to look; it does not have bare stone walls topped with crenellations and a flat roof. Instead it is like a castle for gi-ant fairies with tiled and wood-framed roofs that spray out and upwards like a child's drawing of a Christmas tree. The intricate detail of the roofing and wall tops includes family crests on round tiles on the ends of the eves. Bearsac pointed out that one design looked like the 666 sign of the devil, but I assured him it would have a different meaning.

Himeji Castle was designated a UNESCO World Heritage Site and the first Japanese National Cultural Treasure. It is occasionally known as Hakurojo or Shirasagijo (White Heron Castle), due to its sheer white exterior. From a distance it appeared to stand atop the trees, not unlike a heron. Scenes from the James Bond film 'You Only Live Twice' were filmed here; the castle was used as a Ninja training school by Tiger Tanaka.

It was tiring walking up around the grounds and maze-like paths, and climbing steep wooden steps to each floor of the castle. One has to put on slippers when inside the castle and carry one's shoes in provided plastic bags. Strangely, there were no slippers for teddy bears, but I was carrying Bearsac so they weren't needed really.

From the castle the view of the gardens mimicked a model of a Japanese garden, with manicured lawns and perfectly formed bonsai trees gazing onto glass-like ponds.

The town of Himeji itself is small and reasonably modern, and the castle, found in a park at the end of the town's main road, brings mostly Japanese visitors from other parts of Japan. On the way back to the train station we came by a giant teddy bear standing guard outside a teddy bear shop. Of course photos were taken and words exchanged. The young lady in the shop had never realised that so many of the teddies in her shop spoke until they replied to Bearsac; she seemed most delighted.

Somewhere along the way on the train to Hiroshima, we pass Fuji-san (Mount Fuji), the worldwide renowned mountain, which is an old volcano. It was not possible to see it due to the clouds, black and heavy with rain. I was a little disappointed, as I wanted to photograph Bearsac by the train window with Fuji in the background.

Once at Hiroshima, we took a tram to the park which is home to The A-Bome Dome. Also known as Hiroshima Peace Memorial, and Gembaku Dome, it is a UNESCO World Heritage Site. It was established as such in 1996. The building was originally designed by Czech architect Jan Letzel. It was completed in April 1915, and the new building was named the Hiroshima Prefectural Commercial Exhibition (HMI).

The 6th August 1945 nuclear explosion occurred almost directly above the building (the hypocentre was 150 metres / 490 feet away), and it was the closest structure to withstand the explosion. The building has been preserved in the same state as immediately after the bombing, and is the only building still remaining from that era or before. It now serves as a reminder of nuclear devastation and as a symbol of hope for world peace and the elimination of all nuclear weapons.

Nearby we also saw the Children's Peace Memorial, complete with rope for the bell, which it is customary to ring. I hung Bearsac on the rope for a photograph as a symbol of peace for children, as lots of people see teddy bears as a symbol of peace for children. There were lots of origami paper cranes made by children as symbols of peace too.

In a dog shop, puppies sat in glass capsules with cage openings at the back for feeding and cleaning; it was like a capsule hotel for dogs. They were so happy to have some human and teddy contact, even if it was through the glass. In the ten minutes or so we were in there, three puppies got sold, along with clothes for them. Japanese people seem to love to dress their dogs up like humans and there are many poochy fashions for them. I scanned the display, looking to see if any would be good for Bearsac, but they were all a bit girly for his liking, and that was the boy dog clothes!

We had nowhere booked for tonight but got off the train at Nagoya, where we needed to start our journey the next day. Tourist information was closed by now but the staff of Japanese Rail information were very helpful and gave details of a hostel. We shared the room with two young ladies. I showed our room-mates how to play a drawing game, where each person draws a different part of the body without seeing what the others have drawn, as it is folded over. The result of one drawing was very crazy, as I had drawn the middle part of the body and had drawn male and female parts on the same character. We also drank Japanese green tea until we all went to bed. It was wonderfully quiet in the room and the hostel.

Day 5

On account of not having had any dinner because of my near obsessive drawing, I felt weak and sick the next morning, so much so that it was a real struggle for me to walk the 20 minutes to the train station with my rucksacks. I had to stop three times to buy emergency energy snacks, which Bearsac thought was great as he got to try new yum yums. This did the trick until I got a bento box meal for the 8.43am train to Takayama in the alpine-covered Gifu Prefecture.

Again I was affected badly by sensory overload on the platform, and panicked, scratching around in my bag and panicking further as crumbs and fluff lodged under my fingernails. Once my ear-plugs were in I calmed and my breathing fell back under control.

I was fine unless very high-pitched noises overrode the dulling effect of the earplugs.

Bearsac waved at a young Japanese woman on the train and we went to give her his website card as her train still had a few minutes before it left. She got off a couple of minutes later to give Bearsac some sweets, which of course I put under where his mouth would be if he had one, and proceeded to yum yum yum in Bearsac's voice, before popping one into my mouth and the others into my pocket!

We had no time in Takayama to buy a *sarubobo* in the hope that it would ward off any more sensory overload for me, as the No. 2 bus was about to leave for Ogamachi. *Sarubobo* translates as 'baby monkey', but they are not at all like monkeys. They are cloth dolls with pointy limbs that stick out at about 45 degrees from the body. Usually with no facial features, they are traditionally made by grandmothers as amulets (objects that protect from trouble) and also act as charms for a good marriage for daughters. Takayama is the home of *sarubobo* but they can be found all over Japan.

The bus took one hour and 45 minutes to wind its way down into Ogamachi. Ogamachi, a village in the Shirakawago countryside, rests between mountains and has about 150 *gassho-zukuri* (grass houses). There used to be thousands; those that remain were built between the 17th and 20th centuries. Miles from the nearest train station, steep praying hands roofed *gassho-zukuri* farmhouses; rice paddies trimmed with pretty orange and pink flower beds; roaring aqua river, and pine-covered mountains rising on all sides; make Ogamachi one of the most picturesque and remote villages in Japan. Me and my teddy bear stayed there, cool!

In searching for our *minshuku* (family-style Japanese guesthouse), we came upon a small bus-stop by a paddy field, it seemed so strange to see a paddy field by a bus-stop. Looking out over the lush greenness, I spotted on the other side the *minshuku* where we were booked to stay. . We checked into Yokichi, which I booked because it is a *gassho-zukuri* (grass house) *minshuku*. These differ from the type in England in that the roofs form a steep upside-down V shape, which, I assume, controls the amount of snow that settles on them in the winter. It was a shame we were not here in the winter; it would have been awesome to see the village with its houses with snow-topped roofs.

Bearsac and I introduced ourselves using Japanese learnt from a CD. The lovely lady of the house, Sayeko, spoke very little English but was very hospitable. I had to do all the shoe business, which she thankfully demonstrated very directly, leaving no room for confusion. A thin panelled slide-back door opened onto a large tatami matted room. Sayeko brought me a plastic 'Hello Kitten' mat on which I was to put my rucksacks. The walls of the rooms are thin sliding doors, even between the other guest rooms; so Bearsac had to behave himself and hopefully not snore once we went to bed. There was a safe in the room, but this was not the sort of place where thieving happens.

The roof of the grass-house was about one metre thick. Yokichi is right next to the Sougawa River, which is aqua-green in colour because the water of hot springs is its source. The river could be heard from our room on the other side of the house but we also had a stream outside our room, and we could smell the relaxing aroma of lilies, which helped us sleep well later that night.

I took Bearsac out to explore the village wearing thonged wooden sandals with funny soles, which are raised up on two wood strips. Called *geta,* they make a sound like a horse walking. I just ran around like a lunatic to make the *geta* even horsier, making everyone stare and cover their mouths laughing. People laughed all the more when Bearsac spoke to the colourful windsocks that are plentiful around the village. They are made to look like eels and wiggle in the breeze like eels under water. In the quiet surrounds of the village, simple sounds are pleasurable. Water splashing on the backs of upturned wooden water-scoops - used to scoop water for hand-washing outside a temple – played a tune between them, each resonant of a different note due to its haphazard position. Bearsac was sure he could pick out the rhythm to 'Peter and The Wolf' by Sergei Prokofiev, and started humming the tune.

The cute shops were laden with *sarubobo*, including a giant sun-faded red turning pink one sitting outside a shop, which Bearsac plunged into for a hug. Like Yokichi, lots of the shops and Nagase House Museum are also *gassho-zukuri* style. The museum exhibits were old farming tools and other items. Of course I had exchanged my external for internal footwear on entering. Bearsac was a little scared walking on the wooden floors as we could see through slots to the floor below. These, we were informed, were to let smoke rise up from the cooking. Bearsac was pleased that we didn't come into contact with any silkworms, which in the old days were farmed on the top floor where it was warm from the smoke. Before leaving the museum we took Japanese tea on the floor downstairs, looking out onto the village.

Walking around filming, we came by the biggest butterfly I have ever seen; Bearsac claimed he's seen bigger. I chased the bluey-black butterfly with my camcorder in excitement; its wingspan was as big as my hand length; I could have folded it over and sewn it into a pretty purse.

The suspension bridge from the main part of the village to the bus terminus gives a refreshing and slightly wobbly walk over the gushing river; Bearsac bravely sat on the rail of the bridge, tied securely by his straps so I could take photographs, I was a little worried about him falling in but I had maybe gone overboard on securing him, so there was no real need to worry. I took Bearsac back to a shop to buy *sake*, or more precisely, '*Nihonshu*'. *Sake* simply means 'alcoholic beverage' and is not a drink in its own right. However, the Japanese do tend to use *sake* instead of *Nihonshu* when speaking with foreigners. Top quality gifu water is used to make the region's *Nihonshu* and we were eager to sample some.

Entering Yokichi's dining room was both pleasant and a little disappointing. Sitting on cushions on the floor at low tables was what I had expected. However, I did not expect there to be a TV on whilst we were eating. It spoilt the image I had wanted to create in my mind of a remote village, untouched by the wider world, and I hate having the TV on whilst I am eating.

Dinner was a *Kaiseki-ryori* delight and typical of the Japanese Alps. *Kaiseki-ryori* is like a work of art; seasonal foods displayed on beautifully crafted Japanese china-ware. The meaning of '*Kaiseki*' stems from when Buddhist priests being trained in the discipline of Zen kept a hot stone (*seki*) in their kimono pocket (*kai*) to make fasting easier somehow (I guess it is a bit like me smelling Bearsac's fur to calm me down). '*Rori*' simply means 'dishes'. The *sansai* (mountain vegetables) were so scrummy (or yummy yum yum, as Bearsac would say). I cannot describe what they tasted like. There was one vegetable in particular that was extra, extra scrummy and whose shape was somewhat reminiscent of okra, but shorter and fatter at one end; we saved it until last after the salted river fish and other foodstuffs like chilled tofu, noodle and mushroom soup. A large tub of soggy rice accompanied the fish and vegetables. The meal was lots for one human and a teddy bear but we ate it all between us, as (apart from the rice) it was too good to waste. It was sheer hunger that saw me polishing off enough rice for six people.

A nice Japanese family were also staying as guests in the house; they dined on the table on the floor next to ours. The kids were very cute, even though I'm not too into kids.

After dinner we had more green tea in our room and relaxed to the sound of the stream and the smell of lilies outside, which merged beautifully with the irori-smoke now on my clothes and Bearsac's fur. During the night a cool breeze ran through our room, continuing to waft the aroma of the lilies in waves over my head. This aided my best-ever sleep and touched my dreams.

Day 6

It was still raining heavily when we woke in the grass-house but we were protected by a metre-thick layer of thick stiff grass with bamboo canes beneath, so the rain was not getting through all that! The clouds over the hills added to the beauty and quiet peacefulness of the village in the morning and I wanted to go for a walk to take it in without people wandering around. The rain was just too wet though, that's the only drawback about rain.

The Western-style lavatory in the *minushuku* was a bit flash; it had a button, which, when I pressed, raised the lid and seat. One button warmed the seat and another squirted my bum. There was a blow job option too, but this was in the more literal sense of the word 'blow' and was a method of simply drying the squirted bits. My bum never so clean, I stood up and nearly shit myself when the brainy lavatory flushed itself.

Breakfast was big; we were happy teddy bear and owner. The egg seemed somewhat out of place amid the tofu soup,

Japanese ve*getab*les, simmering pot of *miso*, banana and *nori* seaweed. I shook the egg by my ear to try and determine if it was cooked or not. Thankfully it was cooked, which saved me a lot of possible difficulty asking advice about how long it would need to be cooked over the *irori* (hearth) and did it go in the *miso* pot, which would seem quite strange but was the only visible option. I had the same amount of rice to myself that the guest family had altogether, but in my hunger I ate it all. The only thing I didn't eat was the regional 'hida beef' with shredded vegetables simmering away in a curled up leaf of some type. I offered it to Bearsac, but he turned his nose up at it as he thought eating from a leaf was beneath a teddy bear. Bearsac helped me with the vivid green tea; lovely it was, but rather too much.

The father of the guest family wrote out for me in Japanese 'I do not eat meat' for me to show in places where they didn't speak English. Sayeko gave us a lift to the bus so we didn't get rained upon. I felt awkward with my thank-yous and goodbyes, not knowing if I was appearing polite enough or going over the top; but at least I said them in Japanese. Bearsac's were far more practised than mine.

During our train journey from Takayama to Tokyo we realised that we were on the Noozomi bullet train and not the Hikari bullet train. My JR Pass was not valid but no one asked to see it so I was OK. This was funny really, as on every other train I had been asked to show my ticket and on this train the other people in the carriage were asked to show theirs. I had a feeling that the guard had guessed that the eccentric Westerner and her talking teddy bear would have had a JR Pass and had maybe accidentally got on the wrong train for her ticket, and he didn't want to penalise her for it.

Once back in Tokyo the overwhelming sounds and movement panicked my breathing out of rhythm and the world whizzed around me as it had done before in a sort of slow motion fastness. With my head down, I braved the rush and sonic abuse and made it out of the station, my breathing finally regaining composure.

I had no place booked for tonight but hoped there was a capsule at the capsule hotel we wanted to stay at. The hotel has shoe lockers as you came in; I had to take my shoes off and put them in the locker before going to the reception to check-in. I was escorted up to the women's rooms on ninth floor and shown the tall but very narrow locker for my bags. There was no way I was getting my large rucksack in there and there was no lockable room for large luggage, as stated. The woman was expecting me to put Bearsac in the locker and I was most upset by this! I think she understood when I smothered him in kisses and hugs.

Food was noodles in soup with some fried stuff and spring onion. It looked good for the price in the photograph outside the noodle bar. There was not the same photograph inside, so I took a photograph of the photograph and showed them it on my digital camera. Having hungrily attacked the noodles with my chopsticks, I then picked up the decorative bowl and slurped down the soup; much to the embarrassment of Bearsac but the delight of the waitress.

Bloated with noodles, we left and looked a little around the area before returning to the capsule hotel to use the Internet, have a shower and get into our cool capsule to watch Japanese TV with its crazy programs and adverts. As well as TV, the capsule had a radio, a mirror, alarm clock, basic air conditioning; it was so cool. I changed into the blue cotton guest robe, then emailed Alan from the ground floor, where there were three Internet computers and a printer.

The ladies' capsule dorm was quiet as there were only about three or four other women and we had no direct neighbours to our capsule. It was cool in the capsule, like being in a rocket with our own capsule to sleep and relax in. We watched corny Japanese game shows, which seem to be based on the total humiliation of contestants. There was also some chat-show that kept showing teddy bears, but I couldn't make out what was happening. Japanese TV is in general very bad and everywhere seems to have a bad reception. After I had turned off the light and TV to go to sleep, I kept turning on the light again every-so-often, to give myself visible proof that I really was in a capsule, even though I could sense the comforting compact auric field in the dark.

Day 7

Our bullet train from Tokyo to Ichinoseki was followed by an eight-minute local train to Hiraizumi, where we had booked into the Motsuji Temple lodgings. We met two nice ladies on the train and walked altogether to our lodgings, as they were going to see the temple in the same grounds. There was no-one around to check me in, so I dumped my large rucksack and took my valuables and Bearsac to have a quick look around the grounds and museum.

Before we made it to the large pond across from the lodgings, we bumped into the two ladies from the train and joined them on a 3km trek up the hill and through pretty woods dotted with graceful, swaying flowers, the scent of which emanated over an undernote of damp woodland earthiness. Sunlight flitted merrily through gaps in the dark green canopy of the dense leafy branches above us. The sounds, however, overloaded me and I had to cover my ears; insane insects screamed at us all the way up to the golden temple, where we left the two women and continued down the road.

We found little souvenir and food shops; the car-park for this group of prettily crafted shops contained no brightly coloured cars. White, silver, grey, and a couple of dark blue and maybe one black but no reds, greens, yellows etc. It seemed quite eerie somehow, the way so many of the white cars were parked next to each other, and the same with many of the silver and grey ones – like some sort of car apartheid.

After a look in the shops and the purchase of some mountain vegetables vacuum packed in a touch of salted water, we continued our walk further down the road over the level crossing, at which we witnessed the stopping of traffic and the passing of trains. Down to the river we continued before returning back to the temple lodgings some three hours after having first arrived. We were greeted by a very nice monk who checked us in, laughed at Bearsac's passports which he ran excitedly to show the women in the kitchens and then showed us to our eight-bedded-room, which we shared with just one other person, a young Japanese woman who was in the area taking part in an archaeological dig. We didn't see her much to ask about the dig, it would have been interesting to hear about it.

Motsuji Temple is also known as 'the temple of flowers'. Its gardens are one of Japan's few remaining Pure Land Gardens, which are intended to reproduce the Buddhist concept of the pure land, or 'paradise'. This style of garden was popular during the Heian Period (794-1185). Motsuji was founded in 850, and under the Northern Fujiwara grew to become the Tohoku's largest temple complex with several hundreds of sub temples during Hiraizumi's heyday in the late Heian Period, before being drastically reduced with Hiraizumi's fall.

I washed my clothes, including my Bearsac T-shirt, and hung them to dry. We finally went to see the pond in the Jodo Garden, which we had so longed to see after seeing pictures on the Internet before we came to Japan. Left breathless by the serene beauty of the lake, I was better able to appreciate the soft warm spiciness of incense carried on the breeze from the nearby temple. With the gentle breeze caressing my face and the sound of birdsong, I was whisked to a higher peaceful vibration by the sensory cocktail. Green echoes whispered around the pond as dragon boats and rocks broke its perfect surface.

As well as the pond, a stream lies in the garden. Each year a floating poetry festival is held. What happens is a glass of *sake* is floated down the stream, then each contestant has to recite a given poem before the drink floats down to them on the stream. I If they don't finish the poem before it reaches them, they have to drink the *sake*. This is said to originate from the days long ago when temple owners' guests took turns writing a line of a poem and then floating it down the stream to the next contestant, who would add another line whilst they all enjoyed food and *sake*. I could imagine this event spoils the tranquillity of the gardens. There's a place for boozing and mouthing off, it's called a pub.

After filling up on the scene, Bearsac and I walked to the store to buy dinner and drinks. We had a bit of a 'where from, where to' exchange with other people back at the temple lodgings and then had an early night so we could arise early for the meditation in the temple at 6.30 the next morning.

Day 8

At 5.30am, had a slow walk and quiet sit down around the pond before the 6.30 meditation in the temple. The monk nodded approval for me to take Bearsac in. He took the few people up for meditation in single file to the temple. We each stepped out of our house shoes onto the tatami matted corridor floor, just as he had done, having turned around facing the way we had come first. The sound of rough feet on tatami behind me made me feel like telling the person behind to pick up their feet when they walked. I took in the interior of the temple: strong rich hardwoods, some beams painted lacquer red echoing the exterior. I had a bit of difficulty with my dodgy knees as I tried to kneel. I sat Bearsac to my right; he had to meditate with open eyes, as he has no eyelids. The monk spoke in his soft voice, I assume it was Japanese but it could have been a monk language. My eyes closed, I could hear the careful footsteps of the monk and sense the breeze of his slow movement as he walked across the front of the short line of people attending the meditation with me.

A few minutes later the whoosh of wind followed with a thud. The three footsteps, repeated before the same repetition of whoosh and thuds, brought me slightly back to my consciousness. I kept my trusting eyes closed and my head bent over my body when the footsteps stopped before me and the body to which they belonged turned to face me and raised its arms. Whoosh; thud on one side of my spine. Whoosh; thud, on the other. The monk, I discovered, had used a great big wooden weapon to bang me on the back, each side of my spine, with precision. It was fine; it was part of the meditation and felt really good. The weapon, whatever it was, was beautiful; I had the sense it was an honour to be whacked on the back with such a fine and spiritual clump of wood. I'm just glad he didn't do it to Bearsac.

After the meditation we all followed the monk back to the lodgings in single file, stepping back into our correctful house shoes.

Bearsac and I checked out, thanking and bidding farewell to the monk before I changed into my own shoes in the shoe lobby, then getting to the train station. At Morioka station, in the waiting room, was a giant TV screen, which kept repeating the same five adverts. One of them featured a really cute penguin that seemed to be famous in Japan. Penguin left the Pole with his mobile phone and went to Japan. He was looking a bit lost in one of the train stations and a young woman came to speak to him and then took him with her and bought him a woolly hat, took him on the train and then ice skating, where he felt most at home. It was such a cute advert and we saw it many, many times as we waited for our train. The only thing is was that we lost track of time and missed our train by seconds. The next one was one hour later on the same platform. We went back to the penguin but I set an alarm to go off 15 minutes before the next train was due, so giving us time to get to the right part of the train for unreserved seats.

We got there with plenty of time but as I was stressed out due to the noises of the station, I got us on the wrong train! We got off a couple of stops later, had to wait over an hour for the next train back, then another hour for the correct train once we got back to Morioka. Of course we watched the penguin again but made an extra effort to make sure we got on the right train to Tazawako this time. We got a bus to the Kogen *Onsen* bus stop, then a *ryokan* mini-bus to where we were to stay.

Tazawako is residence to Lake Tazawa, Japan's deepest lake, as well as exceptional scenery beyond description. Yamanoyado-Brekkan *ryokan* was worth all the hassle of getting there, even if it is quite expensive. Far from anything overloading, woodlands and mountains set it in tranquillity with no other buildings around. Our room, which was more of a suite, was crafted with rice paper screens, rich woods and simple Japanese art; I felt like a princess. There was a lockable main door to the hall, then a sliding door to the sitting room, which transformed into a bedroom at night by bedding being placed on the floor as you dined. Further sliding doors opened on to the dressing area and a large window overlooking green surrounds. A large and deep sunken Japanese bath, large basin, drinks fridge and separate lavatory also lead off the hallway. I sat in the wardrobe for about five minutes before sitting opposite Bearsac on the legless chair at the low table to have Japanese tea.

Dinner was in a typically Japanese setting, sitting on a cushion on the floor in our own compartment, sectioned off by sliding doors. The food was even better than Yokichi's. We cooked fish and vegetables over the little coal fire as it was brought in. It was hard to know if there was more to come or when the end of the meal was. As we had arrived a few hours later than we had planned, we had to rush this most splendid dinner ever produced by the earth and its chefs so we could get the Ryokans minibus to the *onsen* at the sister *Ryokan* 1km away. I had lots of trouble asking the waitress if there was more food or if that was the end of the meal, and finally had to mime the action of carrying trays from the sliding doors to the floor.. I showed them the time of the minibus, which they understood, but they just couldn't work out that I was trying to ask if there was more food or not, so I would know if it was the end of the meal, as I didn't want to rush if I didn't need to, but didn't want to take too long if I needed to rush to catch the minibus.

Surely it must have been quite clear what it was that I was asking, even if there was a language barrier. They must realise people don't know how much food is served and when the end of the meal is if it is not their culture; and surely when they understood I wanted to get the minibus quite soon, it must have been obvious that I was asking about the food to see if there was time. It's real weird, as I pointed to my wrist where a watch would have been if I'd had one and circled my finger on it; now, language barrier or not, that means I'm asking the time. They just didn't get it so I had to run to my room to get my phone to see the time. I also grabbed my phrase book and pointed to the words for 'end' and 'more' written in English and Japanese and they still didn't get what I was asking. As the meals were included, we had no bill to signal the end. At last ice-cream and tea were brought in, so end or not, we took that to signal there was no more food. We were not expecting ice-cream at all, considering the food that had come before, but it was served Japanese style, very small and pretty. We finished with five minutes to go before we had to get the minibus, so I rushed back to our room to change into a *Yakata,* under which I was naked. We were meant to be there to relax but I was near having a nervous breakdown!

We did want to walk to the sister *Ryokan* so we could go in our own time and not rush dinner, but were told by the receptionist that it was very dangerous in the dark as there were wild bears in the woods. Bearsac demanded to know what was wrong with bears, but she just laughed and said to him that she wished she had a *kuma* (bear) like him.

Onsen are natural hot springs and these were milky aqua in colour. Having washed thoroughly before entering, I slipped into the steaming water, joining two other women. I eagerly but calmly gave myself up to the luxury of the soothing warmth, letting out a long contented sigh as it caressed my shoulders and silence pervaded my senses. Closing my eyes, I let the missed trains and hours of dragging my large rucksack and Bearsac around seep out of my muscles.

An old Japanese couple we had gone there with bought us a drink as we waited for the mini-bus back. Once back, I left

Bearsac sleeping, had a go at the *Ryokans* indoor hot bath thing and afterwards had Japanese tea in the beautiful room. Bearsac noticed the *Ryokan* didn't provide *Yakatas* for teddy bears; he claimed this was discrimination, but luckily not to the *ryokan* staff. *Yakatas* must be wrapped left over right – unless one is dead, then it is right over left.

Day 9

The breakfast was as beautiful and as large as dinner the night before but we refused the rice, as it would have all been too much and we wanted to get the mini-bus to the *onsen* at 8.15am. At the *onsen* I set up my camcorder on a tri-pod and swam over to the camera to wave at it. I did the same with the stills camera, putting Bearsac in the frame too.

We had to rush to get our train and met two Japanese ladies on the minibus whom we had met the night before, so we all got the bus and train together until Morioka, where we departed. Bearsac and I went to the waiting room so I could set up my tri-pod and camcorder so I could film the penguin advert. I was so happy to get it that I was almost in tears, people were wondering what I was doing when setting up the camcorder but they understood when I was overjoyed at filming the penguin, and some of them appeared to appreciate the advert for the first time. I think they could see how the penguin and young woman were just like me with Bearsac.

Rather than going straight to Tokyo, we took the train to Sendai, dropped off my rucksacks in a locker and then got a local train to Matsushima to go to Matsushima Bay. Matsushima Bay has lots a small islands dotted around, they are said to be shaped like animals. A red footbridge took us over to one called Fukuurajima and I drew Bearsac and wrote his URL in the sand on the small beach of the island. Once we got to the top of the island we could see people looking at the picture of Bearsac and filming it, and the long www.bearsac.com bit, probably so they could have a look at the site.

Outside a souvenir shop hung one of those battery-operated talking parrots. It is meant to keep only the last recording. However, if you have ever had one, you would know that when the battery starts to get low the parrot often holds on to what it records longer than it is designed to. When we first passed it, Bearsac had being saying his website address. When we past it again some time later, it was saying 'bearsac.com, bearsac. com'! So much better the parrot in Amsterdam.

Back at Sendai station we scoffed free samples of various Japanese delights that they were trying to sell, and did the same in the food court of a department store before getting our train to Tokyo. We were to spend the rest of our time in Tokyo as my rail card was just for seven days.

We had booked to stay in the New Koyo Hotel which, from its site, seemed to be more like a flat-share as it looked like flats from the outside in the photograph, and we had our own room and shared the kitchen and bathroom. On seeing the corridor and tiny square windows on the bedroom doors, however, it looked more like a prison! Our room was Japanese style and so small that a cat would get splattered if you swung it, but at 2700 yen (about £13.17), it was the cheapest place to stay in Tokyo and have your own room. There were limited cooking facilities and it cost ten yen for about ten minutes' use of gas on the one gas ring on each floor. Internet was ten yen per minute. But the staff were helpful and that was the Koyo's saving grace really. We weren't too keen on the biting insects in the bedroom but at least we weren't charged extra for them.

We went to Tokyo's Akihabara district (Electric Town) to see if we could get a better adapter so we could charge my batteries and phone, but none worked so we had to buy ordinary batteries. There were no Duracel but the Toshiba ones were OK.

Next we went to Uneo Park, which was full of pesky crows and noisy insects in the trees; I put in my earplugs to muffle to sound.

In a quieter part of the park I took out the earplugs; the gurgling of the stream filled the cavities that my earplugs had vacated. In another part of the park there were lots of blue, home-made tents, which housed homeless people, and lots of them were queuing up in a very orderly fashion for the outside soup kitchen close to the tent city. Not everyone in Japan is well off so I think it's important to tell of this side of Japan.

The main path through the park was lined with trees that must have been made to grow so that the branches arch over the path on either side. Old people sat on benches or low walls arched over in the same direction towards the path. They all returned Bearsac's greeting with a smile or a bow of the head. Younger people pointed him out as Mr Bean's teddy bear and the females laughed behind their hands as they did so.

We visited the Shibuya district to see the famous crossing – not that I'm a road crossing spotter or anything. The queue was too long in Starbucks to bother waiting to get in for the best view of the crossing and film it, and the aroma of coffee gives me sensory overload anyway. I filmed from the station and zoomed in with the lens. It is so crazy when pedestrians from all directions cross the road at the same time, going diagonally.

We went next to check out Tsukiji fish market to find the place we wanted to eat the next morning, as we didn't want to waste time looking for it at 5.30am when it's best to start queuing. I took lots of photos most people would find boring but I found it such an interesting place to take photos. We met a nice Japanese man and I photographed him with Bearsac for his website.

Day 10

We were up and out at 4.40am to get to Tsukiji fish market (the world's biggest) to join the queue for the reputedly best raw fish in the world. A woman showed us the way to the highly recommended 'Daiwa' sushi bar, but advised us to go and see the tuna bidding first before it ended, which we did most readily.

The fluorescently lit hall is enormous and there are hundreds of shiny tunas lying on the ground with tickets on them. Welly-booted men in overalls walk amongst the tunas, lifting them with hooks and looking inside with torches to inspect them. As if at Speaker's Corner in Hyde Park, a man atop a box shouts. This is, of course, not political ranting but is all part of the tuna bidding. Bells are rung; tunas are loaded onto trolleys and taken away, then sold for millions of yen (thousands of pounds). We follow the tuna being led away but only as far as Daiwa, where we give up the chase and queue for breakfast.

Daiwa's queue was the longer of the surrounding sushi bars and we were soon to taste the reason why. First, though, as I sat down with Bearsac on my knee, I was given a steaming cup of green tea and I had my order prepared right in front of my eyes and video camera. Falling over a large chunk of sushi, like a duvet over a bed, the two tuna varieties included the paler Toro fatty tunad which is of the highest quality. It was rich and creamy and just seemed to melt its taste all over my tongue, and generated

221

quivers to my kegel muscles. I almost fell off the stool, but poor Bearsac fell off my lap. I think my cry of 'Aarrrhhh!' at Bearsac's fall was interpreted as slightly delayed orgasmic murmurings by all the staring but smiling faces around me.

Our 3500 yen (£15) set menu included shark. (This we found out after a man asked me if I liked my shark.) Also placed before me on the cold serving bar was sushi topped with a large spread-eagled prawn, which had been flattened with a large knife. Various other raw fish sat in wait for my consumption and large orange fish eggs too, which burst their juices in the mouth, exploding flavour like fireworks. The urchin gonads wrapped in seaweed looked gross but tasted super fine if indescribable. Whilst Bearsac sampled some with his nose, I didn't tell him what gonads are; I thought it best to leave my teddy bear in innocence and let him enjoy.

We were full up after as it was all protein. The queuing system at Daiwa worked for us but could have gone the wrong way. If there are three spaces available at the small bar then a group of three people get asked to come in from the queue; if there is one space made available then one person is asked in. That's what happened so we got in ahead of lots of people. We came out of the back of the shop fuelled up for the day; we had done quite a bit already and it wasn't even 7am yet.

We had a quick look at Tokyo Tower, which is modelled on the Eiffel Tower but taller. A Japanese man in his mid 50s approached me, just as Bearsac and I were about to leave the area. It took me a while to realise the word he was repeating: 'Daiwa', the sushi bar Bearsac and I had breakfasted at. Clearly he had seen me in there. We greeted him in Japanese and he returned in English. After asking me about my time in Japan, he asked me out for a drink. I think he must have been one of the sets of staring eyes that mistook my cry at Bearsac's fall for orgasmic murmurings, and maybe thought his chances with a lone lady traveller were therefore high.

Next we saw the Imperial Palace but you don't really get to get close it and not inside at all. Niju-bashi Bridge acted as an interesting foreground for the moat-surrounded palace, which otherwise would have appeared too small in the photograph.

Back at the hostel we surfed the Internet. Bearsac rested, had a much-needed can of Asahi beer and a break from me, whilst I had a shower before we went out again to Asakusa, where we joined the mass of people at Sensoji Temple. Lots of ladies and some men, dressed in traditional Japanese wear, complete with clip cloppy wooden *geta,* were paying homage to it.

Sensoji (also known as Asakusa Kannon Temple) is a Buddhist temple. Legend has it that in the year 628, two brothers fished a statue of Kannon, the goddess of mercy, out of the Sumida River, and even though they put the statue back into the river, it always returned to them. Consequently, Sensoji was built there for the goddess of Kannon. The temple was completed in 645, making it Tokyo's oldest temple.

Before entering the temple, we first entered through the Kaminarimon (Thunder Gate), the outer gate of Sensoji and a symbol of Asakusa. A pathway of stalls about the length of two football pitches, called Nakamise, leads from the outer gate to the temple's second gate, the Hozomon. Besides typical Japanese souvenirs such as *Yakata* and folding fans, various traditional local snacks from the Asakusa area are sold along the Nakamise. I bought us each a fan and snacks from the stalls and small shops, and got Bearsac a Japanese outfit from the dog clothes shop, well, it fits him so who cares that it was made for a dog, Bearsac doesn't!

Later in the evening we returned to Asakusa for the firework festival. There were so many women dressed in *Yakata*; it is something they wear a lot to firework displays. The women in their *Yakata* looked very feminine but beer cans and fags spoilt the effect!

We found a spot by the riverside with hundreds of people sitting in lines eating and drinking. As the fireworks started, great 'ooohs' and 'aahhhhhs' filled the air and facial expressions of sheer joy shone through the night. I have never seen so many humans go so mad for fireworks, and they weren't even that good.

After a while, we got bored and uncomfortable sitting where we were and went walking amongst the crowds, filming reactions to the fireworks. Suddenly clip-cloppy footsteps rushed up behind us and excited squeals of 'Bearsa, Bearsa!' filled the air; we looked round to see a group of young ladies in traditional costume and glittered faces. We had met them earlier in the day and they had been on the website. They invited us to sit with their group in the middle of the main road and watch the fireworks and share the spread of food and Japanese beer. It was so nice to be invited to sit with them and their family and friends, and it was a shame when the night quickly ended. Had this been a bunch of British people I would have felt a little apprehensive, but I tend to get on better with people of different cultures, as they seem to accept my quirky ways without judgement.

The display ended quite suddenly with no spectacular and obvious end. All of a sudden, thousands of people just got up and walked away! There must have been about a million turnout altogether but the police and train staff had it very well organised and it was quite easy to get to the train station and get on a train. We thanked the lovely people who had made us welcome in Japanese and walked calmly through the orderly crowds to the station, past the police giving instructions into yellow drinks-funnel looking hailers, which where not even battery powered.

Day 11

Most of the day was spent in a quiet park that had hardly any other people in it; it was a most welcome haven from the noisy roads. Large rooks paraded the lawns, making that horrid noise they make; they didn't even fly off when we got too near, even when Bearsac told them to go away. There was a section once used for duck hunting. A wooden wall with gun hole was now only for show purposes and the hole was about the only way to take a peek inside the now fenced-off duck conserve. A stone monument was installed and a memorial service held for ducks as a way, maybe, of saying sorry to the ducks previously hunted. Bonsai trees were all over the park and Bearsac posed in a few for photos. We were there for about three hours before we saw other people and that was just a couple.

From late afternoon we went to Tokyo Bay via the monorail. It was beginning to get dark as we arrived and the giant Ferris wheel lit up, changing colours, its lights reflected in the glass buildings opposite. The lights of Tokyo looked cool and planes flew low and loudly overhead to and from the nearby airport.

We went into the Toyota car show and had a go in the funny-looking squashed car around the track that went in and outside the building. Bearsac did the steering and I the pedals. The car was just automatically set; we weren't really driving it but as a non-driver, I enjoyed pretending. We looked around the shops and met a giant teddy bear with long sharp claws. We spent some time on the boardwalk looking at Rainbow Bridge lit up over the water and spoke to dogs dressed in traditional Japanese costume before leaving and going back to our infested cell.

One curly-furred dog even had chopsticks in its top-knotted fur-do! I thought it might be sexist to assume that this meant that it was a female dog.

Do you think these dogs have mobile phones with clothes?' Bearsac asked me.

Bored with tacky Japanese TV, I lay in the dark listening to bicycle tyres on the pavement and wining dogs. The glow of the street-lights' reflection on the building outside my window filled my small cell, casting faint shadows on the wall. Bearsac looked rather menacing superimposed at several times his size on the wall as I held him in front of the window and moved his head about.

Day 12

I took Bearsac to Asakusa again to help me pick a *Yakata*; I thought I might get one cheap as I guessed they might have them on sale as the festival was over. There was only one place I saw that had them on sale and I got one for 1050 yen (£5.12), which was very, very good. Along the stall mall by the temple an old, tiny lady with a huge great rag-covered wicker box strapped to her back waddled through the crowds. Every so often she stopped and handed out something to people who stopped her; she took money in exchange. I could not see clearly exactly what it was, but it looked like fresh green beans.

Back at New Koyo, I showered and changed into my yakata, having difficulty tying it. I went out to eat wearing it and Bearsac ate using chopsticks to share my raw fish. Taking the train to

Shinjuku - the area to go for the buildings covered in neon lights - I was approached by a woman on the platform. With just a nod and smile as introduction, she proceeded to adjust the sash and bow on my *Yakata* so it sat correctly. I am not one for physical contact, especially so unexpected, but I welcomed the assistance.

We met two lovely ladies in a clothes shop, one of them the designer of the clothes, and took Bearsac's photograph with them. I was asked to go for a drink by a middle aged man but declined him politely in Japanese and we went on our way. The flashing neon lights were surrounded by a multitude of loud noises, but with Bearsac close at hand to smell if I needed him, and my earplugs in, I set about photographing and filming. As much as I hate McDonalds and hate seeing them in every country I go to, it was fun to see it with Japanese writing. By the number of Japanese people inside and around the streets eating its food, McDonalds looks like it is more popular in Tokyo than anywhere else in the world.

Having seen the crossing at Shibuya in the daytime, we returned by night to see it. I was invited for drinks by more men but declined. Bearsac spoke to lots of people on the train back to our part of town and I had my Yakata adjusted twice more. I have a very short waist and my rib cage juts out so it was hard for the wide sash to stay in place elegantly. Once back in our cell, we watched more corny chat shows and game shows and got bitten by bedbugs and fleas all night. Sleeping on the thin mattress on the floor with the fleas took my mind back to when I was nine years old. Our first night at a women's refuge, mother my brother and I slept on seedy flea ridden mattresses on the floor in a damp room filled wall to wall with other women and children. I hoped on this occasion that Bearsac wouldn't become infested the way Teddy Robinson and Panda did then.

Day 13

Today was our last whole day. We checked out of New Koyo and took a train to Narita for Hostel Azure, which is seven miles from the airport. Dropped off my bags and headed out to explore the tranquil park with temples. We met more people on our travels and lots of giant fish. Up to a temple, orderly steps, one behind the other, were being taken by two white kimonoed monks in their *geta*. Despite the awkwardness of such a shoe, they walked with the confident stride of prostitutes in high heels, their clip clops in perfect time with each other. Pagodas, bonsai trees, fountains and streams were all within the park and were thankfully not obscured by tourists. The park was quite empty, which, I'm sure, the wildlife was quite thankful for.

Bearsac got talking to small turtles in a shallow pond; this attracted two little girls and their mother, who came over and all spoke to Bearsac in East European accents. The mother said that they too had seen very few westerners whilst in Japan. Once they had moved on, I sat with Bearsac on my lap on a smooth rock by the pond and two Japanese women came to speak to us as their children did drawings of the pond close by. They offered me samples of various Japanese sweet spreads from jars on wooden sample sticks. I wasn't quite sure if I was to put the stick in my mouth, or take the food with my fingers from the stick (which I wouldn't like to do, having not washed my hands). Sensing my stress, one of the women showed me more sticks, so now clear, I licked off the sweet sticky goo from each stick passed to me. Of course, Bearsac smelt each one first. His 'yummy yum yums' brought over the children who giggled at him shyly and screamed with delight when he bit them.

In the woods Bearsac spoke to an artist painting a picture of a temple-like building, which might have been a large tool shed.

Feeling hungry, we took a black marble bridge to the park exit and in the shops along the way back to the hostel I bought some chopsticks from the 100 Yen shop; some nihonshu *sake*, some Japanese food and green tea to take home. Azure Hostel was nice and clean and had no biting insects, unlike the New Koyo.

Day 14 – Last day

The pungent aroma of incense spilling from shops and the smell of *sake* fuelled our walk around the village, where Bearsac spoke to a parrot in a cage, a dog in a bag and a man in a car who was half-Japanese and half-Italian. The man had the front seats of his car dressed - one in a Japan football shirt and the other in an Italy football shirt.

I bought some calf-length, split-toe ninja plimsolls, some china-ware and food and packed it all carefully away, adding to my already heavy load. With plenty of yen left I got some Japanese vodka, Japanese sweets to take home and a belated birthday present for a friend called Ellen.

On the first flight we sat next to Japanese newly-weds who were on their way to Madrid for their honeymoon. The bride gave us their airline honeymoon biscuits, which I scoffed away at after pretending Bearsac was eating them. We watched three films and cartoons and were so relieved to get off the plane at Malpensa in Italy, where we had to change flights. Bearsac sat on Harry Potter's shoulder for a photograph. It was not really Harry Potter, but a Lego-built Harry Potter holding a hockey stick. I bought some mandarin liquor in the duty-free before our flight to Heathrow.

Bearsac got to sit in the cockpit of the plane and have his photo taken, which he thought well cool.

We got home some time after midnight, greeted by a sleepy-eyed Alan who had been flat-sitting for us, and we all tucked into *sake* and sweets. I made a Japanese meal including sushi topped with salmon and served it on my new Japanese chinaware dressed in my *Yakata*.

Sipping Japanese beer in Tokyo and Sniffing out sashimi in Tokyo

Chapter Thirteen

Trans-Mongolian and More
March 2007

Day 1 – March 14th 2007 - Tallinn, Estonia

Early hours, Stansted Airport was quiet. I lay along a row of plastic seats, studying the ceiling to pass the time with my ear-plugs in just in case of any sudden loud or irritating noises. The earplugs were a wise move as suddenly the peace was besieged by sharp clashing sounds I recognised as belonging to the arcade game where a player stands on each end of the rimmed table and hits a puck with a hand-held hitting device and attempts to score goals. The sliding and clashing sounds grated on my nerves so I hugged Bearsac, smelling his fur until the couple finished play-ing and moved away, the man singing a song of victory.

Bearsac only spoke to one person who told him how much his dog, called Dennis, would like a teddy like Bearsac. I rather thought the man was referring to how Dennis would love to eat a teddy like Bearsac, but I didn't let on to Bearsac.

Normally a teddy bear that jumps up and down with excitement at taking off, Bearsac sat quietly belted in on the seat next to me. I think he was missing his second child, a boy teddy called Bearnado, who had been added to the family just two days be-fore. It was hard to tell as the plane came down to land whether the many huts, some with small greenhouses, were large garden sheds or small dwellings.

Bearsac was a bit more animated on the bus to the harbour and got lots of strokes and paw shakes, especially from old ladies in colourful headscarves. From the harbour we headed on foot towards Tallinn's old town, soon finding the 'City Bike Hostel.' A very small hostel, it is mainly a bicycle hire place but has a few beds and free Internet. We soon dumped my bags and went out to explore.

We met the famous Fat Margaret; I photographed Bearsac with her. Fat Margaret is not a person, though, she is a short fat bastion and gate built in the 16th century to protect Tallinn. Her walls, at the base, are more than four metres thick – must have good sound-proofing. We strolled around in the cold Nordic sunshine; the sky deep blue, like on postcards.

At the Natural History Museum of Estonia, a stuffed bear did not reply to Bearsac for some reason when Bearsac said hello. The female attendants sitting close by looked at each other as if to say: 'This woman is not right in the head and should not be in here'. Bearsac said hello in Estonian, to which they just looked grumpier.

Raekoja Plats (Town Hall Square) was quiet, and the few people in it all seemed to be walking very slowly with their hands held behind their backs; they reminded me of my Dad when we took holidays in small English villages during my childhood. The square has hosted a marketplace since the 11th century and has had a pharmacy operating since 1422, but sadly, not today. Bearsac wanted to look around art galleries; he was given a chin tickle by a woman on the desk of one gallery. Pretty ordinary art galleries, nothing too spectacular but it was a welcome break from the chill.

After a warm-up and Internet session, we took to the cobbled streets again, finding some American girls staying at the hostel, and went with them to see the sights. All in love with Bearsac, they took him up into a tree for a photograph in front of the *Kiek in de kok*, which does not mean what it sounds like, but means 'peep into the kitchen', because soldiers were able to see down onto the pantries of the houses below. Bearsac and I later headed to the harbour; but weren't inspired, so just walked along the disused railway tracks, stepping on all the sleepers, which weren't evenly spaced, so annoyed my Aspie need for uniformity.

We dined across the road from the hostel in the African Kitchen restaurant with sauna. Warmly, we took in the African tribal murals and ambiance of this hip yet cosy, cave-like eating establishment. The kitchen's rich aromas wafted sensuously through to the intimate tables. Greedy Bearsac wanted to try the Peri Peri Antelope, the ostrich and the camel. Being vegetarian, I ordered, and shared with him the kinder silky spinach and carrots in peanut sauce with creamy coconut rice as we chilled out listening to the evocative rhythm of African music. The comforting mango pudding and pomegranate juice brought the meal to a satisfying close. Tiny Estonia is not very knowledgeable about African culture, so the African Kitchen offers more than just an introduction to Africa's food.

Back at the hostel, people spoke about their day as wafts of greasy pepperoni pizza floated throughout. I felt a little awkward trying to talk to the young trendy group of people, but was content listening until I went to bed. With my earplugs I soon got off to sleep. I awoke to use the lavatory and nearly fell off it as it was not bolted to the floor. This gave me a bit a shock and I was envisaging all the germs that I might have fallen onto if I had fallen on the floor, so I didn't sleep too well after returning to bed.

Day 2 – Tallinn - Riga

With very little Estonian money left to buy food and drink for the coach, and with no food shops within walking-with-heavy-rucksack-distance, I was not afforded much choice at the coach-station's newsagent. Hating to eat without having just washed my hands, and not wanting to root inside my bag for my hand-cleansing gel, just to eat a couple of cheesy wafers, I used a little finger that had not touched anything since I had last used the hand gel about one hour before. Once out of the box enough, I took the long wafer out with my mouth. Just then, as we were at the traffic lights, a woman on a coach stopped beside ours stared right at me with a look on her face I took to be snotty. I just waggled the wafer at her with my tongue and she stuck her nose in the air and turned away. I sucked the wafer into my mouth and licked my salty lips with a satisfied smack. The woman looked like Margaret Beckett MP, or at least so thought Bearsac when he pointed at her and told me so. She pretended not to see him.

During the journey I couldn't help noticing the amount of ve-hicles so dirty at the back that the number plates were unread-able; my skin crawled at the very sight of them. The route out of Tallinn was aligned with dark green woods, dotted with wooden houses. It seemed that maybe, rather than destroy the woods altogether, they had left the woods and built lots of well-spaced houses amid the trees. It was a bit like having ten trees in your drive or front garden.

Passing lots of trees some distance on, I noticed that one was abundant with nests, while all the surrounding trees, of the same type, held none. What did that tree have over the others? I wanted to point out this strange phenomenon to passengers on the coach, but we would have passed the tree by the time I had said anything, and I guessed it would be pretty boring to neuro-typical people anyway.

At 2.51pm a stern passport official boarded at the border of Estonia and Latvia. She refused Bearsac's passport for checking when she took mine. Eleven minutes later, the coach started up and passed into Latvia. It is strange passing the border between two countries when the general area is the same place. I soon noticed something not quite the same though. For some reason, maybe political, the grass was shorter almost as soon as we passed the border.

Bearsac was fascinated by a wide river frozen over with only about a five-metre wide gorge of running water. Excitedly, he pointed out the hole in the thick ice and a man ice-fishing from it. He was further excited when, at 3.50pm, we passed the sea with sandy beach; he started jumping up and down on my lap, saying, 'I can see the sea, I can see the sea'. Unfortunately for him, we soon pulled away.

Entering Riga, a debate turned into an argument between two American passengers on whether the tall building to our right was ugly or beautiful; what cause this could be for argument I'm really not sure, but I was thankful when we very shortly arrived at Riga bus station.

Once checked into our hostel, I took Bearsac to buy my ticket for the train to Moscow on Saturday, and some food. On our return I took my free beer, which is given to you on arrival, into the common room to relax, emailed Alan and introduced myself and Bearsac to people. A couple of people didn't really know how to take a talking teddy bear that was better dressed than they were, especially the man wearing combats that looked like they had been gang-attacked by a pit-bull and lawnmower. However, most people took to Bearsac and he got to have quite a few sips of quite a few drinks, getting just a little too tipsy for my liking.

A walk to take in the night scene revealed an assortment of click-ing high heels, giggles and chesty coughs. Nightclub queues seemed to be very thin on males. Maybe it is free for women before a certain time but not for men, or maybe all the clubs we passed in Riga are lesbian clubs or male stripper joints. Either way, Bearsac got lots of waves and a few kisses.

Further down the road, Bearsac calls 'Good evening' to a lady standing in a dimly moonlit shop doorway; she leans against the bay window and sucks on her cigarette seductively. As she exhales a cloud of smoke, she drawls in a husky voice:

'Good evening, handsome teddy bear, would you like a nice stroke?'

Worried that she might try to charge me, I tell Bearsac teddypathically to decline.

'Sorry, lovely lady, but my wife is awaiting my return,' he lies.

The prostitute laughs and blows Bearsac a kiss and I bid her 'Be lucky'.

Day 3

I had slept so soundly with my earplugs that I was unaware that two new people had taken beds in the room. Soon pesky seagulls started their racket; it seemed strange to hear them as I thought of them as being a British thing. Had grapefruit and one of my favourite cheeses, *gjetost* (a Norwegian cheese) for breakfast on some dark rye bread, which is a marriage made in food heaven. I left the hostel at 8.15am to go exploring with Bearsac.

In Bastejkalns Park, many police officers were plodding about. I don't know what was going on but most of them looked miserable; maybe they were always like that. However, three friendly officers took off their gloves, despite the freezing cold weather, to shake Bearsac's paw and take his website card. Bearsac noticed that a bridge in the park was covered in padlocks.

'Some padlocks have baby padlocks locked to them,' he

pointed out, on closer inspection of the bridge. Could protest to something be the significance, or maybe it could be a symbol of marriage.

The Gothic style architecture of the House of the Blackheads compelled me to study its masoned detail and cool mechanical clocks. Constructed in 1344, it was originally the Guild House of Unmarried Merchants. It was partly destroyed in 1941, during World War Two, and its destruction was finished off by the Soviets in 1948. In 2001 it was reconstructed in honour of Riga's 800th birthday. These days the House of Blackheads serves as a museum and sometimes holds concerts. How, considering its destruction, it can be considered old, I don't know, but it is said to be Riga's oldest public building. Old or new, it is beautiful and its reconstruction is in its original style. Bearsac begged me to photograph him by the statue in front of it. We were told by a man in grey that the statue is of the Mythical Roland, but not who Roland was; nor did we discover why he is such a mythical being.

Response to Bearsac thus far in Riga had been a little more confused than in Tallinn, but both towns brought the 'Mr Bean's teddy bear' cry from many people. I wondered if he would get the same thing in Mongolia and China.

With someone asleep back at the hostel, I couldn't retrieve my toothbrush and smelly socks that had fallen behind their bed. At 2pm we went to the market. The market stalls are both outside and inside, the inside stalls housed in old Zeppelin hangers. Divided up in sections based on the food type sold, each hanger offers different smells. I inhaled deep breaths of spicy pickling peppers as I bought *sauerkraut*. We wanted to buy some wine but unfortunately discovered that Riga is full of only sweet wine. All that sweet wine and not a Barsac in sight; Bearsac was most upset, how much he wanted to try a wine so near in sound and spelling to his own name!

The large building of American debate, which can be seen on entering Riga, turned out to be the Latvian Academy of Sciences. Standing in front of this imposing edifice, we scanned for the detail of hammers and sickles, evidencing Latvia's Soviet past, but could not see them. A portrait of Stalin was meant to be part of the décor, but luckily it never got to deface the building. Don't know if we were meant to be inside but it looked interesting and beckoned us in. Dark and spooky; footsteps echoed menacingly down the corridors but no feet followed. The harsh echo of something being scraped along the floor startled me. I ran laughing to the exit, clutching Bearsac to me.

At 8pm Bearsac and I went to see more of Riga in darkness, but as there was not much going on we just got some Latvian booze and some hazelnut curd things from the supermarket, and made dinner at the hostel. In the common room we met a few people, including some young British men on a stag weekend. The others were fine, but the groom-to-be didn't like Bearsac and wanted to pull his head off. I think he had second thoughts about it when I threatened to take *his* head off, with venom no doubt pouring out of my face. How dare this chavvy little worm threaten my darling little teddy bear!

I was rudely awoken at 3.15am by a bald Frenchman. He banged about unpacking and then disappeared for ten minutes, only to return and disturb the quiet some more by drying his underpants with a hairdryer. Being bald, I can only presume he carried the hairdryer for drying clothes. I suggested he give his raggy underpants a blow job in the hallway and not in the bedroom. He pretended not to understand English. If I hadn't been on the top bunk I would have got out of bed and pulled the plug out.

Instead, I just put in my earplugs and sat Bearsac staring at him, hopefully menacingly.

Day 4 – Riga to Moscow

I got up quite early, making plenty of noise, as the only other person in the room at the time was the Frenchman who had made lots of noise with his underwear. Don't think the man dared say anything to a madwoman talking to her teddy bear, asking him which items of clothing he wanted to wear today.

Once Bearsac was dressed and I was satisfied we had both made enough noise and had bashed the man's bed enough with the metal under-bed storage boxes, we went to the market. I purchased stuff for the train and to give as presents for the Mongolian family we hoped to find in the country in Mongolia. Took a long walk through the park where Bearsac walked on the frozen river with the ducks. We also discovered what the padlocks on the bridge were about. Newly-weds put a padlock on the bridge to symbolise the eternity of their love for each other; the smaller padlocks are added when they have children. Bearsac wondered if the padlocks are removed in the event of divorce. Thankfully he didn't ask any of the wedding party that had assembled on the bridge for photographs.

The rustic décor of the Latvian taverna with its crooked tables and cosy atmosphere was a delightful and peaceful place to lunch. Locally brewed brown beer, served by a barmaid dressed in an old-fashioned barmaid costume, came in a face-shaped mug and complemented very well the carrot pie. I surmised that the pie base must have been made with dark rye bread compressed into shape. Bearsac and I shared three Latvian cheeses on sticks, enough cheese for ten humans, let alone one human and a teddy bear. Hoping I would be able to make the carrot pie back home, we left, leaving a good tip, and then headed back to the hostel to collect my bags and catch the train to Moscow.

We shared a section of the common carriage with a Russian family. My upper berth permitted me a little privacy whilst the family sat on the lower berths, but I thought I should make the effort to join them for a while. The little boy offered me some Russian bread – very hard and chewy bread, I should add. I was a little apprehensive to take it as he had not cleaned his hands and I had not cleaned mine. My research on Russian culture informed me as to the deep offence my refusal of Russian food would likely cause, so I took the bread with the sides of my finger*s* rather than fingertips and put the untouched end into my mouth, making yummy sounds as I chewed hard, hoping my teeth would stay intact. The saltiness of the bread became more intense the nearer I got to the touched bit, or so it seemed. I made out I was about to sneeze and lose co-ordination, thus dropping the bread on the floor and apologising profusely in Russian.

When later I was offered more food by hand, I had worked out how to say *hygiene* from my Russian dictionary and tried to demonstrate, by way of English words and gestures, that I cannot eat with my own unwashed hands, and therefore, logically, not from other people's. That is part of having Asperger's syndrome for me, nothing personal to them. I think they understood after the explanation, but if not, they certainly did after I used disinfectant sheets to clean my hands as I couldn't find my hand gel and there was a queue for the lavatory. I started to come up in a slight rash where I had used the disinfectant sheets on my skin, but I think it was more the panic than the disinfectant.

The bunks were constructed so that the ends went from window to aisle. On the other side of the narrow aisle were more beds (non bunks) that ran along the length of the windows. During the day, they were two seats and a table; at night they folded down into one bed. These offered less privacy even than the bunks. Opposite our section of bunks resided a Russian granny with a bad wig. I think she had the idea that the more Russian she spoke to me, the more I would understand. Maybe my pronunciation of *'ya nye panimayu'* (I don't understand) was not understood by her like it had been by other people.

Bearsac and the little boy played the 'shaking hands and biting' game, from which Bearsac always gleans so much delight. This involves people shaking his paw and him biting them, and it is a game that is understood worldwide.

I took a trip to the lavatory in the dim lighting and nearly kicked over a potty full of wee and poo, which, for reasons best known to the parents of its little owner, had not been emptied. Wee splashed on my foot and I nearly puked up over the man snoring in the bed opposite the bunks; but it was thankfully a vomit-free heave. On the way back, I nearly got my foot stabbed by the stiletto heels on a teenage girl's boots. Turquoise in colour, the knee-length boots reminded me of vehicles in Italy. With her sparkly tights, hot-pants and cropped top, I wondered whether the train might have its own lap-dancer.

Back in my section with the Russian family, it almost felt like I was home. My first ever sleep on a train was fine; with my earplugs and eye mask, I almost forgot I was on a train and slept my usual four hours.

Day 5

I woke after my first ever sleep on a train and looked out onto the snow outside. Of course, as sod's law has it, snow lay all the way to Moscow but when we got to Moscow it had all been snow-ploughed away.

I wasn't sure which train station we were at, so couldn't use the map to attempt to walk to the hostel. I tried asking a man which station I was at, pointing to the map and at the station floor, and trying to assume a 'which' and 'where' expression on my face that I had learnt from people at my lip-reading class. He said 'Get metro', but I tried to explain I had not yet changed my money and didn't yet want to, as I didn't know how much I needed until I got to the hostel. He didn't say which station it was but started asking people questions and not getting much luck from them. An old lady in a large furry hat then gave him money, so I realized he had been asking them for money for me; I felt embarrassed and tried to say no, which I worried was insulting. I went up to the old lady to thank her and she squeezed Bearsac's face between her gloved hands and made a noise people normally make when squeezing the cheeks of children.

In Russian, I thanked the lady again, and the man, and headed for the metro. My brain was addled by guilt, so I was relieved to find they had given me only a little more than the single metro fare. Two women with a child walked me to the road the hostel was on; they expressed their amazement that a woman would travel alone and were fascinated by the idea that I was taking my teddy bear with me and photographing it for its website.

The four flights of steep stairs to the hostel reeked of cigarettes; I was out of breath when I reached the top, having had to run up as that hurts my knees less. I didn't have the energy to take off my heavy rucksack, so was thankful when a young man, seeing my struggle, helped me off with it. It was as much as I could do to give him the thumbs-up in place of speaking my thank you.

Once I had sorted out my things, Bearsac and I hit Red Square. Wow, we were in Red Square! My attention was taken first by the colourful onion-domed roofing of St Basil's Cathedral. At 13 degrees centigrade, it was very warm for Moscow in early spring, warm enough to be gloveless – a relief for taking photographs and camcorder footage of Bearsac. I even found a few flat surfaces to use as a pod so I could be in the photographs as well as Bearsac. Bearsac was worried the photos would be spoilt by my presence. Nice to know how my teddy bear feels about me!

Moscow's communist past and growing capitalist present clash violently in various parts of the town. Just off Red Square resides a modern department store; I felt somewhat bored by it but Bearsac was happy to stop and say hello to people sitting in giant tea-cups that served as seating. A cliché is that Moscow is a city that breathes in history and exhales pollution; we certainly found that to be true as we continued our walk through the polluted haze around the outer wall of the Kremlin and Red Square, me with my small hair scarf over my nose and mouth. Bearsac told me that the Kremlin has the world's largest bell, *Tsar Kolokol*; not that it works or anything. It is 6.14 metres in height, 6.6 metres in diameter and weighs 216 tons. Where does my teddy bear get his knowledge from?

At the Tomb of the Unnamed Soldier, we were just in time for the changing of the guards. I wasn't the only person photographing a cuddly toy in front of the monument and guards; two men had placed a bunny on a pillar to photograph it. The bunny was called 'Nozzel' or something like that and the men, like me, take him on their travels. Bearsac gave them his website card and encouraging suggestions to make Nozzel a website. The men and Nozzel were from Austria.

All five of us laughed as the guards performed something reminiscent of John Cleese's Nazi walk in Fawlty Towers. Maybe John Cleese is known worldwide, like Mr Bean's teddy bear. Two of the guards openly hugged each other on their exchange of duties; I was surprised, but pleasantly so, to see this display of affection between two male guards; I'm sure it wouldn't have been common practice, but it would have been all the better if they'd had a full-on snog. The crowd had been stunned into silence by this mutual exchange of affection, which clearly was more than a simple friendly greeting. Bearsac broke the silence with a rip-roaring 'Ooooooooooooww!' followed by a cheer, but neither of the guards looked his way.

When we had done the full circuit of the Kremlin wall we fell upon a nasty sight. Two men with two small monkeys, a bigger monkey and two large birds of prey, were exhibiting them to the assembled crowd, charging for photographs. The monkeys were dressed as humans and the bigger one made to sit on a chair and smoke; it ate the cigarette end after smoking it. The birds were very struck by Bearsac and turned their head when Bearsac did, mimicking his movements. The monkeys weren't scared of him like the wild monkeys in Sri Lanka had been, which was a shame really, as it was not natural.

One of the birds tried to fly off and pulled the large metal perch it was chained to, pulling it along the ground. I was triumphant that it was showing that it was not happy being chained to its barless prison. The men wanted to hold Bearsac with the monkeys but I held him away to demonstrate 'no way', and they said 'Not touch bear OK'. I doubt they realized it was because we were upset about the monkeys and that I didn't want to fund their monkey's smoking habit. A loud, middle-aged American woman wined to her equally loud husband until he relented and paid for her to be photographed with one of the monkeys. Holding it like

244

it was baby, she rocked it and sang a lullaby to it. The monkey looked almost relieved to get back to the familiar arms of its captor; what else would the poor thing know?

One thing I noticed throughout the day was how many adults were walking around with cuddly toys; Bearsac ran us up to most of them to say hi and gave them his website card. I assume they had just been won in Gorky Park, and it was not that all these people were taking their cuddly toys out like I do with Bearsac. I think, from his worn out appearance and clothes, it was clear to people I had not just won him!

Back at the hostel I met one of my room-mates and exchanged the usual where-froms and where-goings. I then went back out in search of money exchange and food. When I saw the price of food in the supermarket, I realised I should have got more money exchanged.

I spent most of the evening talking to people about travel, Bearsac, and Asperger's syndrome and the pros and cons of it. I explained that I talk quite a lot about those three subjects and don't recognise when people get bored with it, so to tell me if I was going on too much. They said it was fine. I had to tell myself to let them speak and to also ask them questions. I even explained to a man I was talking to that I have to manually tell myself to let others speak and to ask them about themselves. The man knew people with Asperger's, so he understood.

By 11.30pm I was overloaded by all the surrounding noises: TV, fridge, different conversations and other sounds, so I retired to bed. I got up again at about 3.35am and took advantage of the fact that no-one else was up to use the Internet and typed up my notes of the trip. It's 4.31am as I type this bit right now, so I am going to check something out on the net and then email this to myself.

Day 6

I thought I'd avoid the shower rush when I got up to use it at about 7.13am, but it was mayhem out there. About 15 suited women in the lobby had their baggage sprawled everywhere. They behaved as if they owned the place and had commandeered the showers, lavatories and kitchen, where they were washing themselves. They just pushed around past the rest of the back-packers, who could not sleep due to their noise and a stuck-up attitude.

I started washing my clothes in the basin next to the shower, which was occupied, so whoever was next didn't realise I was waiting for the shower and so was not being protective of her place in the queue. When the occupant of the shower came out I rushed in, leaving my clothes in the basin. The woman who had pushed me earlier with her nose in the air stormed in, as the lock was broken, shouting in Russian. I just told her, not caring if she understood, that I was adding two minutes to the time I was in there for this and for any further interruptions. I normally only shower for about a minute, but as she interrupted a further time, I hung in there for about four minutes after I had finished dressing.

Once out, I continued to wash my clothes whilst she was in the shower. A young man asked me if anyone was in the shower and I replied there was not. An almighty scream emitted from the shower. I smiled to myself with satisfaction and scrubbed my clothes harder on the energy, similar to the way footballers run around faster for a few seconds after play reconvenes after a goal has been scored.

I headed to the Cosmos Hotel, where my train ticket was be-ing held for Mongolia. After leaving the office with my ticket, I plunged into a large comfy armchair in the hotel lobby to study the metro map I had got from reception. It had taken an hour and a half to walk here, so there was no way I was walking back. Once back at the hostel, I made lunch, and Bearsac and I talked to a couple from Norway. They were going to be on the train to Mongolia too, and were talking about going out to try and change US $10 bills for $1 bills, which would be better in Mongolia, where they accept the US dollar as currency

Seeing as I had brought dollars rather than pounds with me, I asked if I could come along. Once I had finished eating, we all went out on the hunt. One bank that was happy to change $10 notes for $1 notes only had three $1 notes, so it was no good. The exchange place we tried misunderstood the Russian instructions we had asked the hostel staff to write for us, asking to change $10/$20 bills to $1 bills, and just showed us the exchange rate for roubles. We returned with the notes we had left with and I stayed in the rest of the day and evening, as I was exhausted and it was raining.

Later in the evening a noisy group of young men struck up an in-depth discussion on how ties should be tied and whether the Windsor knot or another was better. The Italian amongst them, who had really badly bleached hair and mismatched clothes, insisted his way of tying a tie was the latest way and the Windsor should not be used as it was out of fashion. He insisted that he knew best as he was Italian and was therefore more fashionable. Another, arguing the case for the Windsor, went to get his 'tying ties guide' and started instructing others on how to do the Windsor. The hostel owner pointed out that that was the normal way to tie a tie but the tie guide owner insisted it was a relatively new method. It was the way I used to tie my tie at school and the only way I have ever seen a tie tied. The tie posse started Googling about tying ties with much animated enthusiasm. I just wanted to tie their ties around their necks tightly, the quickest way that would strangle them.

I think the hostel owner was maybe getting as annoyed with the petty discussion as the rest of us there because he asked me Bearsac's website address and asked me to show the tie posse his passport. People then gathered around the computer monitor to see Bearsac photographed with celebrities and the annoying tie discussion was thankfully forgotten.

Day 7

Arose at 2.34am to use the Internet, then again at 6.20am and hit the metro in order to take photographs before it got crowded. The Russian metro system has some of the most amazing stations architecturally; it is like an underground art gallery. Halls with chandeliers hanging from domed ceilings, walls tiled in colourful mosaic, classical painted ceilings that command one to endure neck-ache to peruse them. By 7.50 it was unbearable for me as I was getting stressed by the noise, smell, dust, and rushing about of people. Metro trains seared my ears.

I couldn't find the post office to send my postcard to my cousin, despite the hostel owner having told me it was opposite McDonald's. . I asked lots of people, in Russian, but only one person spoke to me and they didn't know where it was. Took a walk down the riverside to the Red October chocolate factory and bought some chocolate – just for Bearsac's sake, of course! A bit further down is an iron statue of Peter the Great and The Church of Christ the Saviour; with its golden domes shining in the sun, it beckoned us over. From there we went to the Kremlin. It is only open to groups, so Bearsac prompted me to mingle into a group of students and we got in as far as a presentation room where the presentation was in Russian and the slides of boring egg ornaments, so we snuck out, not wanting to wait a long time to see if we could follow the group on the rest of their tour. It was now getting close to 11am, so we headed back to the hostel for me to shower, pack and check-out.

I was allowed to stay at the hostel and still use the kitchen and Internet, so I popped out with Bearsac to get food for lunch and for the train journey. Got what I thought would be cherry milk-shake but was happy when it turned out to be a yoghurt drink. I was sitting waiting for the cleaner to finish emptying the bin and move away from the door, so I could take my lunch into the common room, when she started telling me to 'sitting' when I got up. I tried to explain that the washing machine was too loud for me to eat in the kitchen, and that I was not a child, but an adult. I think she understood about the washing machine by me throwing my hands to my ears and pointing to the washing machine with my foot; but don't think she understood the rest. I ate in the common room, wondering what I would have to look like so as not to be told what to do by someone not even in authority.

I rested for a while before going to St Basils, or Baz's gaff, as Bearsac prefers to call it. Beautifully painted with flower detail inside, it has small crooked corridors and uneven floors. The pretty spiralled cathedral was authorised by Tsar Ivan the Terrible, its building taking place between 1555 and 1561. Legend says that once the work was finished, Ivan The Terrible ordered that Postnik Yakovlev, the architect, be blinded so he could never create anything as beautiful again. (But thankfully he did go on to build another cathedral in Vladimir, despite his loss of sight!)

Trans-Mongolian

Late afternoon I struggled into my rucksacks and set off for the Trans-Mongolian train. It was not clear which of the two neighbouring stations was the one I needed, as neither used the name as it was written on my maps or in my book or ticket. Once at the correct station, I debagged my back and ceased my panic. I noticed that the glass jar of cassoulet beans in tomato and onion sauce had smashed and its contents leaked over the rest of the food.

Once the platform was announced I went and waited beside a number six painted on the platform edge, hoping that, like in Japan, it meant that was where a door for carriage six would stop. Once the train stopped, a Chinese train attendant held up a card with number nine on it. Something about his smile made me realise he was jokingly holding it upside down! Bearsac and I were the first to board, and greeted the all-male Chinese train attendants in Mandarin.

It was sauna-like in the couchette, so sorting my luggage was a challenge. Once I had copied out into my notebook, like a true Aspie, the train stops schedule from the shared sheet of paper, I joined the other three couchette-mates on the lower berths. I probably should have introduced myself first but, also like a true Aspie, I had got the notebook routine set in my head and become absorbed within the task.

I made the mistake of asking a Belarusian man about his book. It started a half hour explanation in Russian, drawings and frantic rooting through the Dutch/Russian phrase book belonging to the Dutch couple who made up the other two occupants. He drew what looked like a dolphin and then, under the waves, what might have been a submarine or robotic dolphin. He pointed out each character on the front cover of the book, repeating their names several times. He then went on to communicate what might have been an explosion and a secret name as he crossed his fingers. Once we realised that the dolphins were seals, we worked out that the book was about navy seals using pseudonyms. I was thinking how Aspie-like it was to go on and on about the book the way he was.

When the Belarusian offered me vodka, I declined it in Russian as I don't like vodka but mainly as it was too hot for alcohol anyway. He asked a few more times, which angered me. I know it can cause offence by declining offers, but I really hate people not accepting the choices I make for myself. He then started over-offering me coffee; I tried to explain the sensory overload I get from just the smell of it. The Dutch couple were partly able to make him understand, and he took the coffee from under my nose and placed it on the far side of the small table, which I thanked him for in Russian.

The train ride so far had been very bumpy and jerky. The lights went out for a few seconds a few times, with the more violent jerks plunging us into darkness and high-pitched screams from further down the carriage. I really hoped it wouldn't be like this for the four-day duration.

The Norwegian couple from the hostel in Moscow are a couple of doors down the carriage. I wonder if I should go and say hello or not; can never really tell if people mean it when they say about getting together for a chat if you see them again, or if it is just a small-talk thing. The train should make its first stop in 20 minutes, according to the train schedule, but the times might be wrong as the Dutch woman says it's from last year.

However, it did just stop at the timetabled time and I got off to get some fresh air and stretch my legs. The train attendants were playing on the platform with a toy car that lit up; they chased Bearsac with it when he got down on the platform to talk to the cars. He is crazy; he really thinks toy cars can speak! I have a crazy teddy bear.

Why do people drinking bottled beer look at the bottle so often? OK, once or twice to read the label, fine, but several times seems unnecessary, surely. It is not just the Dutch man who I have seen do this now, but many people over time. Why? It can't be to see if it is still alight, like when people do that with a joint. I never see people do it with soft-drinks, so it must be something to do with it being alcoholic; the logic, if there is any, eludes me though. Is it the same as when people walking down the street open their carrier bags and look inside but don't really look, or when people look at their watch but need to look again if Bearsac asks them the time. I conclude that these are simply neuro-typical nervous tics that have no logic. When later I was given a bottled beer by my Belarusian friend, I tried looking at the label several times to see if I could fathom out the reason for this strange ritual, but was none the wiser for my effort.

Day 8

Took off my eye mask to a blast of brightness, too bright for the time, and saw snow – yippee! I wanted to go out and build a snowman, or snowbear, as Bearsac would prefer, but I somehow don't think they would have stopped the train. My couchette-mates and I did the looking at each other's passport bit. When I showed the Belarusian Bearsac's passport, his eyebrows knitted together and deep vertical creases between them made him look like something out of Star Trek. The strange man started pointing at his belly and pinching it, lord only knows why; I didn't dare entertain an explanation from him by asking him.

Having passed lots of open space and then lots of bare trees, wooden houses started appearing, just the odd few with paths dug out of the deep snow. What did these people do for work? A couple of dogs were doing it, doggy style, alongside the tracks, oblivious to the train's invasion of their territory.

Further east people walk down the rail tracks to escape the snow; they are mostly heading towards industrial buildings, but some seem to roam nowhere in particular. The train crosses a frozen river; it is wide but has just a narrow gorge of running water in the middle and a few people nearer the edges ice-fishing from a hole dug out of the surface. I am lying on my front, looking out of the window and writing my notes as the Dutch couple sit on the lower berth and the Belarusian man snores gently below me with the occasional snort. I take Bearsac from the hook above my bed and change his clothes and he shows them to the Dutch couple, the snoring Belarusian is still asleep so misses Bearsac modelling his attire. I then wedge him between the bed and window so he can see out; really, I do! At a level crossing he waves at the crossing attendants, he has his wave returned so he is happy.

A little later the train jolted wildly and Bearsac was dislodged from between the bed and window. Before ending up on the floor, Bearsac managed to knock a tub of salt off the table. It emptied all over the oblivious Belarusian, who just turned over, still asleep, unaware of his saltiness. I left it a few minutes before getting down from my berth to retrieve Bearsac. The Dutch couple weren't in the couchette so I could just say that the train jolted and the salt fell off the table and not mention that Bearsac was the culprit.

About 20 minutes later the now salty Belarusian awoke and discovered that he and his bed were covered in salt. I told him honestly that the train had jolted and the salt fell off the table, it wasn't a lie. I had to leave the couchette as I was finding it hard not to laugh at the poor man with salt in his hair. I will now refer to the Belarusian as 'Salty'. I actually think he was called Mikal, but am not sure and giving him a nickname is more fun anyway. On my recomposed return, Salty was sweeping up salt with a piece of rolled up lavatory paper, still shaking salt from his hair. I had to leave again to laugh.

10.05am saw us take a ten-minute stop at Kirov; although there was snow the short stop meant we were permitted less than five minutes off the train, so no time to build a snowbear. I would have liked to build a snowbear at every station. I was also disappointed not to see any babushka selling home-made food and drink on the platforms. Rather, there were young people with barrows all selling the same nuts, chocolates, and other packaged junk. I wasn't in desperate need of supplies yet, even with the loss of my cassoulet beans. From the train window I watched the vendors restock their wares. I was reminded of Sri Lanka, when one vendor restocked her barrow with red-skinned bananas. After the samovars were restocked with coal, we were off.

I am writing now sitting in the restaurant with Bearsac on the table. Blue and green tapestry tablecloths dress the tables and leather tiebacks for the curtains form the shapes that children draw in house windows. I'm not sure if we are allowed to eat our own food in here, but I am tucking into a very large apple the size of a grapefruit. From the Russian money I still have, I have a budget of just under £3 a day. Hopefully I will have enough of that left to buy something from duty-free when I change flights in Moscow on my way home at the end of my trip. Such is the life travelling on a tight budget.

I have just finished my giant apple and am hiding the evidence from the waitress, who has just told a man off for eating his own food in the restaurant. I spot the Dutch couple from my couchette and the Norwegian couple from the hostel but do not know if I should go over and sit with them or not, I never seem to be able to read situations like that. I am happier to be alone really and it's nice to have some space to myself from the cramped shared conditions of the couchette, so I stay where I am in companionable solitude with my thoughts and my teddy bear.

A young man's order is brought over; it's a dried up piece of white bread with a miserly bit of plastic-looking ham on top. He also has a nice little bowl with handles, the liquid it contains is thin and dark; it must be cold as he eats it straight away without blowing on it to cool it. I guess it must be *borsht*, but my curiosity to be exactly sure gets the better of me and I ask what it is. He thinks it's *borsht* too, but he should be surer, he ordered it and is eating it. He says it's OK but does not sound too convincing.

As the Norwegian couple pass, exiting the restaurant, I put my head down to write; not because I don't want to speak to them, it's just I am not sure if I am meant to make contact with them and small-talk isn't an Aspire strength anyway. Bearsac now lies on the table with a plastic bag in his tummy containing the apple core that I will bin once we leave the restaurant. I hope I remember to; otherwise it might still be there in a few days or even weeks, going all mouldy in my beloved teddy bear.

I spot the waitress admiring Bearsac with her head on one side and a smile. I wave his paw at her; her smile widens. I consider Bearsac for a moment. He seems so real somehow, in a way I can't explain. I suppose I have made him a real character, the way TV characters are real on TV although not in real life. He really is a very beautiful teddy bear, no wonder people take to him.

Becoming too hot in the restaurant, I return to my carriage and sit for a while on a pull-down chair in the corridor, watching a snow-laden Siberia rush by. Another river within a river comes into view, this time no ice-fishers but evidence in the shape of holes and footprints in the snow suggest there have been. A few wooden houses, variant in size, crop up with roofs shaped like the roof on the spooky house on Amityville.

Bored and in need of a lay down, I get back on my berth to read my Trans-Siberian book. I wedge Bearsac again between the bed and window but this time secure him by his straps so he doesn't fall and wreak any more havoc on poor old Salty, who is snoring for Belarus in the Snoring World Champion; I put in my earplugs to block it out. I get to thinking about how there are so many books entitled *101 Things To Do With (whatever)*. I wonder if anyone has written *101 Things To Do To Wile Away The Days On A Very Long Train Journey When Sharing A Couchette With A Snoring Man With Salt In His Hair.*

The snow deepens as we pass into noon, most of the wooden houses with a very thick layer of snow decorating their roof. They must have good insulation, or is it just that is it so cold out there that the snow just won't be melted by household warmth exiting through the roof. It would have been nice to stay in one of these small wooden houses for one night in the middle of nowhere but I am on my way to Mongolia and looking forward to visiting one of the least visited countries in the world. This is the land of feared ruler Genghis Khan.

1.40pm, we stop at Balezino and are greeted by babushkas, younger people and lots of smoked fish with dead eyes. I'm not sure what breed my little fellow is, but I can't wait to eat him, he looks well tasty. Two young men try to sell me woollen shawls as a blanket for Bearsac. Bearsac explains it is too hot on the train for a blanket.

Once satisfied with getting my toes nicely wet in the snow, we were back on the train watching the babushkas. The two young men were under the window, still trying to sell the shawl to me for Bearsac, pointing at him. One got out his phone, gesturing that he wanted a photograph of Bearsac and me. Although I suspected it might be a ploy to try to sell to me more directly, I took Bearsac to the door to see if they really wanted a photo. They did, and asked all about him, saying that he looked like Mr Bean's teddy bear! I wonder if Rowan Atkinson is aware of just how global his Mr Bean and Bean's teddy bear are. The young men asked Bearsac what football team he liked; Bearsac gave them his website card and told them that he had photographs of himself with Arsenal players. This seemed to be totally amazing to them and they wanted to stroke him and take more photographs; Bearsac, of course, loved all the attention. They asked why I was not flying, I explained about train journeys being something people do for the journey and not simply getting to the destination. This was clearly an alien concept to them.

Back by the windows waiting for the train to depart, people laughed and looked my way, for some reason, at the very large cuddly toys on a barrow being wheeled down the platform. Even I wouldn't buy a teddy bear that size and have it taking the tiny bit of space on the train. Would anyone bother? They were rather tacky-looking anyway, like the sort of thing won at fun-fairs.

The carriage attendant started hovering. Bearsac danced in front of it, moving back as it edged too close, daft bear; think he was getting a bit bored. It is a challenge keeping a nine-year-old teddy bear amused on a train for so long.

Before tucking into my fish, I had to first wash my hands before washing the fish under the samovar. Things would be so much easier if I wasn't a hygiene freak. Happy that I now had some omega-3 in me, I joined it with some vitamin C from a clementine.

I had a bit of a broken English chat with Salty; he started touching my knuckles for some reason, and showing me his. I have very prominent bony knuckles, whereas his were quite flat. He then started doing boxing gestures; I guess he was saying my knuckles would be good for boxing. He then started squeezing my wrist to see how hard I could take it; this was getting weirder by the second. He was going on and on about boxing, knuckles and wrists; I realised he must be an Aspie, the way he went on endlessly about the same thing. Some would argue it was just a cultural difference, but I don't think so. This man's behaviour was just too bizarre.

I decided to do some stretches and exercise up and down the carriage; I think people thought it a bit weird, but I think it more weird to sit on a train for four days or more and not take any exercise. I was soon exhausted from the heat, so lay down and used my fan, which I normally just use to run down my batteries before recharging them. At 4.45pm, Salty came in and gave me a cone-shaped packet of sunflower seeds, which was very nice of him, then left again. I didn't even know that I was the only person in there until then, so I had privacy and didn't even know it; it didn't feel like I'd had privacy before then. Salty came back in with a bottle of lager for me. I prefer dark beer, but this was another kind gesture and I welcomed the alcohol, and it went fine with the sunflower seeds.

At 5.33pm the train made a 23-minute stop at Perm 2, quite a large town with tower blocks. The change of scene brought people to the windows and then we all trundled onto the platform to get food, drink, and air. All on offer for a non-meat eater were vegetable noodles; I photographed the packet in the window, showing it on my camera to the woman so she knew what I wanted. A train attendant took Bearsac and strapped him over his shoulder; he had really taken a shine to Bearsac. He looked after him whilst I skipped around the platform for exercise. Back on the train,

Bearsac had his waves returned by people on the platform. As the train departed, it was getting dark but we could still see a couple of snowmen on the roofs of a garage and block of flats.

I thought I had locked the lavatory door properly but it opened mid-poo! I quickly closed it again and continued pooing, stinking out the intruder, no doubt. Back in the couchette, Salty played with Bearsac, making him dance for about 15 minutes; even I get bored after about two minutes of making Bearsac dance and stuff, and I'm a confirmed Aspie. Salty made Bearsac talk in Russian, but when I asked Bearsac to say in English what he had said, he was dumb-struck; I don't think I have ever heard Bearsac go so quiet so quickly! Salty started getting a bit rough with Bearsac, but not intentionally. I showed him the bald patches on the back of his head to demonstrate that he needed to be gentle with him, but he was still rough until I cuddled Bearsac and pretended he was crying. I think he finally understood.

9.52pm, we have now been on the train just over 24 hours and are about a quarter of the way through the journey to Ulan-Bataar in Outer Mongolia. Bearsac and I have survived a whole day on a train; only three more to go! I hope the Swedish blokes next door don't play the annoying, repetitive music they have just started to play for the next three days, it's driving me more potty than I already am.

Day 9

I'm surprised how well I'm sleeping, what with the train full of people snoring competing with the rumbling of the train; it is the earplugs that permit this . I did a few yoga stretches on my bed: cat pose, dog pose, the plank, child pose and salute to the sun. Washed and dressed in the lavatory with now dirty floor. It's hard trying to dress whilst standing on your sandals and stepping into each trouser leg, trying not to fall over, or have your feet touch the urine-enslimed floor, or bash your hips into the basin whilst the train jolts about. I discovered a few bruises on my legs and a dirty great big one on my left wrist. I don't remember if Salty squeezed that wrist, nor do I remember banging it. Although I bruise easily on my legs, even without feeling anything; I don't easily bruise on my arms.

Russian bread and pink grapefruit made up breakfast; the smell of the grapefruit cleansed the stale air. Today Bearsac is wearing his multi-coloured striped jumper; he calls it his jelly baby jumper, as its colours are similar to jelly babies. I'm starting to notice a pattern at level crossings. The pattern seems to be that at each level crossing one vehicle waits to cross, unless they are army vehicles, in which case there are two.

Train stops no longer match the timetable, but we are slowing, so maybe we are stopping. It's 8.45am; according to last year's timetable we should have stopped at Shim at 7.46am for 12 minutes. I'm guessing we are past there, but really it's anyone's guess what part of the white Siberian wilderness we are running through.

The slowing down was not for a stop but we did stop at 9.25am. I made a snowbear on the platform with Bearsac strapped to me but did not get time to give it arms. It got a few laughs from people on the platform, but they could have just been laughing at me because I was out in the snow in a vest top, thin trousers and sandals when they were all in thick coats, hats, scarves, gloves and boots.

'I wonder how long Snowbear will last; I hope his ears don't fall off,' said Bearsac.

My bed-sheets are getting filthy from my feet getting dirty by wearing sandals on the platforms, and also from eating on the bed. I hope they have a powerful washing powder wherever the sheets get washed. I want to shake off all the crumbs, but don't think Salty will like crumbs in his hair as well as salt.

After some time sitting on one of the pull-down chairs in the corridor watching Russia rushin' by, I exercised, running up and down the corridor and doing shadow boxing and press-ups. Bearsac lazed on the bed staring at the ceiling in that teddy bear sort of way. Two of the Swedish men from next door started doing dips between the bed bars and press-ups, so looked like I had started a trend. The Dutch couple did suduko and Salty read.

The couchette, smaller than a prison cell, has narrow beds both sides top and bottom; and a small table between the lower berths by the window. Apart from a few short stops, we are locked away; but that's fine as it gives me time to think. I consider the question of tolerance. When you're locked on a train or any confined area with other people, tolerance is a gift – a gift I am not naturally blessed with, but one I have to work at. Having time to think has led me to look at how, in trying to be tolerant in my life, I have overdone it and tolerated too much. It might be my Aspieness that makes me less able than average to judge what I should and should not tolerate, and my limited ability to assert myself in a way that will not be taken for aggression, and which is both understood and respected.

I think about strange things sometimes. Finding myself thinking about the shagging dogs of many miles back, I wonder if the female of the species ever goes on top. Do male dogs ever lie on their backs with their front legs behind their heads, thinking of England, Russia, Mongolia, or whichever part of the world they come from? Does the male animal lie there staring at the sky as she gyrates all around him? Do animals have same-gender sex? Reading my mind, Bearsac tells me teddy bears do.

I am starting to get a deep crease under my chin where I rest it on the pillow when lying on my front looking out of the window; I hope it doesn't stay with me, like the way my mum used to say my face would stick if the wind changed when I pulled faces.

Some time after noon we stopped again; there were no Babushkas, and small kiosks sold all the same dry food items. The coal-truck men swapped the empty for full baskets of coal, and we were off. I had lunch, sharing with Bearsac tinned marinated smoked salmon fillets (not bad for a tin) and some dark green, shredded pickled vegetable with a slight gherkin taste, more Russian bread and sunflower seeds. The chocolate I had bought at the Red October factory had now all broken up so it was not worth keeping to take back home to Alan and the rest of the teddies, so Bearsac thought it would be a good idea for us to have some. Sorry, Alan and other teddies, if you are reading this.

To each side of us lay the Baraba Steppe of Barabinsk, a flat, tree-filled plain of white with green bits poking out here and there. There was not a snowman or bear in sight; Snowbear was left behind, now a distant memory. When we stopped I asked one of the train attendants to take a photograph of me and Bearsac in the train doorway; he chopped my head off so I took one on the self-timer, placing the camera on the stairs opposite. We were both in the frame this time, but as per usual, I looked awful!

Darkness started closing in as we left the station. I had a nice poo, leaving Bearsac on the bed. When I flushed, I noticed dying daylight, so I guessed droppings of my poo had polluted the tracks from Moscow. I hoped no-one would step in it while crossing the tracks.

So far no party atmosphere has visited us. Maybe things will perk up later tonight. Thankfully, no armed gangs have raided the train, as I have heard sometimes happens. Salty has been very quiet today, hasn't said a word yet, just a nod. I'm relieved though, and I'm sure the Dutch couple are too. Maybe he has no more books to over-explain.

I am using a lot of ink; my pen has nearly run out, I have never run out a pen before. Of course as you read this it will be in type and not handwriting, which is just as well, as my handwriting is scruffy and illegible. As I'm writing I am running down my rechargeable batteries from my digital camera in my blue and yellow fan so I can recharge them. The fan sounds like a vibrator, hope no-one thinks I'm using a vibrator. I could just say that it's Bearsac's if anyone suggests such a thing.

Later, at 7.22pm, the train stops at Novosbirsk. It is snowing as opposed to simply having snow on the ground. In childlike excitement, I run along the platform, making my presence known by frenzied footprints in the virgin snow; I am triumphant that I am the one to take the snow's virginity.

The guide book stated that the station has a grand interior, so I took Bearsac and went to video it. I had been in there no more than ten seconds when a man in an orange tabard gestured me to get back on the train. I gestured back: 'ten minutes'. He insisted, as did I. He was not Chinese and I had not seen any train attendant on our train wearing an orange tabard. After further frantic and opposing gesturing from each of us, he pulled me towards the train, clearly thinking I was on his train. Panic rose within me; I pushed him then ran. In my haste I nearly got on the wrong train, which probably would have been his, but saw my couchette-mates on the correct platform.

Calmer, I went to buy peach juice. The fridge was outside the kiosk and locked; it needed to be opened by remote control, and you then took out your desired item. I was going to give the woman a 50 and two ten-rouble notes for the 70 roubles, then realised it would be better for me to give her a 100-rouble note and get small change for buying stuff from the Babushka's. She saw my tens and wanted them, refusing the 100 with a waft of her calloused hand and trying to grab my tens (not to steal them, but for payment). I insisted, so did she, so I grabbed back the 50 I had already given her, Bearsac growled at her and I gave her back the juice from the fridge, leaving her to put it back. I got back on the train and drank my now cooled water from the samovar. Clearly being stuck on a train all this time and then being let loose onto the virgin snow had got the better of me.

At last a party of sorts on the train. I took Bearsac and a beer and tried some Ukrainian honey and chilli vodka, which I rather liked. I don't usually like vodka. Nine of us at a time (or ten if you count Bearsac) were crammed into the lower berths of the couchette where the party was, but there were about 15 in all. It turned out the Norwegian couple I'd met in the Moscow hostel were just good friends. The party was a real international affair; as well as the Norwegians there were Belgians, Swedish, Belarusian, Ukrainian and a late comer from another carriage who was from Kazakhstan. I don't think I have met anyone from Kazakhstan before. One of the Belarusian men took a shine to Bearsac and strapped him to his shoulder for most of the time, plying him with alcohol and asking him if he was an alcoholic; I think Bearsac was too inebriated to reply. Apart from one of the Swedish men, everyone loved Bearsac and wanted to hold him and ply him with further alcohol. I could see I was going to have one very drunk teddy bear.

It's funny with so many different nationalities crammed into this small space trying to communicate on common ground; but we all did quite well, and my Russian got a little better; the Belarusians and Ukrainian spoke Russian. I didn't feel the usual amount of discomfort I often feel in a group; I seem to do better with people of other nationalities than with British people.

Day 10

I awoke to brightness, my watch displaying 2.10am. It was still on Moscow time so really it was four hours later, I think, but it was hard to be sure with all the time zones. No-one other than myself, Bearsac and one of the train attendants were up.

At 6.53 (Moscow time), we stop at Krasnoyarsk, where a steam engine stands on display. Bursting with enthusiasm, I grab Bearsac and run over to it through the snow in my sandals and photograph and video Bearsac in front of it. I exercise by light jogging up and down the platform before re-boarding and having grapefruit and water with grapefruit juice for breakfast. We are starting to lose the snow; I hope there is some in Mongolia when we get there in two days' time.

11.21am saw us stop for 20 minutes. A line of babushkas with home-made food at last! And I could buy it as some was vegetarian – some clearly so, some not. I was trying to ask if certain things had meat in and had forgotten the Russian for 'I don't eat meat'. A long train of oil tankers roared by, I could not co-ordinate my pointing and speaking. Then, with the overload worsening, I had to cover my ears for what seemed like an eternity until the train of oil tankers had ceased to roar its menacing presence and leave the station.

On recovering my composure and co-ordination, I took my hands from my ears and pointed again to the food and then at Bearsac, attempting to paste a questioning look on my face. I was hoping they would understand that I was asking: does the food have animal in it? But I guess that may have been a bit too much of an abstract way to ask. With a sudden burst of eureka spirit, one babushka bent down and promptly produced a bottled lager with a picture of a bear on it! I'm not sure if she was more disappointed that I did not buy the beer or that she had misunderstood what she thought she had sussed out.

Thankfully someone else bought some of what I had been enquiring about and they spoke enough English for me to ask them if it had meat in it. To my intense disappointment, the dumplings did contain meat, so I moved on. I thankfully got some red cabbage, beetroot and potato salad, some veggie noodles and grape juice. I wanted a nice dark beer, but there were only lagers on display. I tried to say 'dark', pointing again at Bearsac, which was really a silly thing to do as even when I had done this in relation to food with another babushka, it resulted in her thinking I wanted the lager with a bear on the label. So, of course, another bottle of bear-bearing lager was produced from a tattered box.

Back on the train, I did another stint of carriage-jogging whilst Bearsac slept. When he awoke he was asked by one of the Swedish guys next door if they and Bearsac could be photographed together for Bearsac's website.

Small snowflakes start to kiss the window fleetingly; everything is so white out there. By comparison, my Trans-Siberian guide book is starting to look like a colouring book as I continue to use highlighting pens on words and sections I wish to keep special note of. I often buy second-hand guide books from charity shops and find, if they have them, the hand-written notes and highlights from the previous owner very useful. Of course I bear in mind price increases and that some information will be outdated; but historical facts stay the same; and with the use of the Internet, new names of accommodatios and updated information stemming from the guidebook is easily found.

At 4.34pm Moscow time, and still probably four hours ahead in the time of our position on Earth, we stop at Nijneudins. This was meant to be a 23-minute stop, but we were called back after just five minutes, giving me no time to find veggie food or buy booze. The train still stayed at the train for the 23 minutes, it may have been even more. We are normally called back with five minutes to go, not within five minutes of being let off.

I have just spilt the sachet of sunflower oil from a packet of noodles on the bed sheet; mine must win any competition for the dirtiest bed sheet on the train. As well as various food stains, there are ink spots; I don't know how they got there. Overall the sheets, which were pristine white when given out, are grey with random splashes of colour; almost like a Jackson Pollock! Thankfully I have not yet spilt any of the beetroot on them. However, still having some left and having to pour it from the flimsy plastic bag onto my plate; there is still a high risk of this happening if the train jolts suddenly, thus adding purple to the spectrum of colours.

6.28pm Moscow time - that was more than just a jolt, that was a full scale emergency stop. Oops, no, two emergency stops, the second not as hard as the first as we had already slowed down from the first. Now mine may no longer be the dirtiest bed-sheet as the lower berths would no doubt have had any food and drink on the tables spilt on them; looks like I won't win that competition anymore. Contents from the table have fallen on Salty's bed, but thankfully no liquids or damp foods. Twice more the train has jolted as I write, but no more emergency stops. I wonder what the reason for making the emergency stop was; a bear or wolf on the line, perhaps. At least it's different from the British 'snow or leaves on the line' excuse.

I left Bearsac snoozing when I got off the train at Zima and jogged up and down the platform; lots of people from the train asking where he was. I was half expecting him to be bear-napped and held to ransom when I got back on, but he was thankfully where I had left him, he had not moved an inch. I sat on the lower berth for a while, comparing the English/Chinese to Dutch/Chinese phrase-books; the Dutch one did not have an entry for teddy bear like my English one.

The male of the Norwegian friends did what I would have loved to do, and probably would have done by now, if ours had not been full of luggage – he got inside the overhead luggage space that was above the corridors and opened from above and at the foot of the upper berths. Maybe I will get a chance once the luggage is taken down before I get off in Mongolia.

Day 11

It is 2.50am, Moscow time, I don't know which time-zone we are in to know if it is four or five hours ahead of Moscow time and my watch. We have just gone through a tunnel. All this time on the train, and this is the first one. From the timetable, I guess we are somewhere between Irkutsk and Sliudianka, where we are scheduled, according to last year's timetable, to stop at 3.12am Moscow time. We have just come out of another tunnel, so I guess we are going through mountains; so I am now defiantly getting out of this pit to have a look from the corridor. Why didn't I get up as soon as I woke? I am probably missing Lake Bikal.

I am in the corridor with camcorder and my notebook, I could kick myself as I have only got a glimpse of Lake Bikal and we are edging away at speed.

Wait! Yes! Thankfully we are now coming round the other side; we were just going around a very large bend. It is one very large ice rink covered in snow. They could hold hundreds of 'Holiday On Ice' shows in one go and still have room for several winter Olympics without even covering a fraction of the ice. Someone has written something in the snow with their feet, the sort of thing I would do if I had the chance. I, of course, would have written www.bearsac.com. Our short three-minute stop meant we were not let off the train. Oil tankers blocked our stationary view of the world's biggest ice rink.

We have now been going past Lake Bikal for about one hour, there's still no sign of its being a lake rather than an enormous snow-topped ice rink. I have just waited 20 minutes for a vacant lavatory; people are now getting washed and dressed. Once one is free, I cannot use it due to the intense stench of poo emitting from it. I'm feeling panicky as my hands are filthy and teeth furry, and I need stodgy food. I trek through other carriages to find a vacant lavatory; when I finally find one the tiniest trickle of water dribbles from the taps, but at least I wee and clean my teeth. The Samovar and flannel facilitate cleaning of my hands.

The soot on my lungs was stressing me out, but at least now I could have some food. I shared with Bearsac some bread, garlic and chilli olives, chocolate and grape juice for breakfast. Now comfortable on my bed, having had enough of Lake Bikal, Salty told me 'Lake Bikal, Lake Bikal!' I nodded and turned back to what I was doing. He repeated, pointing, 'Lake Bikal, Lake Bikal, Lake Bikal.' He wasn't going to shut until I got down from the bed and looked, as if I had not seen it for an hour already. I swung over the bed bars, jumping down, hurting my foot on the opposite bar and stomped to the window. Grabbing hold of the window bar, I pulled myself promptly to the window and sarcastically looked out with wide-open eyes, with an 'I am looking at the f*****g lake, OK?' stance, before immediately turning back and stomping back up to the bed to continue what I was doing!

Salty is now driving me bonkers. It's like being in the Big Brother house, minus the constant cameras, and it is smaller. I want him evicted! I think he might have realised he is getting on my nerves as he has now gone back to bed, sulking. Poor Salty; I suppose he was just being helpful and that he didn't want me to miss the lake. He wasn't to know I'd already seen it for an hour and got bored. I find rude people easier to deal with than too-nice people; they are easier to ignore than the over-nice ones.

With the Dutch couple still sleeping, and Salty sulking below me, we have just been the closest to the lake so far, about ten metres. I now want to see what it is like as a lake, not an empty expanse of snow-clad flat land; that's what I would think it was if I didn't know it was a lake.

My goodness – the Swedish one who doesn't like Bearsac just smiled and said hello to me; maybe because I don't have Bearsac with me, as he is on the bed with my eye mask on, having a nap.

Hip hip hurray, my batteries charged OK, I can take some more photos now. The train attendants have just put on some Chinese music; no they have now turned it off again as I write, which is a shame as Bearsac, who has just woken up, was getting into the groove dancing. Now they have put on some French-sounding music; the female singer is really throwing her tonsils about, it's overloading me a bit so I think I'll put in my earplugs and cuddle Bearsac.

At Ulan Ude, army tanks roared past on a flatbed train: I wanted to photograph them but by the time we got off there was a long oil tanker train in the way, yet again. I hate the things; they spoil all my photo opportunities.

New people get on the train – new house-mates have entered the Big Brother house on wheels! I'm being evicted tomorrow, along with lots of others; the remaining house-mates will continue to Beijing.

Wow! I just saw a cow; a solitary cow! Apart from the cat tied up in the doorway of a stationary train and a few dogs running along the tracks, this is the first animal I have seen. Bearsac's wave was too late for the cow to see, but don't suppose it would have waved back anyway, cows don't usually do that sort of thing, do they?

At last, I have stained my greying white sheets with beetroot; I knew I would. Bearsac and I are currently sitting alone in our bedroom on wheels, watching a frozen river pass the dirty window, and low clouds hug the hills. I wonder what creatures the hills hold. A window in the corridor has now been unlocked; fresh air. It's sometimes the simple pleasures that we take for granted that are the most welcome. The train attendant has even wiped the top of the window frame so we don't get dirty leaning our arms on it to take photos.

Bearsac has just flown without the aid of an aeroplane or helicopter. I strapped his straps twice around my arm and held with the hand tightly as I hung him out of the window. He was taken into horizontal flight by the gush of wind and I filmed him in his adventure. People were quite surprised to see me risk losing him, but there was no risk as his straps are secure. If he had a mouth, I'm sure he would have been smiling. He came back in very excited, if a little cold.

Now I had to start using up some of my roubles, I thought I'd treat myself to something in the restaurant. I had just sat down with the menu when a man I had not seen before came to my table, even though there were so many empty ones, including the one he had vacated. He gestured if he could sit there and I gestured it was fine and turned back to the menu, not looking at him. I could see, though, that he was waiting for me to look up at him. I was about to order some caviar and other stuff when he got out a cigarette and lit it up. Now it is a smoking restaurant but if you move from an empty table to sit with another person, surely you ask, even just by gesture if there is a language barrier, if they mind you smoking. I got up and sat at another table but because I was angry at his ignorance, I was stressed out and the smell of the cigarette became overwhelming and I had to leave the restaurant carriage. So now I'm back on the bed eating bread and olives.

A couple of hours after seeing the first cow, there are now lots, some on a football pitch, which reminds me of my school-days, when the headmaster used the school football pitch to house his wife's horse. A football lies near the cows. However, they seem more interested in eating the brown grass than bending it like Beckham. According to last year's timetable, we will be stopping for passport checks in 15 minutes at 1.08pm, and will remain stationary until 3.32pm.

It is 3pm now, just waiting for the return of the passports. The nice lady passport official has taken Bearsac's passport with all the others, after showing it to a colleague. Bearsac asked them to stamp it, so I'm hoping it comes back with one. We have had a nice walk around a dusty wooden village; a cow loose along the road reminded me of Sri Lanka. I got some vegetable noodles, smoked fish and dark beers in a small wooden shop. Nuts and juice I found in a bigger shop that had an abacus to work out the money instead of a till. Bearsac attracted the attention of a small dog that followed us back to the train. It was too small to climb aboard though, which was a relief. After a bit of whining, it went off with another dog that was also on the platform.

It is now 4.50pm, have only just got back our passports and, sorry to say, there is no stamp in Bearsac's. This is not just to mine and Bearsac's but to the disappointment of most people in our carriage. Whilst waiting for the return of the passports, I met three of the new house-mates and sat with them in their couchette. We are going back to sit with them now the passports are back and bags checked.

I have just discovered a variety of vodka which I like. It is a classic one with a blue label and square bottle. I could do with some now to have with the smoked fish and its extremely rich roe or liver; not sure which. After feeling very full from the protein of the large fish, I joined the party with the original train-mates until Mongolian passport officials got on and we had to all return to our couchettes. This lot laughed at Bearsac's passport. Back at he party we had some mild tasting caviar, for lots of us this was like the night before eviction from the Big Brother train.

Day 12 – UlanBataar – Mongolia

The day started earlier than I had expected, as I thought our arrival time was 7.35am. (I was still using Moscow time but it was of course using Ulan-Bataar time; silly me.) Rather than a few more hours, the train attendant alerted me to the fact that there were about 40 minutes until arrival.

I stripped my bed of its filthy sheets and hid them under a pile of others in the corridor. I managed to get into the lavatory to wash and dress before the two Russian ladies who had been wearing the same multi-coloured blouses for four days. They neither of them looked too happy about it.

Not one to make a fuss of goodbyes, I just waved from the platform at the BB train-mates still on-board as I held up Bearsac to alert my host family to my arrival, just as I'd said I would in my email. A man approached with a card bearing my name; he greeted me and Bearsac. Mejet warned me of possible muggings if I went out at night, not that I had any plans to.

The family lived in a block of flats with rasta colours on the stairs, which had a weird smell; I later realised it was dried cheese pellets. Once in the flat I was greeted by Mejet's sleepy wife, Billet, and the two boys aged six and ten, and later by their gran. The boys seemed playful and well behaved. They loved Bearsac the, younger one especially taking a shine to him. The flat was just like a flat in the UK.

After days on a train with no shower, I was in sheer desperation for one. It would be nice to speak of pleasing sensations and a release of tension intensified by delayed gratification, but I was more than a little frustrated to find the water trickle out of the shower-head. I had never seen water falling from my hair as dirty as this. I felt near human after the shower but I could have really have done with feeling fully human, having had proper water pressure. Of course later it was fine!

I was offered some bread and jam; I'd not had bread and jam in years, so it took me back a few years in memory. I could have done with some peanut butter to go with it, though. The younger boy favoured bread with butter coated in sugar; it made my teeth ache just to watch him eat it. Mejet drove me to the bank to change up some of my dollars. I It was approximately 1160 Torog for a dollar, and I got $50 changed. I hate having so many notes and having so little money, but at least it would go quite a long way in Mongolia.

Now on my own – well, alone with Bearsac at least – I went to find the Legends office, where I was to pick up my Train ticket for the train to Beijing in a few days. It took much hunting to find it and I went into the American cultural building as I guessed I would find some English speakers in there. I did, and was directed to the Legends office, which was just round the corner and which I had passed. The Internet instructions on how to find it showed the name in English, but on the wall of the building it was in Mongolian, which was why I hadn't spotted it at first. If they had put the Mongolian as well on the Internet I could have recognised the pattern of the letters even if I could not read it, and would not have spent so long looking.

Being Sunday, the office was closed but Bearsac introduced himself to the building's reception and security staff, who each shook his paw when he offered them it. One of the women said he looked like Mr Beans teddy bear and took a photo of him with her phone. Satisfied that I now knew where exactly to go tomorrow and that I wouldn't have to spend ages looking for it, I left the building and took Bearsac to the State Department store, which is meant to be *the* place to go, for some reason; not that either of us could work out why. Not really into fashion and jewellery, it quickly bored me.

We easily found Sukhbaata Square, not that it's much to write home about; in fact UB is just one ugly capital. The people make up for it though; with their friendliness. Lots of folk walk around in *del*, which is the national dressin Mongolia, though most people wear western clothes. I was setting up my camera to take a photo on self-timer when a lady offered to take the photo for me. She chopped my head off, so I waited for her to go before doing what I had tried to do in the first place and got a photograph of Bearsac and me including my head.

The National History museum was closed, so we would have to see that, if there was time, when we got back from the countryside. We had a look around Choijin Lam Temple, which has a handful of small buildings enclosed by a wall. The Buddhist art on display includes paintings by a religious reformer of the 1600s, Ts. Zanabazar, and of course the usual Buddah statues. Bearsac was scared by the ceremonial masks but tried on a Mongolian hat.

Wandering around, Bearsac did his usual waving and saying hello; his waves and greetings were returned with no surprise. He even got to meet a rabbit rucksack on the back of a little girl in a tiny purple *del* with pink bobbles in her hair. After the two cuddly rucksacks had shaken paws, we moved on.

Walking towards us, on our way to the supermarket, was a little old lady in a rather worn out brown *del*; she was hobbling due to the weight of what she was carrying . I had seen people queuing for milk at various places, having their milk urns filled. However, this little lady was hugging a large, wicker-encased demijohn – which is more normally used for refilling with wine in some parts of Europe and the Mediterranean. I smiled at her, greeted her *sain-ban-uu,* then nodded down at the demijohn. Smiling back at me with her few remaining long brown teeth, she held it out slightly and said 'demijohn', then something I didn't understand in Mongolian. She didn't understand when I asked her where she got it, using the Mongolian word for 'where'. I'm guessing she had milk in it. Even though it may not have been as practical for refilling as a milk urn as it only had the usual demijohn narrow opening, she seemed pretty proud of it. Seeing as she knew the English word for it, I guess that a traveller might have given it to her as a present, or that she might have been in a country where she got it herself. I held up Bearsac in the same fashion as she had with the demijohn and said 'teddy bear'. The brown-toothed lady tilted her head back and laughed and spoke in Mongolian, then gave a strange, double-toned droning throat sound before hobbling away! I assumed this to be throat singing. It's amazing the things people share with me because of Bearsac.

In the supermarket, a western woman was confidently filling her basket with all manner of foods not before seen to me, so I asked her if what I had in my hand was fermented mare's milk. It was. The woman has been living here for a couple of years. She said she thought me very brave for trying the fermented mare's milk and putting things in my basket when I had no idea what they were. Bearsac made friends with the supermarket staff but bit a couple of them, which they didn't seem to mind; in fact, they called over their boss to get bitten by him too.

I couldn't find any place to eat that served vegetarian food, but got from a baker's shop what I can only describe as a dry, crunchy, yet soft cake filled with a bean paste, that couldn't decide if it was meant to be sweet or savoury; it was quite filling though. I walked back to the flat in the snow eating my snack, forgetting to share it with Bearsac; it somehow tasted better for it! Bearsac didn't notice anyway, he was too busy being pointed at amid shrieks of 'Mr Bean's teddy bear!'. Once back at the flat we had a Mongolian tea, so as not to be rude, but I couldn't make out if I liked it or not. It has a strange taste but not altogether nasty. It is hot milk with finely shredded Chinese green tea-leaves floating in it, and tastes similar to Ovaltine.

Watched sumo wrestling on TV, it was Mongolia against Japan. Sumo may be Japanese, but a disproportionate number of the top sumo wrestlers are Mongolian, or so I was informed by Billet. I kept nodding off for a few seconds, not due to boredom but from sheer tiredness. Don't think Billet noticed my many very short-lived snoozes, though; she was too busy reading emails.

About 6pm I made myself dinner and afterwards sat with Billet and the two boys for the evening with a few appearances of Billet's mother. Mejet came back about 9pm and showed me photographs and books of Mongolia.

Billet and the boys read their horoscopes; they seemed to be really into it and teased each other about them when it said something bad. The boys got on well together and grew a little less shy as the evening went by. There was no difference I could see between the family and Western families, just that the boys were maybe better behaved and the family more a family. I felt awkward not knowing when would be a suitable time to go to bed. Too early might be rude and too late inconsiderate. My problem is I can't read subtle cues. Tired and in dire need of time to myself, which I had not had in days, I drew the courage to stifle a fake yawn and say that I should take myself off to bed.

I am alone in the bedroom now – well, alone as a human, that is. The younger boy has twice stuck his head around the bedroom door with a smile. I will turn of the light after sorting my clothes for the morning and hope for a good sleep undisturbed by cute smiling face. I'm looking forward to staying with a family in a *ger* tomorrow; feeling a little apprehensive about it but I'm sure I'll be fine; Bearsac will be warmly greeted, I'm sure.

Day 13 - Terelj

My internet research back in the UK had told me that there was only one bus a day to Terelj National Park during winter, at about 4pm. So I was glad when the family told me that they thought there was a bus at 10am. I went with Mejet when he took the younger kid to school, then took me to get my train ticket for Beijing on Thursday, and to catch the 10am bus to Terelj.

We waited in the car by the bus stop until 11am but no bus. Mejet rang Billet, who rang someone else and finally found out there was just one bus at 4pm. So back to the flat we went. This turned out to be advantageous, as it bought me time to go and buy a del.

Mejet took me to what is called the black market, near to the flat. It can be a dangerous place for westerners, so Mejet said, and I could also get ripped off buying the del. I saw a beautiful maroon del; it was very good quality and the quilted lining was just as beautiful as the outside. It was £25,000 torog (about £11) and the yellow silk sash was 3000 torog. Something of its like and quality in the UK would likely be over £300, so right price or not, I was very happy.

After lunch I played ball with the younger boy who was back from school. We each invented ways of passing and catching the soft spiky ball between us; even Bearsac joined in. It was soon time to leave.

Taking the crowded local bus out to the nation park in Terelj finds us up close with the friendly locals who give up their seats willing to foreigners. The dusty road through Terelj bares no bus-stops, but the merest grunt at the driver, or tiniest of gestures, ensures that he will stop. The bus pulls up promptly, and I am summoned off with friendly sounds from all aboard.

As arranged by Mejet, waiting at the roadside is a little lady. Orsta, quiet and wise, in her 60s leads the way from the bus to the ger enclosed within a wooden perimeter fence with two other gers. A half-wild Mongolian dog stands on guard. The family's cattle is shut away on the outside. We take care not to commit the crime of stepping on the threshold.

Entering the ger, I am hit by the heat of the stove in the middle. It is more than tall enough to stand up in, and is spacious with its four beds, table, sink (unplumbed), catering cabinet, sacred chest, other furniture and personal items.

Light enough to transport on the backs of cattle, the parts that make up a ger are easy to erect and this can be done so within an hour. Beds are painted in patterns and have ethnic style blankets. Furniture painted in colourful patterns and personal items are placed around the ger in traditional order. Rugs hang on the wall behind each bed giving decorative insulation.

The materials that make up a ger are felt covered in canvas which insulate from the cold and wet. The circular walls are constructed from criss-crossed chestnut wood trellising, with the roof supported by poles also made of chestnut wood, which connect into an eight-holed crown made of oak. This is oiled and painted and is the crowning glory of the ger. A hole in the roof lets out the metal chimney of the stove, which is fuelled by wood or animal dung, and a roof window lets in light during the day. Doors are usually made from Flanders pine and are usually painted in bright patterns. However, the door to this ger is not quite as elegant, but the beauty inside more than makes up for that.

Animal shelters appeared to be built from animal dung. Bearsac wondered how many pooing animals it takes to provide an adequate shelter and does the poo from one animal lend itself more adequately than that of others to the building and maintenance of poo shelters.

I was worried about farting in front of the family in their ger, but soon realised that I had the four-bedded tent to myself – and Bearsac of course. I have a bed on the right as I am a woman. Bearsac being a teddy bear is not expected to sleep on the left just because he is male, he will accompany me in my bed.

After having a look around the *ger,* I sit back down for a few minutes, not knowing what I should do. Am I to wait for something or not? Am I expected to go find Orsta or not? After much internal debate, I venture outside with Bearsac; we get barked at by the half-wild family dog, which is thankfully tied up.

As Bearsac and I step outside the enclosure, we are both attacked by a dog; the attack, though, is of the licking variety and not of the biting. I had read during my research about the furiousness of Mongolian dogs and how they are not pets. This one is not the family's but a wild dog that has adapted to living around humans and is the friendliest dog I have ever met. As much as I like friendly dogs, I hate having my face licked; but this dog is determined to lick my face, and whilst I am off balance because of its weight pushing me, it manages to lick Bearsac's face. Yuck, now I cannot kiss Bearsac's face until I wash him; the thought of it has me spitting on the ground as though I have germs in my mouth. However, my beautiful *del* has thankfully survived the greeting from the world's most friendly dog.

Orsta soon enters with a large thermos and some dried-up looking items I assume to be food. I take the offering of Mongolian tea with both hands. As well as the dried stuff, there is thankfully some hot, non-dried food; it is a cross between ravioli and Polish dumplings, and, as briedfed by Mejet on his arranging my stag, Orsta has made sure they are vegetarian. The 'dumplings' are adequately tasty but there is enough for –four to ten people; I really hope I am not expected to eat them all.

When Orsta enters again to stoke the stove, I ask where the *jarlong* is (lavatory). I am escorted out into the dark, where it is most likely – minus eight degrees C or colder. Many stars pierce the sky, far more than in the UK! Orsta gestures towards a tiny wooden ramshackle hut; it has no light but I am aware that it will be a hole in the floor and pray I will not miss it. The sound tells me my wee has not missed, which is quite a good effort on my part, as I am finding it hard to balance as my knees are playing up from sitting in the same position on the bus for so long. I have to hold my nose due to the stench, which smells as though the cattle might also use this as their *jarlong*! The horse neighing just behind me doesn't help my balancing act but I manage not to get a foot stuck in the hole. There is no lock on the door but I have no fear of anyone entering, as they would have heard me laughing and farting. Thankfully, I manage not to wee on my *del*. I get barked at again by the unfriendly dog as I return to the *ger*.

As I sit in my *del* on a beautifully painted stool, Orsta stokes the stove. It is so hot; I am fully dressed underneath my *del* but I do not know if it is appropriate to take it off in company, so I just sit there getting hotter and hotter. After tending to the stove, Orsta makes me up a bed. It takes her 15 minutes to put the duvet cover on the duvet. When she sits down on a brightly patterned stool, it is not for a rest, but to take from the bridge of her glasses a length of thread. Silently, she threads a needle in one go, despite the dim lighting, then takes the pillow and sews up the opening of the pillowcase. After undertaking this seemly unnecessary task, Orsta winds the remaining thread back around the bridge of her glasses and, with her hands rubbing her knees, nods at her handiwork with a satisfied smile. It is as if she has blessed the bed for its guest.

Orsta wanted a look at the Mongolian/English dictionary that Mejet had lent me. As I was eagerly waiting to see what she wanted to say, a man I took to be her husband came in. It sounded as if he was having a go at her, as he was shouting. I soon realised that it was because the stove had gone out. She paid no attention to his ranting, only to the dictionary. He carried on ranting at her, even when he went outside to get more wood, and continued when he returned with the wood. As soon as he spotted Bearsac sitting on my knee, he stopped ranting and went Orrrrrrrrrrrrrrrrrrrrrrrrrrr! Bearsac said '*Sain-bain-uu*', to which the man stood up and replied the same back to Bearsac. He then said the same to me. As soon as the stove flamed up, he left the *ger* singing! Orsta left five minutes later and I walked around the stove clockwise several times to get this *ger* rule and custom ingrained into me.

I am now in cooler clothes to sleep in; I don't know if anyone will come in again. Ha ha, just as I write that, Orsta comes in, she is again stoking the stove fire. I try to look up the words for diary and journal in the dictionary, but they are not there. I find the word for book and hope she won't think I am asking for a book; she understands I am writing and indicates, with her finger*s* scanning the words and pages, that she wants to know how many words I have written so far. I write 15,000 and point to my diary; then I draw a book and write 47,000, then a plus sign to show that they should be added together to give the total amount so far. She gives me the thumbs up and points to herself, no doubt asking if I have mentioned her in it; I return her thumbs up and she nods her smiling approval. She takes the dictionary and spends quite a while looking through it. As she studies it, she sits with her feet under the stool. Mongolian custom dictates that legs must not be out in front and that the soles of the feet should not be seen. I am hoping I have not yet done anything incorrect.

I am thinking as I write, that maybe Orsta or someone else will keep coming in whilst my light is on, which makes me feel guilty. So when she leaves, I will turn off the light and lie listening to the crackling fire until it goes out. Before leaving, Orsta covers the remaining food, goes to take away the thermos but, on realisation that it still contains tea, gestures for me to sit at the table. Oh no! I have drunk so much of this tea (or at least hot milk with a tiny bit of tea in it and maybe salt). The thermos is huge; I have never seen one so big and full of liquid. I know I will have to drink the rest of the tea but this thermos must hold three litres of the stuff. I have already drunk about two-thirds since I arrived but that still leaves about one litre! Help! You'd have thought Bearsac would help me drink it but he is just sitting on the bed staring blankly at the rugged wall of the *ger*. Some friend he is! I know I will have to venture out into the dark with my torch during the night to wee out all the tea, so if the unfriendly dog barks and wakes Orsta, then it will be her fault!

Orsta has now gone. She has left me the thermos, no doubt trusting that I will sink its contents. Sink its contents, now there's a thought. I go to investigate the sink, by torchlight now, as I have turned off the light; but as I suspected, there is no plumbed drainage, just a large bucket in the cupboard under the sink. Maybe I could take it to the lavatory and pour it down into the depths of the hole, but it might not be as deep as it sounded and the milky colour of the tea would give me away. This is something I hadn't thought of during my planning; I will know, next time I stay anywhere where I might be expected to eat or drink excessive amounts, to take something to decant unwanted liquids and foods into. Let this be a warning to anyone that might find themselves opting for such hospitality! Take a non-transparent receptacle to rid yourself of excess or horrible beverages. How any human can possibly drink three litres of tea in just three hours, God only knows.

The sounds of animals occasionally break the otherwise surrounding silence as I drift into peaceful thoughts and turn off my torch.

Day 14

At 5.30, Orsta enters to light the stove, which is good as it is freezing. She actually came in three times after I had turned out the light during the night. One of the times I shone my torch for her, but there was no need as the woman has bat-like ability to find her way around in the dark. Anyway, she is now lighting the stove and the smell of lighter fluid fills the *ger*; the familiar sound of flaming inspires my freezing body with the thought that it will soon be warm enough get my arms out of the covers and read. However, it takes another two visits from Orsta stoking the stove and about 35 minutes before it is warm enough to do so. I wonder if I am expected to get up now that I am quite clearly awake.

I remember the two remaining veggie pasta dumpling things and get up quickly to eat the evidence of the fact that I did not finish the feast for ten people the night before. The remaining tea, now no doubt cold, will have to be found unfinished by Orsta when she no doubt brings a fresh lot with breakfast, whenever that will be. Mind you, her gesturing me to the table last night to drink the tea could have just meant I should have a bit before I go to bed, rather than meaning I should down the entire contents. Asperger's syndrome means I take things quite literally, so I can sometimes make wrong assumptions about what someone has meant.

I am happy it is light as I can now see by daylight the hole in the floor of the lavatory, though only by holding the door ajar. The smell of the latrine takes any last traces of sleepiness from me; it's like a slap in the face. Now I have seen the deepness of the hole, I am happy to release my poo into it – and there is a lot of poo to release into its thankful depths. As I squat with painful knees, I wonder just how much poo mine is joining. I wonder how deep the hole is and how much it has been filled since its original depth. As I return back to the *ger,* I take a few deep breaths of the fresh, bracing air.

A strange sound breaks the silence; I assume it is some type of bird call but I can't be sure. I see just sparrows sitting on the perimeter fence; it would be disappointing to find it is only they that are the owners of such an exotic sound.

I dress Bearsac in a green corduroy jacket today; Orsta nods her approval of it when she brings in a metal kettle of water so that I can wash. She pours some into the tiny tank that has a small tap and leaves the kettle on the floor beside the sink. Shortly, a fresh thermos of hot tea is brought in and I am gestured to the table. Orsta gently shakes the old thermos but her face bares no reaction that I recognise to its non-empty status.

As I drink my hot tea and eat the crunchy things remaining from yesterday, I wonder what the day will bring for me and Bearsac. If I do horse-riding, should I wear my fancy new *del* or not? It would be more authentic to wear it, but it might end up smelling of horse; I will most likely decide at the time. I want to leave the *ger* and perimeter but don't know if I should just yet. There is all day, so I tell myself to calm down; I'm like a child when it comes to checking places out. I'm going to tidy up instead.

At 7am, some hot sticky rice, cold beans, and the garlic and chilli olives I gave Orsta as a present are brought as my breakfast. I offer Orsta an olive; I'm not sure if she's had them before, nor if she will like them. However, she licks the spoon after she has eaten an olive with it, so I conclude she does. The baked beans were what Billet gave me to bring in case there were no vegetables available. I'm not over keen on baked beans, I prefer plain beans, but what worries me most is that I'll be farting all day. If I do horse-riding then at least they will assume it's the horse! Normally Bearsac takes any blame for my farts.

After I had finished eating, Orsta gestured walking, so off Bearsac and I trundled, deep in thought. We first headed into the trees where snow still lay on the ground as it had not yet melted. The crunching sound of the snow and the fact that it was up to about two feet deep excited me. Like a child in wild fascination, I ran through it, laughing and squealing. Even though I had two pairs of socks under my hiking boots, my feet became so cold I could hardly feel them; but they soon warmed again once out of the snow.

Bearsac wanted to head up to the top of the opposite hills to see what he could see, so up we trekked until we came to an *Ovoo*, which to most people would just look like a pile of stones; or perhaps to arty-farty types, maybe a geological work of art. However, the *Ovoo* is a symbol of worship to the mountains and sky. You must never touch it, but must walk three times around it; you should never pass an *Ovoo* without doing this. So of course we walked around it three times, hoping it was not the wrong way if there was only one way to do it. For some reason this *Ovoo*, and the ones I had seen in photographs on the Internet, had sticks covered in what looked like blue plastic poking out of the stones. I can see the stick might mean something, but what is with the blue plastic? Bearsac suggested it might represent the sky.

Resting on a rock, I realise that for the first time in days I am alone (as a human, that is). It is wonderful to have the feeling of solitude. However, it is a short-lived feeling.

From further up the hill we hear singing and whistling. At first we don't see the owner of this happy voice. Then suddenly, we see horses galloping in the distance, coming over the top of another hill. A human figure appears as the voice gets louder. Bearsac's eyesight is better than mine and he says that the horses are quite small and funny looking. Soon they are at the top of the hill we have started to descend, then gallop past us kicking up dust. Bearsac says *sain-bain-uu* to a young man who bids us the same, and the horses and their herder are soon as far down the hill as they were up the other hill when we first spotted them. It turns out that they are being taken to the family's patch of land, so I realise that if I go horse-riding I will not be alone; I'm not sure if I want to meet other tourists or not, as I'm enjoying the solitude. I know from my research that tourists who go horse riding are often taken to meet a nomadic family and to spend time in their *ger*.

I return to my *ger* to find out whether I am to go horse-riding in a group, and to tidy my *ger* in case my fellow riders come to see it. On the table is another large bowl of crunchy dough things. I really am praying now that the tourists will be shown my *ger* and eat most of the crunchy things for me. I quite like the strange-tasting dried cheese pellets, but some other things in the bowl with them are quite nasty-tasting and look like some type of stuck-together breakfast cereal thing. I guess that if they are to be shared by others, I will be the only one who likes the cheese pellets; and no-one will like the other things but they will hopefully eat them out of politeness. I weigh up in my mind solitude versus ridding myself of crunchy things, and surmise that solitude can wait until later if its disturbance rids me of crunchy things.

The husband has just come in and touched his head to the brightly painted chest and spun the prayer wheel in the north part of the *ger*. This is the sacred part of the *ger* and his action a ritual. When staying in a family's *ger*, expect no privacy, even if you have it to yourself. After his ritual, the husband points to Bearsac and himself and then the camera; he then holds Bearsac, rocking him like a baby, and stands proudly, jutting out his chin. He likes the photos when I show them to him on the camera. He says 'tourist,' and I say 'yes' in Mongolian, assuming he means do I want to go horse-riding. I offer him an olive; his expression, which, I can't read, is followed by a thumbs-up, which I can.

I follow him out of the *ger* and find a group of tourists just pulling up in a minibus. It seems strange seeing Westerners, it is almost like I have been here for years and not seen any in all that time. They are impressed by my *del* and I think that they wish they too had got to stay with a family in the middle of nowhere rather than in a tourist *ger* camp.

The horses are saddled up and mounted, but there turns out to be none left for me. I see off the group and take another walk, hoping that there will be a chance for me to go riding when they return an hour later. Content to just walk until then, Bearsac and I head off in the same direction as the horses and then take our own route off the beaten track. We carefully walk on the frozen river; at no point does it crackle.

Into the woods, large poos are strewn around. They are not of the horse variety and are too big for dogs or wolves; I guess they could be yak poos, but we see no yaks.

After a while we see a fence on top of an embankment. Curiosity gets the better of me and we find a way up. It turns out to be a tourist *ger* camp and hotel. The arts exhibition is closed. However, I am told by two women picking up litter that the hotel lobby has a shop. One takes me to it; I am hoping that there might be a teddy bear in a *del* about the same size of Bearsac, but there is not. I thank the woman and head back a mile down the road, this time back to my *ger*. If I were to retrace my footsteps it would be more than a mile and I would miss the tourists returning from their horse-riding. I want to ask how their time in Mongolia has been, and to promote Bearsac to them. I have missed the return of the first lot by the time we get back to the *ger*, and a second lot have already headed off.

One pathetic looking horse remains. A young Mongolian woman nearby on horseback talks to the family. I'm asked if I 'tourist horse'; so on to the pathetic looking one I climb. Once mounted, I get Orsta's husband to take a photo of me and Bearsac on the horse, but when I see the photo, I notice that he has not got the horse's head in! Surely he must have realised I wanted a photograph of me on the horse and not just a photo of me. But I can't be bothered to try to explain, so just thank him in Mongolian and the young woman and I set off.

Holding the reins in one hand, I strapped Bearsac to my front with the other and then got out my video camera to film my first ride on a Mongolian horse, and first ride on a horse at all in over 25 years. Seeing my confidence, the young woman suggested we could catch up the others if we galloped. The gallop was a short thrill as we were not more than a minute's gallop behind the others. As there were a lot of first-time riders, the group was just riding at walking speed. I noticed there were a couple of dogs with the group, though I didn't know if one of them was the friendly dog or not.

It was quite frustrating just walking. I started to lag behind a bit so I could create a bit of a gap so I could go faster. But the horse I had was the oldest of them all and couldn't, or maybe wouldn't, respond to my '*Tchoo tchoo*' (which is the Mongolian equivalent of 'giddy up'). I finally coaxed it into a trot and passed some of the horses, but once back with the horse it seemed to be mates with, there was no shifting it.

Once out in a large clearing, one of the experienced riders on a young and bigger horse got a chance to gallop up and down with one of the Mongolians; there was no shifting my one though, it would not even respond to the young man I had seen herding them earlier smacking its bum.

Once I relaxed back lazily into the saddle, I became overwhelmed by the surrounding scenery: variant greenery on one side and red mountains on the other set against contrasting deep blue sky. I swapped between video and still camera as I breathed in the pure air. The air was pierced by aggressive barking. One of the dogs running with us was being attacked by five other dogs that had appeared from nowhere. I did not see it return, and the Mongolians didn't seem bothered, so I guess it was not the family dog, which means it could have been the friendly wild one.

After the horse riding, the group took Mongolian tea in my *ger*. I discovered from one of Mongolian guides that what I had thought was blue plastic on sticks on the *Ovoo* was actually silk - not having dared get too close, it had looked to me like plastic. Someone in the tour group said that one of the girls had brought a teddy bear with her, but it was at their camp, so Bearsac did not get to meet Yellow Teddy. It turned out that the group would be on the train on Thursday like me, so they could meet then. As I had guessed, the group were not over-impressed by the crunchy things but ate some to be polite. I suggested they take some back to their camp and gestured this as I spoke. The gesturing was more for Orsta's sake (indirectly). Orsta jumped up and took some of the crunchy things and packed them in paper to give out to the group, who by now, I guess, hated me! Proud of myself, I chomped on a crunchy thing and said 'yummy' whilst rubbing my tummy!

Once the tourists had left, the husband came in with two glasses and a Mongolian beer for me to share with him. He gave some of his to Bearsac, without any prompting from Bearsac. He gestured to his mobile phone, saying 'UlanBataar'. I realised he meant we should phone the family in UB about coming back next day. It was confirmed that there would be a bus at 8am. After the husband had finished his beer, he left Bearsac and me to rest after all our exercise that day.

6pm brought stove lighting and dinner, pretty similar to the dinner the night before and just as much. On the whole, Mongolian food is quite bland but can vary between adequately edible and nasty. Even the dried cheese pellets I strangely quite like are not something to rave about. I am looking forward to more tasty food in Beijing, and really want to try some insects.

Few children live in the national park as there is no school, so during the week in term-time, the kids live in UB, and some come home at weekends. Bearsac hopes the toys and Bearsac T-shirts I brought over from the UK will find homes. It is 6.45pm, my bed has just been made, and I am ready for it already. The husband has just come in to spin the spinning prayer wheel on the sacred chest and nod at the photograph on the mirror, so I can't get into bed just yet. Just as I write this he leaves, so I will get into bed now. I have left the light on in case they think I am being rude turning it off so early, but thankfully I have my eye mask.

Day 15

The stove was lit earlier this morning, 5am, as I am leaving on the 8am bus. Again breakfast was hot gooey rice, cold beans and the olives I had meant for the family. I was given a doggy bag of the crunchy things and I paid up, giving extra and a postcard of Borehamwood (where I live). On it I wrote 'Thank you' in Mongolian, using Cyrillic letters. I drew my face next to my name and Bearsac next to his; Orsta liked that and put some more crunchy things in the doggy bag! I will love to see the faces of the group from yesterday when I see them on the train and pull out the doggy bag and offer them crunchy things!

I was surprised when the grandson pointed to his watch and said 'bus' and then took my bag. I looked at my watch; it showed a quarter to seven. He showed me his and it said a quarter to eight. The clocks usually change that day but this year they didn't; maybe in the national park they didn't know this. Orsta hugged and kissed Bearsac and we headed off for the bus. It was a tremendous privilege to have shared the culture and way of life of Mongolian nomads. The bus came just before 8am on my adjusted watch and the grandson and me and Bearsac got on, he getting off at the first village (the grandson, that is, not Bearsac). Bearsac was greatly admired and lots of people, mostly old, wanted a go of holding him or sitting him on their lap. As the bus bashed its way down the bumpy road, past hills and yaks, Bearsac jumped up and down on their laps. He looked most funny; I am not used to seeing him from this angle.

I was happy to find the shower worked properly once back at the flat in UB. Billet washed my clothes and I took Bearsac out to the supermarket. I got some chocolates for the family and some food and Mongolian beer for the train and, at last, some fermented mares' milk, which I could not wait until I got back to the flat to try, but opened as soon as I left the supermarket. It was thankfully not as nasty as accounts on the internet had led me to believe, though it would definitely come into the acquired taste category. It tastes somewhere between plain yoghurt, lemon juice and Andrews Liver Salts! Maybe I can share it on the train tomorrow, along with the crunchy things!

When we got back to the flat, Bearsac was presented with a present. It was a red Korean silk Mongolian sleeveless jacket with Mongolian stamps on it; it was beautifully lined in white silk, and fitted him perfectly. It turned out that Gran had made it for him. It was amazing how she had made it the exact size. Bearsac was over the moon and I felt bad for giving them just the box of chocolates. I had given them a bottle of drink on the first day, but nothing could have said thank you for this.

Bearsac and I played more ball with the younger boy and I took Bearsac to bed about 10pm. As my mind and body drifted into slumberland, I looked forward to showing people on the train his new clothing.

Day 16

It felt a bit awkward saying goodbye. Like I often do, I don't know if I am showing enough appreciation in my voice, or if I'm overdoing it in trying to express the appreciation I do actually feel but don't know the way to express. I have been so privileged to stay with such nice people over the last few days. On reflection, I think I did really well. Staying with families is hard enough, I should think, for anyone; but for someone with Asperger's syndrome maybe much more so.

The couchette on this train is nicer than the one on the train from Moscow to UB; it has wood veneer panels on the walls and the lavatories even have hand disinfectant and liquid soap. Included in the price of my ticket was lunch, not that it was anything to write home about. I left the meat, but then so did most of the meat eaters; at least it wasn't Mongolian crunchy things!

I am sharing with a quiet Korean man and two British women from London. I would have preferred to again be the only Brit on the train, but the two women – Teresa and Jan - are nice and about my age, which I don't usually get on my travels. I feel a bit sorry for the man; although his English is very good he is sharing with three women that speak the same language, so no doubt as a quiet type, he will soon tire of us. One of the women is a psychologist and knows about Asperger's syndrome, so I speak to her about it, telling her to tell me if I go on about it too much.

After a while I go to find the Norwegians that I met in the hostel in Moscow, who were on the last train. I go up and down the carriages to no avail; lots of doors are closed. We did though find the group that had the girl with the teddy bear. Bearsac and Yellow Teddy were briefly acquainted and Bearsac promised to return later for photographs. Yellow Teddy, we discovered, is a rather flat teddy; years of being slept on have left him in this state.

From afternoon the train has been ambling through the Gobi Desert; I am a bit disappointed at its flatness, well at least so far. To the west lies flat, almost grey sand, to the east is flat, almost grey sand, behind us is flat, almost grey sand, and ahead of us, for some time, will likely be flat, almost grey sand. We did pass by a little 'almost' dune detail, but it was desperation that got my camera out rather than anything worthy of the action.

I later took Bearsac to the restaurant car to spend the last of my *torogs*. We were both mesmerised by the wooden fretwork partitions and table legs; even the walls and ceiling were covered in it. A group of Mongolians, I think, were sitting on the table next to us. They were singing, or rather wailing – it didn't sound like words as such. Bearsac joined in with them, wailing along to the general rhythm. They loved that and gestured to us to join them, giving us some vodka. They videoed Bearsac and took photographs, so Bearsac was in his element.

Bearsac's passport got a Mongolian exit stamp. He has been invited for drinks with Yellow Teddy, so we will take our Mongolian beer, fermented mares' milk and crunchy things when we go after the return of the passports. 9.15pm saw us stop at the Chinese border but this time the miserable passport woman just handed back Bearsac's passport without reaction; so no Chinese entry stamp. Quite a few people gathered around, waiting to see the reaction of the passport officials to his passport too, so there were quite a few disappointed humans and not just a disappointed teddy bear. Much slagging off of said woman took place when she had gone.

As we were held on the train we had the misfortune of having the music from the film 'Titanic' pan-piped to us over the speakers on the platform – what a treat! Another rug was laid down over the existing rug and sewn down at the ends, for health and safety, I assume. It reminded me of Orsta in Mongolia sewing up the end of the pillow case and I smiled warmly to myself as the image of her winding the thread around the bridge of her glasses paid a visit to me.

At Erlian the train was shunted into the bogie shed for the great bogie change. Excitedly I filmed from the open window. Someone asked what bogies are; Bearsac explained.

'Bogies are nothing to do with congealed snot; they are the chassis or framework carrying the wheels of the train.'

'Thank you, Bearsac, for that explanation, I feel well informed now.'

The tracks are different widths. China uses the standard gauge while Mongolia and Russia use broad gauge. Each carriage is first separated and placed precisely, between four enormous hydraulic jacks. They are then slowly each raised to about 10-foot off the track so that the bogies can be slid out and changed. This took a long time and a lot of banging before and after the bogie change. We couldn't feel anything happening but at least got to see what it looked like by watching the carriage on the opposite track being raised up and down. I felt like a bit of a train-spotter videoing this event but I enjoyed it, so who cares.

Day 17

Awoke after little sleep; murkiness outside robbed me of any inspiration to video the interesting villages where people pedalled around on bicycles and tricycles, some with dogs tied to the handlebars. My enthusiasm had not yet woken, so I just lay on my front with Bearsac sat in the corner of the bed next to me, looking out of the dirty window.

At 7.15am we stopped at dusty Datong, a mining village. Skinny people walking, heads down; all in the same direction towards a large soot-stained building with smoking chimneys. The scene was somewhat reminiscent of LS Lowry's Salford but with fewer buildings and more donkeys. Not that I have seen any donkeys in Lowry's art. But here a donkey pulled an empty cart covered in coal-dust out in the murkiness that was Datong.

A few miles out of Datong are the Yungang Grottoes, which would have made an interesting visit. Caves cut along the mountain 1km long, sporting more than 51,000 statues; the largest, a 17-metre high statue of Buddha. They are the largest groups of ancient caves in China. It is a shame we will not get to see them.

My Lonely Planet book informs me there will soon be interesting scenery, so I take Bearsac and park my bum on one of the pull-down seats in the corridor in preparation. I forgot to get out clothes for Bearsac to wear today, so just reverse his red Mongolian jacket Gran made so that it is on the white side and looks like he is wearing something else. This system will help me identify what days I took the photos on when I get back home and sort through them for the website and this book.

The sight of farmers wearing conical straw sedge hats, ploughing fields the old fashioned way, with ox and furrow ploughs, brought my childhood memories of National Geographic to life. Overall wearing men with spades over their shoulders are led to work by a spadeless, suited cigar-smoking man half their age; he walks with a swagger. I surmise that he acts the big dick as he probably has a small penis. The scenery is getting more beautiful but is spoilt by the weather, which does not improve as we start to see the first glimpses of the Great Wall. We stop at Badaling and a trainload of people trundle out and take feeble photographs and video footage from the platform. After this little break the train goes backwards; Badaling was not on the timetable, so it would appear that the train was taken there purely for the sake of seeing the wall, which was very nice of the train company.

At last we arrive at Beijing. Bearsac and I say our goodbyes, but I am just dying to offload my bags, change money and eat. I have nowhere booked to stay tonight but head to the hostel where I am booked in for tomorrow night and the following two. Thankfully there is a bed for tonight, but they don't have my booking for the following nights, even though I had emailed to confirm I was still coming whilst I was in Russia. There are plenty of beds and I am in a six-bed, all-female room. Of course they are all young trendy things, so I am limited on conversations with them, but they all seem nice.

My hunger getting the better of me, I simply went to a place next to the hostel and had noodle soup with scrambled egg and tomatoes in it, due to very little vegetarian choice. My hunger satisfied, I took Bearsac walkabouts. On constant lookout for maniacs on bicycles rushing past us on both sides along noisy main roads, I found the Sanlitun Yashou Clothing Market, which was mentioned in the Lonely Planet book. I wanted something Chinese to wear for the Beijing Opera, but got chased by stall-holders trying to sell me their overpriced western rubbish. The Chinese clothes were similar to prices in London; not even worth bargaining with them. In the supermarket they refused my 50yuan note, so I left my weird assortment of food and walked out. I purchased food in one of the two 24-hour shops next to the hostel; they didn't bat an eyelid at the 50yuan note. After an invigorating shower, I had an early night to catch up on sleep lost and prepare for the early rise next day.

Day 18

After leaving the remaining Mongolian crunchy things in the kitchen with a note reading 'If going to Mongolia, practise eating these', I left the hostel with sleepy-eyed Bearsac at 4.50am for the 5.30am bus to Badaling. To our annoyance we found that the first metro was 5.08 and that the subway did not open until 5.10am! We would not make the 5.30 bus. Around 20 people stood patiently outside. Bearsac shook the gates and yelled 'open up'; this, for some reason, prompted much laughter from my fellow waitees and remarks of his likeness to Mr Bean's teddy bear.

It took about one hour to get to the great wall, which was half the time my research had told me, so I was happy. The wall was quite unimpressive on entry, but once we had a full view, we were both awestruck by its sheer greatness and silent vibration. Almost empty, we set out upon it with much enthusiasm. My enthusiasm was soon dampened by having to battle against the strong wind and twats trying to sell fake Russian hats with cardboard inside covered in teddy bear fur. Bearsac was not impressed and began to lecture on how cruel it was, and the rights of teddy bears. Unfazed by this strange demonstration of teddy power, one man followed us, still trying to convince of to buy his tacky wares. He pretended he wanted to know more about Bearsac just so he could follow on with his dead teddy bear hats;

he even put one on my head, it was far too big but he still asked me to make an offer. I took it off my head, placed it on his, patted the top of the hat and walked off. Still he followed and for over half a mile. '*Bo dwee, xie xie,*' I repeated several times (No thank you). At last I had had enough. I stopped, turned to him and at the top of my lungs and for about 20 seconds I yelled on the Great Wall of China 'Noooooooooooooooooooooooooo!'

'You no scare me,' he laughed. But he left me alone from there on.

I'm quite a fit person but I have a knee condition called *Chondromalacia Patellae*. Stairs aggravate the condition and cause pain, so it was a bit of a struggle for me as I started getting stitches in my knees. Despite the knees and wind I carried on, pleasure in my soul now I had rid myself of the dead teddy bear hat-seller. I robbed Bearsac of the elastic band that held on his sunglasses so I could use it to tie back my hair, as I could no longer cope with it being blown in my face and was getting angry. Bearsac didn't seem to mind, he was more bothered about getting blown about in the wind when I held him up to take photographs of him.

The Great Wall is 4000 miles long, extending from the dry Gobi Desert, all the way to the wet sea in Shanhai Pass, on the eastern edge of China. The Chinese built it to keep out the Mongolians. It is the longest man-made structure and the only man-made structure visible from the moon.

About one and a half hours after arriving at the near empty wall it was beginning to get quite busy; a stream of people soon turned into a multi-coloured river. From this multi-coloured river, streams of green slithered into a river of algae. Green uniformed Chinese men came walking along past us, some running up the steep stairs. A few posed for photographs with Bearsac. I'm not sure if these young men were police or army, but they made for good video footage.

After another hour we again saw the dead teddy bear hat-seller; we just looked at each other and laughed, but he knew better than to take it as a cue to rekindle his love of salesmanship. Three hours was enough for me, so we headed back to the bus stop via some souvenir shops where I spotted teddy bear with Chinese clothing. I asked if there were any clothes in Bearsac's size. The assistant, who had started hassling me as soon as I stepped through the door, went to grab a far smaller teddy to take off its clothes and knocked over her freshly bought cup of tea. Satisfied it had not scalded the teddy bear, I left before they could see laughter on my lips.

The bus ride back to town took two hours, this time due to the heavy traffic. We sat by a lake for a while before getting the subway. The wind blew the surface of the water, and ripples raced each other out of sight. The scent of algae drifted into my soul as it followed us down the lake and I held it within. We exited back onto the road and took the subway to go and check out the location of the theatre and buy tickets for the Opera.

As so many roads were unnamed it was difficult finding the theatre. Four Chinese men helped us, one using his mobile to phone a friend to ask where it was. The map was of little use to them or the people they stopped and got to look at it. A rickshaw rider who, assuming he had got a fare, had a near collision with a car, reluctantly told them the exact route and up to the door the four men escorted me. I thanked them and photographs with Bearsac and me were taken. As I went to get one of Bearsac's business cards from my bag, one said:

'No money, just helping English tourist.' I had known they would not expect any money, even for the phone call, but I did offer for the phone call. They said no, it was a pleasure to meet English woman and talking teddy bear.

We stepped through the heavy deep red doors of Zhengyici Theatre and were greeted by three happy faces. After finally finding the theatre, it turns out I could not buy tickets there. They gave me a phone number and a calendar and let us have a look around.

Entering the main hall, it took time for my eyes to adjust to the dim lighting, but on doing so, a sense of silent shouting of colour - mainly red and green - permeated my inner being as I took in the detail of the walls, ceiling and furnishings. Patterns picked out in contrasting colours, protected under layers of lacquer. Paper lanterns hung from the ceiling and beams. Singular high-back wooden dining chairs, echoing the high ceiling and set beside tables, stood where one would expect padded, low-backed fixed theatre seating. Originally a temple built in 1688 during the Ming Dynasty; it was converted into an opera theatre in 1712 and is the oldest tea house theatre in Beijing.

The theatre was on part of one of the *Hutongs*. *Hutongs* are the narrow alleys and lanes of tatty but charming housing and shops. They look much as they did hundreds of years ago. I was intrigued by the amount of power lines, and took lots of photographs of them. I'm sure most people would find the photographs boring and repetitive but I love the pattern of the power lines criss-crossing above the scruffy little buildings. The buildings are laid out according to the principles of *feng shui*. It's a shame though, for the people that live in them, that *feng shui* didn't think to make them bigger! It was good to see this aspect of Beijing and not just the tourist parts.

As Beijing prepares for next year's Olympics, the shops are filled with weird cuddly toy characters sporting the Olympic logo;

I reckon that China's own strongest sport would be spitting. Everywhere around me, it seems, people are spitting; I myself am starting to get a build up of phlegm from the pollution. It's not the sight of it so much but the awful sound that accompanies it that grates on my nerves so.

I nearly get run over by an old lady on a rusty tricycle as I dump my Borehamwood Tesco carrier bag with banana skin and apple core into a bin. A man approaches me, I assume to see if I'm OK. The man, though, proudly tells me he makes the Tesco bags in the factory where he works in another part of China; he speaks perfect English, a surprising rarity in Beijing so far. I wonder why with his good English he makes carrier bags, but he seems happy in his work as he relates it to me. It is funny to think how the carrier bag I got in Borehamwood has done the full circuit and returned home to its country of origin. When I relate this story later, though, to one of the women working at the hostel, I find out that they return to China anyway to be recycled – but instead end up as heaps of dirty junk. It is absurd that in our bid help the environment by recycling, we pollute it by transporting carrier bags on a two-way journey halfway around the world, and then they just get left around polluting water and poor areas.

Talking of Tesco and Bejing, Tesco has recently opened its first Beijing branch. The opening has caused concern from animal rights people in Britain as the Beijing store sells live turtles and frogs. There is rumour that they were considering killing chickens in-store.

We went in search of Gondalia's vegetarian restaurant but were told, by some Germans we'd asked directions from, that it might have gone, as the road was being developed for the Olympics next year. Coming by a small market we took a look. As soon as we set foot within the row of market stalls, we were besieged by stall-holders and their cries of 'What do you want?'

'Give me a chance to look and I might see something, hassle me and I'll go somewhere else,' I'd reply. This of course was either not understood or just totally ignored. I got chased by calculators and stall assistants pretending they wanted to stroke Bearsac.

I spotted a silk blouse on a stall that was one of few with prices displayed. It fitted me, as did the silk trousers the assistant suggested would go with it rather than the one skirt I thought would go with it. The blouse was marked at 90yuan, which was more than four times less than I had seen very similar blouses. I offered 50yuan; Bearsac pipped in 'that sounds like a fair deal' and made the poor woman jump out of her skin. Once recovered, she did all the stroking and kissing the perspective customer's teddy bear bit and said I could have both trouser and blouse for 90yuan. Satisfied; I gave her the money and one of Bearsac's business cards and hit the street again.

Too exhausted to visit Tiananmen Square and the Forbidden City, which were just nearby, we headed back to the hostel and booked a ticket to the Opera with the hostel, as the one they go to has subtitles in English and a minibus there and back. Too exhausted to go too far for food, we checked out the hostel/hotel restaurant and had chilli tofu and rice. The rice arrived ten minutes after the tofu and, after waiting five minutes and having asked twice for the rice, I just started tucking into the spicy sauced tofu. There was so much tofu that it made no difference that the rice arrived late as I still had mounds of it left. It was just a shame that the taste was not as big as the portion. I needed a lie down to rest my bulging tum, so to our room we went, hoping for some peace and quiet. The other girls were in there squeaking away, but my earplugs muffed that and when they spoke to me I think I murmured yes and no in the right places, but I was beyond caring. I just lay smelling Bearsac and chilling out.

Later I went to one of the nearby large shops but got annoyed by the assistants pestering me, and by not being able to find my way out.

I was shouting, to myself in part amusement and part frustration rather than to anyone,

'How the hell do I get out of this god forsaken hell-hole of a shop?'

I was instructed to go all the way around the shop to exit. Overloaded by the buzzing sounds of wobbly toy robots and police cars with flashing lights and sirens that patrolled the floor space and maybe arrested drunken robots, I was desperate to escape. I saw that if I got over the glass-topped counter (like the ones in 'Are You Being Served'), I could save about three quarters of the trek round the shop. I gently sat on the counter top and swung my legs over it; this was much to the amazement of both shop assistants and customers, but no-one dared utter a word!

Day 19

The morning started with an attempt to buy a selection of the small cakes I'd had the day before. I chose different ones but only wanted one of each. They weighed OK but I was told by way of gestures that I couldn't just have one of each. If they thought they would succeed in selling me more by telling me that, they soon discovered that they were going to lose out. Cakeless, I turned on my heel and walked out, but closely followed by three assistants saying 'Just one', 'Lady, lady, just one.'

Bearsac growled at them and one screamed and ran away! I didn't know whether to scream, laugh or apologise.

We headed to the world's biggest square, the one we were too tired to visit yesterday; Tiananmen Square. The square is 440,000 square metres. Bearsac nearly got tangled up in the string of a kite when he got too close to where it flew down. We lost count of the number of times Bearsac got pointed at by people saying 'Mr Bean's teddy bear' – it seemed to be said all around us. No matter where we go in the world he gets pointed at amid cries of 'Mr Bean's teddy bear!' Maybe he could make money as a look-a-like or stunt double.

After a roam around the square we had a sit down on the grass to change my batteries and speak to some maroon-robed monks. The monks, we found, were Burmese and knew a little English. They laughed at me when I fell about on the grass laughing when one of them pointed at Bearsac, saying 'Mr. Bean teddy.' Is there anyone in the world that does not know of Mr. Bean's teddy bear, and is there anyone that does not think Bearsac looks like him? I'm not that convinced that Bearsac looks like him, but if I had a pound for everyone that has ever expressed a likeness, I would be rich. I held Bearsac's paws together within my own hands and nodded goodbye to the monks, who returned the same (minus a teddy bear).

The large picture of Mao adorning a wall alerted us to the Forbidden City. I didn't really need to walk as I got floated along by the mass of bodies pouring through the gates. Once inside the outer southern gate, Tiananmen gate, my feet touched ground again and Bearsac was safely still wrapped up in my arms. I let him decide which way to go, as I hadn't a clue. The work that goes into the shaping and painting of the buildings is amazing; there must be renovations constantly being carried out. The roofing alone was amazing; Bearsac especially liked the little animals along the corners and wanted to have a few words with them; and I desperately wanted to sniff at them and feel the texture against the tip of my nose; but I don't think it would have been appropriate to climb up to do so.

As well as admiring the architecture, I made my fun people-watching and filmed the kids playing in knitted dresses and silk outfits. They loved Bearsac and so did the adults that gathered around to listen to him talk to the kids. It was like being in Covent Garden as a street entertainer. Bearsac was given sweets galore by his audience, which I ate as he can't. There were mostly Chinese tourists groups, each group identified by different coloured baseball caps or T-shirts promoting the tour organisation. There were a few Japanese tourists; but very few Westerners.

Around the Forbidden City's long moats were far fewer people, so we had a chance to relax. A woman was selling pineapple on sticks; I sat and watched to see how much she charged the Chinese. When I gave her, like them, a 1yuan note, she held up two fingers; I took a pineapple on a stick from the bunch in her hand and put up one finger, and walked off. I'm sure it tasted all the more fresh for my having done so! Bearsac helped me eat it, which I know makes no sense when I have just said he can't eat sweets as he is a teddy bear, but my imagination is not very consistent and changes its mind a lot. Lots of people wanted their photograph taken with Bearsac but also with me, as a Westerner.

We perused Chinese costume and art exhibitions but were almost attacked by a cat. This cat was not of the alive and furry variety, but of the gold, red and black plastic with paw moving up and down variety. Of course it was not the cat itself that chased us, but the little old lady, in red shoes, trying to make me adopt it and shouting 'lucky cat, lucky cat.' After seeing enough plastic waving cats to last us several lifetimes, I manoeuvred Bearsac and myself rapidly away and left the cat maybe feeling a little unlucky by now with its rightful owner. Bearsac wanted to stay and speak to it but it's not as if we'd not seen our share of the same tacky cats in Japan last year; and at least in Japan we didn't get chased by one. I wonder if Japan and China argue over their claim to these tacky felines in the same way both Turkey and Greece argue over their claim to kebabs.

Hungry, we found a restaurant away from the fray for lunch. Unable to sit at the small table near the open doorway to which I was directed, due to the sound of mopeds buzzing past, I was moved to a large table at the back. This meant that I was soon sharing the table with other people. This was fine, as I got to hear all about the travels of the first two Chinese men that shared my table for their meal, and with the second pair of Chinese men that told Bearsac all about panda bears and gave him a glass of their tea. Filled by my oyster mushrooms and tofu in oyster sauce with rice, we set off again and just wandered around aimlessly with Bearsac getting pointed at and no doubt being called Mr Bean's teddy bear; with my earplugs in I could only guess, but I doubt I was wrong.

As is often the stereotype with Chinese food, just half and hour later we were both hungry again. This time we opted to try a Chinese crepe. In the queue, we met some Americans who did not quite understand Bearsac, and some that did and wanted their photograph taken with him to be on his website.

Back at the hostel the two Danish girls who were in the room said that they had seen where there were insects to eat and showed me on the map. After a rest Bearsac and I headed off to the general area to hunt out the insects I was determined to try. I don't see them in the same way as animals and was very enthusiastic to try some.

As the sun was sinking in the direction we were headed, silhouettes of cyclists were cast, inspiring photographic action. I asked directions for where I could find insects to eat from a traffic officer. I think Mr Traffic Officer quite enjoyed my miming; my stepping on imaginary cockroaches (complete with crunching sound effects) and then eating them from a kebab stick with eating sound effects. He laughed, said in Mandarin he understood and pointed me to turn right, then left.

Bearsac first spotted the insect stalls; we could see only two. At first I just stood videoing the first stall, seeing what Chinese people were paying. Bearsac started speaking to the scorpions, which were still wriggling about on a wooded kebab stick. After much hassling us to try them, one of the stall workers took a wriggling stick of scorpions from its potato holder and shoved it almost in my face. Whilst I recoil from the intrusion of scorpions, a sweaty little man pushes up my arm to try to make me take it. . Then, taking his hand from under my arm, he thrusts his hand out for money.

On his third attempt at this I lost my temper and pushed him, yelling and gesturing at him not to touch me. He stumbled into the stall, but luckily did not knock it over or burn himself. I stormed off to the other stall where it was less hectic and the staff calmer and non-hassling. Thankfully I was not being pursued by angry Chinese man wielding wriggling scorpions.

The only thing that really looked filling enough was cocoons. It turned out they were silkworm cocoons, so I gave them a try. Bearsac was made a fuss of as we waited for our cocoons to cook and people videoed him talking to the scorpions that were also alive on this stall. Once our silkworm cocoons were cooked I sat at a table, set up my video camera on its tri-pod and videoed both Bearsac and me eating them. With initial trepidation, I swept my hair away from my face and munched on the first fat cocoon. Crunchy on the outside, soft inside and slightly sweet; the cocoon spurted out a little sticky juice onto my glasses. I gave the thumbs up to the stall workers and both Bearsac and I tucked into the rest, despite the fact that we were lost in a sea of onlookers with video camera and phones filming me and Bearsac.

With excitement at having eaten such weird food I took back to the streets with a spring in my step, kissing Bearsac with my greasy lips. I noticed a bargain shop with lots of people inside spilling onto the pavement and went to see what the fuss was; I still wanted to get some shoes for the Opera. I saw no shoes, but there was some nice jewellery that was too cheap and too unusual not to buy.

Walking back to the hostel, past many red lanterns that were now lit, I started feeling a bit hot, and my hands became somewhat itchy. I assumed I was just a bit excited. However, quite soon the palms of my hands became very hot and extremely itchy. I looked at my palms, they were bright red. My face started feeling very hot and blotchy and my hands became even itchier. I had to scratch my palms continuously but my hair falling in my face irritated me so much that I had to stop every so often to sweep away my clinging hair from my sweaty face. The few seconds I stopped scratching my palms were unbearable each time.

Once back in the hostel my hands, not satisfied to itch alone, were joined by the soles of my feet. I started panicking, but by some miracle I did not feel any sensory overload from the cat-like singing on the TV or the overpowering smell of perfume one of the girls was spraying. One of the girls suggested I try her antihistamines, but they were prescription ones so I didn't think it a good idea. Another suggested having a shower, but I was so bad that I couldn't refrain from scratching long enough to get my stuff together for a shower. The girl that suggested I try her antihistamines gave me Vaseline and kept telling me to rub in more and more. I was worried about using all her Vaseline but she firmly told me to carry on rubbing it in. This helped a lot and I was able to just lie down as still as I could and control my breathing.

A new girl entered the room, asking if we all were suffering sunstroke; the two Danish girls were a bit sunburnt as they were very fair skinned and had been out in the sun and wind all day, but I must have looked like a lobster! A couple of hours later I felt OK enough to get up and look at my face; I did look like a lobster. My face was swollen with large red blotches and was bigger even than it normally is. It was shining and my hair clung damply and possessively to it. Rather than go into full-scale panic, I just lay back down and cuddled Bearsac but found that when I kissed him his fur just irritated my face. Offering silent apologies to silkworm heaven, I asked them to forgive me and let me be OK. I finally just fell asleep, still dressed. Maybe my apologies had been accepted by the great silkworm god.

Day 20

Felt itch-free on getting up, but still had a couple of small blotches on my face. I set off with Bearsac for Summer Palace with relaxation on the agenda. By now I was buying metro tickets and locating the correct platform like I had been living in Beijing for years; but I just still had not got used to the winy high pitched PA system.

Located about 12km from the centre of Beijing, Summer Palace, first built in 1750, overlooks the western hills. As its name would suggest, Summer Palace was used as a summer residence by China's imperial rulers as a second home to the 'Forbidden City'. Its temples, pavilions, ponds and lake are beautiful and peaceful, with wind-chimes musicing softly on the air. The gardens that make up Summer Palace date from the Jin Dynasty (1115-1234). Doors to one building we liked were large and heavy with 49 gold bolts; I know, because Bearsac could see there were nine rows of nine and told me that that made 49.

It was more fun to scramble up the rocks to the temples than take the orderly path. The green and yellow tiled Temple of the Sea of Wisdom is the home of a gilded Buddha statue. Why Bearsac even bothered to greet him I will never know. When we accidentally found our way to Kumming Lake, we stood silently with the wind in our hair and fur, to take in its splendour. From the top, the lake looked still and as reflective as a mirror; but standing by it, the ripples raced diagonally with the directional wind. The lake was man-made and its soil taken to build the 60 metre high Longevity Hill from which we had first viewed it.

We were at the north side of Kunming Lake, where the Long Corridor is located. All 728 metres of its length are decorated. Lake scenes and images of Chinese mythology are too perfectly intact to be original, but are beautiful restorations. We sat for a while, admiring the artistic flair, before coming by the marble boat and being swamped by young Chinese and Japanese women who wanted to photograph, not Bearsac, but me. Empress Dowager Cixi used to dine out on the boat during summer evenings.

Walking around the lake and its bridges, we met on our travels many people. Further young women wanted their photograph taken with me; it was like I was famous. Bearsac was feeling a bit jealous as it is normally he that people ask to be photographed with. Of course Bearsac was in the photos too, but it was the Western woman that they were really interested in.

It was proving hard to enjoy the beauty of the scenery and six bridges because it was so windy. I was almost halfway around the lake, which had taken 45 minutes; I could take the wind no more but knew it would take so long to go back the way I had come and that it would maybe only save five minutes compared to carrying on the way we were going. When we came to bonsai cherry blossom trees I just had to photograph Bearsac in them. Bearsac got some attention – the usual pointing and Mr Bean's teddy bear comments.

Towards the full circuit was a café, where I was relieved to eat noodles with shredded cucumber and soy sauce. It was refreshing, and the sit inside out of the wind for 15 minutes helped me recover from the unrelaxing walk around the lake. Bearsac thanked the ladies working in the café, who *ooohed* and *ahhhhhed* over him, and then we got the bus back to town.

The mini-bus was bit late picking us up for the opera, which kicked my Aspie trait of time panic into overdrive. However, we got there with enough time to watch the tea pourers pouring tea for people at tables downstairs from metal teapots with 5-foot long but very thin spouts. They made a great song and dance about pouring the tea and it looked more like a martial art performance.

At last the curtain drew back. I was very glad that I had brought my earplugs as the singing and speaking sounded like cats being strangled – even the men! People in the audience were trying not to laugh, but laughing couldn't be helped. Bearsac told me off for being such a philistine; he was wearing his plum velvet suit and bow-tie and he usually becomes quite snobby when wearing it. The acting though was good and the acrobatics superb. The main woman kicked the ends of long batons with the grace of a prima ballerina and the precision of a world-class footballer; she performed back-flips and forward-flips, not once missing the many batons that were tossed to her. It was nothing like a

Western Opera but it was entertaining, even if the singing was screechy and gave me cause to use my earplugs.

Back at the hostel, I was ready for dinner. It was my last night so I wanted some decent Chinese food. So far, the average Chinese food I had eaten in England had been better than anything I'd had in China. After 45 minutes of walking around, Bearsac and I were back near the hostel and found three restaurants next to each other. We entered the nicer looking of the three and sat down, too wound up from the search to bother waiting to be shown to a table. The waiter brought the menu and smiled at Bearsac. As soon as I opened the menu, the waiter had his pen and order pad almost in my face. I said in English, with clear gestures in-case he did not understand:

'Could you please give me five minutes to look at the menu.'

He just stood there nodding, but with pen and pad poised, waiting for my order. I had only just opened the menu and had not even read a word. I gestured for about three minutes by pointing to my wrist (where my watch would be if I had one), holding up five fingers and waving him away from the table. Still he stood with pen, pad and inane smile. Annoyed, I snatched his pen and pad from his hands. I drew a face with glasses (me) looking at a menu, a man with pad (him) next to an arrow pointing away from the menu to a clock with a large number 5 and a small section between the 12 and 1 shaded. Baffled, the waiter took it to his colleagues and they all puzzled over it. He returned and stood as he had done before with his order pad nearly in my face. I closed the menu. He turned 45 degrees away from the table but stayed on the spot. I opened the menu and he turned back with the pad. I closed it again; he turned away but still on the same spot. How he knew when I had it open, I don't know. This went on for about a minute or more. I took the menu and went into a small room I had spotted and closed the door. He opened the door and stood there with pen and pad poised! I stormed back to the table, determined I was not going to walk out as I was hungry and wanted some proper Chinese food. He came back to the table, stood just as he had done before. I got under the table with the menu. He crouched down and lifted up the long tablecloth! I sat back on the chair but lifted the tablecloth and put my head under it to look at the menu. He lifted the tablecloth again. That was it. I lost my temper, frisbeed the menu across the restaurant, grabbed Bearsac and my camera bag and stormed out.

After I had crossed the footbridge, I realised that I had left my jacket in the restaurant so had to go back! As I approached the restaurant a woman - who had been standing outside when I had stormed out - told them I was coming back. The waiter approached the door, wariness in his shaky but determined stride, and my jacket - which he had folded neatly - in his upturned hands, as though carrying jelly on a silver platter. He presented it back to me; I said thank you in Mandarin and went and got a pot noodle!

Day 21 – Last day

On the airport bus they repeatedly played the song 'Got To Say Goodbye For The Summer.' Bearsac and I now know all the words, and Bearsac got a few people singing along with him.

Two young kids sat near us on the first flight to Moscow; although they weren't too noisy, their high-pitched, squeaky voices meant I wore my earplugs most of the flight. Worse though was my overload of the strong-smelling meat being eaten by people around me; even when they had finished I was still overwhelmed by the smell of its traces in the containers. I sat with my hands over my nose and blanket over my head, shielding my intense headache. The smell of meat doesn't normally bother me that much but this was really disgusting and strong. The overload to the meat smell made me even more sensitive to sounds. I just had to sit huddled up under the blanket, smelling Bearsac. The woman sitting next to me asked what was wrong and got the flight attendants, who brought me an antibacterial pollution face mask. Having explained I have Asperger's, I was asked by the flight attendant 'Are you travelling alone?'

'No,' I replied; 'I am travelling with my teddy bear!' Of course I knew they meant: *why is someone like you, travelling alone, are you allowed to?* They also asked if there was any medication I should take, as if I wouldn't have the ability to think of it myself if there was!

I finally got to spend the roubles. At the airport in Moscow I bought a bottle of honey and chilli vodka. Bearsac spoke to people, including a young woman from Adelaide who had a teddy bear in her luggage called Snuggles. Unfortunately Snuggles was in her hold luggage, so Bearsac and he did not become acquainted. Bearsac expressed concern at Snuggles being in the hold but the young woman assured him that there was plenty of air and candy inside. Talking of candy, Bearsac was given some lovely candy by a man that he had been speaking to. Bearsac must have been given more candy on this trip than all the others put together.

The flight from Moscow to Heathrow was fine and we met lots of people on the tube home who shared their holiday stories and duty free chocolates with Bearsac. Of course, I had to eat the chocolates for Bearsac; he is just a teddy bear, after all!

Our ger in Mongolia

A bear in Red Square with his owner

Sitting with Kiek in de kok – Tallinn

Taking a break on our 4-day Trans- Mongolian train trip

Me and Bearsac Opera House – Riga

Resting in Tiananmen Sq. before visiting the Forbidden City - Beijing

Afterthoughts

The places I've been and things I have done have been an experience. One of the main pleasures, though, has been the people that I have met along Bearsac's and my travels. I have met wonderful characters that I would not have seen if I had followed the 'Don't talk to strangers' rule that is ingrained in us all during childhood, for good reason, but often gets carried through into life as a responsible adult, for no good reason.

Travelling as a lone human, even without Asperger's, is a challenge at times, and something so many people never do. That is such a shame. The world opens itself up to you more as a lone traveller; especially if you have a rather cute teddy bear with you.

Openness breeds openness and closedness brings closedness, which is why two people can take the same trip and report very different experiences.

Lone travel frees you from the everyday roles you play, from the expectations of people known to you that box you into their way of seeing you. It is a chance to release yourself from the box, from the patterns of your interactions with these people, that don't see the real you, but what it suits them to see. Why take that burden with you on your travels? Leave it at home and set yourself free.

On the Trans-Mongolian train I thought about *tolerance* and how I no longer want it to imprison me. I have made the decision to move on in my life; if that has lost me friends, then so be it. I feel released.

Though not a very demonstrative person, I here express my gratitude to the many people that have shown me kindness and understanding and have shared with me, and with Bearsac, their wisdom, appreciation and their curiosity.

My memories will be cherished forever, long after Bearsac has worn and faded away.

To see photographs of our trips and other features see Bearsac's website

www.bearsac.com